Summary of Contents

SIMPLY RAILS 2

BY **PATRICK LENZ**
SECOND EDITION

Simply Rails 2

by Patrick Lenz

Copyright © 2008 SitePoint Pty. Ltd.

Expert Reviewer: Luke Redpath **Editor**: Hilary Reynolds
Managing Editor: Simon Mackie **Index Editor**: Max McMaster
Technical Editor: Andrew Tetlaw **Cover Design**: Alex Walker
Technical Director: Kevin Yank
Printing History:
    First Edition: January 2007
    Second Edition: May 2008

Published by SitePoint Pty. Ltd.

48 Cambridge Street Collingwood
VIC Australia 3066
Web: www.sitepoint.com
Email: business@sitepoint.com

ISBN 978-0-9804552-0-5
Printed and bound in the United States of America

About the Author

Patrick Lenz has been developing web applications for more than ten years. Founder and lead developer of the freshmeat.net software portal, he and his Rails consultancy and web application development company, limited overload, are responsible for several community-driven web applications developed using Ruby on Rails. Patrick also authored some of the first articles to appear on the web about architecting and scaling larger Rails applications.

Patrick lives in Wiesbaden, Germany, with his wife Alice and his daughter Gwendolyn.

When not working in front of a computer, he can often be seen with a camera in his hand, either taking artsy pictures or documenting the progress of his baby girl conquering the world.[1] He also enjoys cars, music, and extended weekend brunches with friends.

His weblog can be found at http://poocs.net/.

About the Expert Reviewer

Luke Redpath is a programmer with over seven years' experience in the web design and development field. A recovering PHP and ASP developer, Luke has been using Ruby and Rails professionally for nearly two years and has released and contributed to several Ruby libraries and Rails plugins, including UJS—the Rails unobtrusive JavaScript plugin.[2] He currently resides in North London with his long-term partner Julie.

About the Technical Editor

Andrew Tetlaw has been tinkering with web sites as a web developer since 1997 and has also worked as a high school English teacher, an English teacher in Japan, a window cleaner, a car washer, a kitchen hand, and a furniture salesman. At SitePoint he is dedicated to making the world a better place through the technical editing of SitePoint books and kits. He is also a busy father of five, enjoys coffee, and often neglects his blog at http://tetlaw.id.au/.

About the Technical Director

As Technical Director for SitePoint, Kevin Yank oversees all of its technical publications—books, articles, newsletters, and blogs. He has written over 50 articles for SitePoint, but is best known for his book, *Build Your Own Database Driven Website Using PHP &*

---

[1] His pictures are regularly published to Flickr and are available at http://flickr.com/photos/scoop/
[2] http://www.ujs4rails.com/

MySQL.[3] Kevin lives in Melbourne, Australia, and enjoys performing improvised comedy theater and flying light aircraft.

About SitePoint

SitePoint specializes in publishing fun, practical, and easy-to-understand content for web professionals. Visit http://www.sitepoint.com/ to access our books, newsletters, articles, and community forums.

---

[3] http://www.sitepoint.com/books/phpmysql1/

*To my daughter Gwendolyn and
my wife Alice.*

Table of Contents

Chapter 5 Models, Views, and Controllers 119

Preface

Ruby on Rails has shaken up the web development industry in a huge way—especially when you consider that version 1.0 of Rails was only released in December 2005. The huge waves of enthusiasm for the new framework, originally in weblogs and later in the more traditional media, are probably the reason why this book is in your hands.

This book will lead you through the components that make up the Rails framework by building a clone of the popular story-sharing web site digg.com. This will give you a chance to get your feet wet building a simple, yet comprehensive web application using Ruby on Rails.

While the first edition of this book hit the shelves shortly after Rails 1.2 was released, the Rails Core Team quickly hurried off to work on an even better and even more polished version of the framework—a version that was released in December of 2007 as Rails 2.0. Although seen as an evolutionary (rather than a revolutionary) update, Rails 2 features improvements in almost every corner of its comprehensive code base, hence the requirement to update this book. And the improvements continue: as we go to press, the 2.1 release of Rails is imminent.

Without going into too many boring details, rest assured that with Rails 2 you have the fastest and most secure, concise, fun and rewarding version of Rails in existence. You get a secure web application almost out of the box; using the latest web technologies such as Ajax has never been more accessible; and it's just as easy to produce a well-tested application as it is not to do any automated testing.

If that's all Klingon to you, don't worry. I'll get you started, and by the time you finish this book, you'll be able to discuss all things Web 2.0 with your friends and coworkers, and impress your dentist with geeky vocabulary.

Who Should Read This Book?

This book is intended for anyone who's eager to learn more about Ruby on Rails in a practical sense. It's equally well suited to design-oriented people looking to build web applications as it is to people who are unhappy with the range of programming languages or frameworks they're using, and are looking for alternatives that bring the fun back into programming.

I don't expect you to be an expert programmer; this isn't a pro-level book. It's written specifically for beginning to intermediate web developers who, though they're familiar with HTML and CSS, aren't necessarily fond of—or experienced with—any server-side technologies such as PHP or Perl.

As we go along, you'll gain an understanding of the components that make up the Ruby on Rails framework, learn the basics of the Ruby programming language, and come to grips with the tools recommended for use in Ruby on Rails development. All these topics are covered within the context of building a robust application which addresses real-world problems.

In terms of software installation, I'll cover the installation basics of Ruby and Ruby on Rails on Mac OS X, Windows, and Linux. All you need to have preinstalled on your system are your favorite text editor and a web browser.

What You'll Learn

Web development has never been easier, or as much fun as it is using Ruby on Rails. In this book, you'll learn to make use of the latest Web 2.0 techniques, RESTful development patterns, and the concise Ruby programming language, to build interactive, database driven web sites that are a pleasure to build, use, and maintain.

Also, as web sites tend to evolve over time, I'll teach you how to make sure you don't wreak havoc with a careless change to your application code. We'll implement automated testing facilities and learn how to debug problems that arise within your application.

What's in This Book?

Chapter 1: Introducing Ruby on Rails

This chapter touches on the history of the Rails framework, which—believe it or not—is actually rather interesting! I'll explain some of the key concepts behind Rails and shed some light on the features that we're planning to build into our example application.

Chapter 2: Getting Started

Here's where the real action starts! In this chapter, I'll walk you through the installation of the various pieces of software required to turn your Mac or PC into a powerful Ruby on Rails development machine. I'll also show you how to set up the database for our example application, so that you can start your application for the first time, in all its naked glory.

Chapter 3: Introducing Ruby

Ruby on Rails is built on the object oriented programming language Ruby, so it helps to know a bit about both object oriented programming and the Ruby syntax. This chapter will give you a solid grounding in both—and if you'd like to get your hands dirty, you can play along at home using the interactive Ruby console.

Chapter 4: Rails Revealed

In this chapter, we start to peel back the layers of the Rails framework. I'll talk about the separation of environments in each of the application's life cycles, and introduce you to the model-view-controller architecture that forms the basis of a Rails application's organization.

Chapter 5: Models, Views, and Controllers

In this chapter, we'll generate our first few lines of code. We'll create a class for storing data, a view for displaying the data, and a controller to handle the interaction between the two.

Chapter 6: Helpers, Forms, and Layouts

This chapter starts off by looking at how Rails's built-in helpers can reduce the amount of code required to create functionality for your application. I'll show you how to use one of the helpers to create a fully functioning form, and we'll style the end result with some CSS so that it looks good! I'll then show you how to write unit and functional tests to verify that the application is working as expected.

Chapter 7: Ajax and Web 2.0

Let's face it, this chapter is the reason you bought this book! Well, it won't disappoint. I'll walk you through the steps involved in adding to our app some nifty effects that use Ajax to update parts of a page without reloading the entire page. Along the way, I'll explain the different relationships that you can establish between your objects, and we'll make sure that our application uses clean URLs.

Chapter 8: Protective Measures

In this chapter, I'll show you how to keep out the bad guys by adding simple user authentication to our application. We'll cover sessions and cookies, and we'll see firsthand how database migrations allow for the iterative evolution of a database schema.

Chapter 9: Advanced Topics

This chapter will give our example application a chance to shine. We'll add a stack of functionality, and in the process, we'll learn about model callbacks and join models.

Chapter 10: Plugins

In this chapter, I'll show you how to add a plugin—a component that provides features that expand the functionality of your application—to the example application. We'll also talk about some of the more advanced associations that are available to your models.

Chapter 11: Debugging, Testing, and Benchmarking

This chapter will cover testing and benchmarking, as well as the reasons why you should complete comprehensive testing of all your code. We'll also walk through a couple of examples that show how to debug your application when something goes wrong.

Chapter 12: Deployment

Now that you've developed a feature-packed, fully functional application, you'll want to deploy it so that other people can use it. In this chapter, I'll introduce you to the options available for deploying your application to a production server, and walk you through the steps involved in taking your application to the world.

The Book's Web Site

Head over to http://www.sitepoint.com/books/rails2/ for easy access to various resources supporting this book.

The Code Archive

The code archive for this book, which can be downloaded from http://www.sitepoint.com/books/rails2/archive/, contains each and every line of example source code that's printed in this book. If you want to cheat (or save yourself from carpal tunnel syndrome), go ahead and download the files.

Updates and Errata

While everyone involved in producing a technical book like this goes to enormous effort to ensure the accuracy of its content, books tend to have errors. Fortunately, the Corrections and Typos page located at http://www.sitepoint.com/books/rails2/errata.php is the most current, comprehensive reference for spelling and code-related errors that observant readers have reported to us.

The SitePoint Forums

If you have a problem understanding any of the discussion or examples in this book, try asking your question in the SitePoint Forums, at http://www.sitepoint.com/forums/. There, the enthusiastic and friendly community will be able to help you with all things Rails.

The SitePoint Newsletters

In addition to books like this one, SitePoint publishes free email newsletters including *The SitePoint Tribune* and *The SitePoint Tech Times*. In them, you'll read about the latest news, product releases, trends, tips, and techniques for all aspects of web development.

You can count on gaining some useful Rails articles and tips from these resources, but if you're interested in learning other technologies, or aspects of web development and business, you'll find them especially valuable. Sign up to one or more SitePoint newsletters at http://www.sitepoint.com/newsletter/.

Your Feedback

If you can't find your answer through the forums, or if you wish to contact us for any other reason, write to books@sitepoint.com. We have a well-staffed email support system set up to track your inquiries, and if our support staff members are unable to answer your question, they'll send it straight to me. Suggestions for improvements, as well as notices of any mistakes you may find, are especially welcome.

Conventions Used in This Book

You'll notice that we've used certain typographic and layout styles throughout this book to signify different types of information. Look out for the following items.

Code Samples

Code in this book will be displayed using a fixed-width font, like so:

```
<h1>A perfect summer's day</h1>
<p>It was a lovely day for a walk in the park. The birds
were singing and the kids were all back at school.</p>
```

If the code may be found in the book's code archive, the name of the file will appear at the top of the program listing, like this:

```
                                                          example.css
.footer {
  background-color: #CCC;
  border-top: 1px solid #333;
}
```

If only part of the file is displayed, this is indicated by the word *excerpt*:

```
                                                    example.css (excerpt)
  border-top: 1px solid #333;
```

Some lines of code are intended to be entered on one line, but we've had to wrap them because of page constraints. A ➡ indicates a line break that exists for formatting purposes only, and should be ignored.

```
URL.open("http://www.sitepoint.com/blogs/2007/05/28/user-style-she
➡ets-come-of-age/");
```

Tips, Notes, and Warnings

 Hey, You!

Tips will give you helpful little pointers.

 Ahem, Excuse Me ...

Notes are useful asides that are related—but not critical—to the topic at hand. Think of them as extra tidbits of information.

 Make Sure You Always ...

... pay attention to these important points.

 Watch Out!

Warnings will highlight any gotchas that are likely to trip you up along the way.

Acknowledgments

Thanks to the great people at SitePoint for giving me the chance to write this book. In particular, thanks to Technical Editors Matthew Magain and Andrew Tetlaw for their crisp, sharp commentary, and Managing Editor Simon Mackie for applying an appropriate measure of brute force to me and my drafts—dedication that ensured that this book is in the best shape possible. I am truly grateful for this opportunity.

To the people in the Rails Core team, for making my developer life enjoyable again by putting together this amazing framework in almost no time, bringing outstanding improvements to an already great foundation, and laying the base on which this book could be written, thank you.

Special thanks to the makers of the Red Bull energy drink, without which the countless nights that went into both the first and second edition of this book wouldn't have been as productive as they were. In a related fashion, my sincere thanks to the rock bands 30 Seconds to Mars, Linkin Park, Fall Out Boy, Placebo, Billy Talent, and Good Charlotte, among others, for orchestrating the late-night writing sessions.

Finally, thanks must go to my family, especially Alice and Gwen, for giving me so much strength, motivation, and confidence in what I'm doing. Thank you for bearing the fact that I was rarely seen away from a computer for way too long. Many thanks to my dad, for the foundation of my professional life and for teaching me so many things that could fill an entire book on their own. Thank you!

Introducing Ruby on Rails

Since Ruby on Rails was first released, it has become a household name (well, in developers' households, anyway). Hundreds of thousands of developers the world over have adopted—and adored—this new framework. I hope that, through the course of this book, you'll come to understand the reasons why. Before we jump into writing any code, let's take a stroll down memory lane, as we meet Ruby on Rails and explore a little of its history.

First, what exactly *is* Ruby on Rails?

The short—and fairly technical—answer is that **Ruby on Rails** (often abbreviated to "Rails") is a full-stack web application framework, written in Ruby. However, depending on your previous programming experience (and your mastery of techno-jargon), that answer might not make a whole lot of sense to you. Besides, the Ruby on Rails movement—the development principles it represents—really needs to be viewed in the context of web development in general if it is to be fully appreciated.

So, let's define a few of the terms mentioned in the definition above, and take in a brief history lesson along the way. Then we'll tackle the question of why learning Rails is one of the smartest moves you can make for your career as a web developer.

- A **web application** is a software application that's accessed using a web browser over a network. In most cases, that network is the Internet, but it could also be a corporate intranet. The number of web applications being created has increased exponentially since Rails was created, due mostly to the increased availability of broadband Internet access and the proliferation of faster desktop machines in people's homes. It can only be assumed that you're interested in writing such a web application, given that you've bought this book!

- A **framework** can be viewed as the foundation of a web application. It takes care of many of the low-level details that can become repetitive and boring to code, allowing the developer to focus on building the application's functionality.

  A framework gives the developer classes that implement common functions used in *every* web application, including:

  - database abstraction (ensuring that queries work regardless of whether the database is MySQL, Oracle, DB2, SQLite, or [insert your favorite database here])

  - templating (reusing presentational code throughout the application)

  - management of user sessions

  - generation of clean, search engine-friendly URLs

  A framework also defines the architecture of an application; this facility can be useful for those of us who fret over which file is best stored in which folder.

  In a sense, a framework is an application that has been started for you, and a well-designed application at that. The structure, plus the code that takes care of the boring stuff, has already been written, and it's up to you to finish it off!

- **Full-stack** refers to the extent of the functionality that the Rails framework provides. You see, there are frameworks and then there are frameworks. Some provide great functionality on the server, but leave you high and dry on the client side; others are terrific at enhancing the user experience on the client machine, but don't extend to the business logic and database interactions on the server.

  If you've ever used a framework before, chances are that you're familiar with the model-view-controller (MVC) architecture (if you're not, don't worry—we'll discuss it in Chapter 5). Rails covers *everything* in the MVC paradigm, from database abstraction to template rendering, and everything in between.

 Ruby is an open source, object oriented scripting language invented by Yukihiro Matsumoto in the early 1990s. We'll be learning both Ruby *and* Rails as we progress through the book (remember, Rails is written in Ruby).

Ruby makes programming flexible and intuitive, and with it, we can write code that's readable by both humans and machines. Matsumoto clearly envisioned Ruby as a programming language that would entail very little mental overhead for humans, which is why Ruby programmers tend to be happy programmers.

What Does Ruby Look Like?

If you're experienced in programming with other languages, such as PHP or Java, you can probably make some sense of the following Ruby code, although some parts of it may look new:

01-ruby-sample.rb *(excerpt)*

```
>> "What does Ruby syntax look like?".reverse
=> "?ekil kool xatnys ybuR seod tahW"
>> 8 * 5
=> 40
>> 3.times { puts "cheer!" }
cheer!
cheer!
cheer!
>> %w(one two three).each { |word| puts word.upcase }
ONE
TWO
THREE
```

Don't worry too much about the details of programming in Ruby for now—we'll cover all of the Ruby basics in Chapter 3.

History

Ruby on Rails originated as an application named Basecamp,[1] a hosted project-management solution created by Danish web developer David Heinemeier Hansson for former design shop 37signals.[2] Due largely to Basecamp's success, 37signals has since moved into application development and production, and Heinemeier Hansson has become a partner in the company.

When I say "originated," I mean that Rails wasn't initially created as a stand-alone framework. It was extracted from a real application that was already in use, so that it could be used to build other applications that 37signals had in mind.[3] Heinemeier Hansson saw the potential to make his job (and life) easier by extracting common functionality such as database abstraction and templating into what later became the first public release of Ruby on Rails.

He decided to release Rails as open source software to "fundamentally remake the way web sites are built."[4] The first beta version of Rails was initially released in July 2004, with the 1.0 and 2.0 releases following on December 13, 2005 and December 07, 2007 respectively. Several hundreds of thousands of copies of Rails have been downloaded over time, and that number is climbing.

The fact that the Rails framework was extracted from Basecamp is considered by the lively Rails community to represent one of the framework's inherent strengths: Rails was already solving *real* problems when it was released. Rails wasn't built in isolation, so its success wasn't a result of developers taking the framework, building applications with it, and then finding—and resolving—its shortcomings. Rails had already proven itself to be a useful, coherent, and comprehensive framework.

While Heinemeier Hansson pioneered Rails and still leads the Rails-related programming efforts, the framework has benefited greatly from being released as open source software. Over time, developers working with Rails have submitted thousands of

---

[1] http://www.basecamphq.com/

[2] http://www.37signals.com/

[3] Highrise [http://www.highrisehq.com/], Backpack [http://www.backpackit.com/], Ta-da List [http://www.tadalist.com/], Campfire [http://www.campfirenow.com/], and Writeboard [http://www.writeboard.com/] are other hosted applications written in Rails by 37signals.

[4] http://www.wired.com/wired/archive/14.04/start.html?pg=3

extensions and bug fixes to the Rails development repository.[5] The repository is closely guarded by the Rails core team, which consists of about six highly skilled professional developers chosen from the crowd of contributors, led by Heinemeier Hansson.

So, now you know what Rails is, and how it came about. But why would you invest your precious time in learning how to use it?

I'm glad you asked.

Development Principles

Rails supports several software principles that make it stand out from other web development frameworks. Those principles are:

- convention over configuration
- don't repeat yourself
- agile development

Because of these principles, Ruby on Rails is a framework that really does save developers time and effort. Let's look at each of those principles in turn to understand how.

Convention Over Configuration

The concept of **convention over configuration** refers to the fact that Rails assumes a number of defaults for the way one should build a typical web application.

Many other frameworks (such as the Java-based Struts or the Python-based Zope) require you to step through a lengthy configuration process before you can make a start with even the simplest of applications. The configuration information is usually stored in a handful of XML files, and these files can become quite large and cumbersome to maintain. In many cases, you're forced to repeat the entire configuration process whenever you start a new project.

While Rails was originally extracted from an existing application, extensive architectural work went into the framework later on. Heinemeier Hansson purposely

---

[5] The Rails repository, located at http://dev.rubyonrails.org/, is used to track bugs and enhancement requests.

created Rails in such a way that it doesn't need excessive configuration, as long as some standard conventions are followed. The result is that no lengthy configuration files are required. In fact, if you have no need to change these defaults, Rails really only needs a single (and short) configuration file in order to run your application. The file is used to establish a database connection: it supplies Rails with the necessary database server type, server name, user name, and password for each environment, and that's it. Here is an example of a configuration file (we'll talk more about the contents of this configuration file in Chapter 4):

02-database.yml

```
development:
  adapter: sqlite3
  database: db/development.sqlite3
  timeout: 5000
test:
  adapter: sqlite3
  database: db/test.sqlite3
  timeout: 5000
production:
  adapter: sqlite3
  database: db/production.sqlite3
  timeout: 5000
```

Other conventions that are prescribed by Rails include the naming of database-related items, and the process by which **controllers** find their corresponding **models** and **views**.

 Controllers? Models? Views? *Huh?*

Model-view-controller (MVC) is a software architecture (also referred to as a design pattern) that separates an application's **data model** (model), **user interface** (view), and **control logic** (controller) into three distinct components.

Here's an example: when your browser requests a web page from an MVC-architected application, it's talking exclusively to the controller. The controller gathers the required data from one or more models and renders the response to your request through a view. This separation of components means that any change that's made to one component has a minimal effect on the other two.

We'll talk at length about the MVC architecture and the benefits it yields to Rails applications in Chapter 5.

Rails is also considered to be **opinionated software**, a term that has been coined to refer to software that isn't everything to everyone. Heinemeier Hansson and his core team ruthlessly reject contributions to the framework that don't comply with their vision of where Rails is headed, or aren't sufficiently applicable to be useful for the majority of Rails developers. This is a good way to fight a phenomenon known among software developers as **bloat**: the tendency for a software package to implement extraneous features just for the sake of including them.

Don't Repeat Yourself

Rails supports the principles of **DRY** (Don't Repeat Yourself) programming. When you decide to change the behavior of an application that's based on the DRY principle, you shouldn't need to modify application code in more than one authoritative location.

While this might sound complicated, it's actually quite simple. For example, instead of copying and pasting code with a similar or even identical functionality, you develop your application in such a way that this functionality is stored once, in a central location, and is referenced from each portion of the application that needs to use it. This way, if the original behavior needs to change, you need only make modifications in one location, rather than in various places throughout your application—some of which you could all too easily overlook.

One example of how Rails supports the DRY principle is that, unlike Java, it doesn't force you to repeat your **database schema definition** within your application. A database schema definition describes how the storage of an application's data is structured. Think of it as a number of spreadsheets, each of which contains rows and columns that define the various pieces of data, and identify where each data item is stored. Rails considers your database to be the authoritative source of information about data storage, and is clever enough to ask the database for any information it may need to ensure that it treats your data correctly.

Rails also adheres to the DRY principle when it comes to implementing cutting-edge techniques such as **Ajax** (Asynchronous JavaScript and XML). Ajax is an approach that allows your web application to replace content in the user's browser dynamically, or to exchange form data with the server without reloading the page. Developers often find themselves duplicating code while creating Ajax applications: after all, the web site should function in browsers that *don't* support Ajax, as well as those that do, and the code required to display the results to both types of browser is, for the most part, identical. Rails makes it easy to treat each browser generation appropriately without duplicating any code.

Agile Development

More traditional approaches to software development (such as iterative development and the waterfall model) usually attempt to sketch out a long-running and rather static plan for an application's goals and needs using predictive methods. These development models usually approach applications from the bottom up—that is, by working on the data first.

In contrast, **Agile** development methods use an **adaptive** approach. Small teams, typically consisting of fewer than ten developers, iteratively complete small units of the project. Before starting an iteration, the team reevaluates the priorities for the application that's being built; these priorities may have shifted during the previous iteration, so they may need adjustment. Agile developers also architect their applications from the top down, starting with the design, which may be as simple as a sketch of the interface on a sheet of paper.

When an application is built using Agile methods, it's less likely to veer out of control during the development cycle, thanks to the ongoing efforts of the team to adjust priorities. By spending less time on the creation of functional specifications and long-running schedules, developers using Agile methodologies can really jump-start an application's development.

Here are a few examples that illustrate how Rails lends itself to Agile development practices:

- You can start to work on the layout of your Rails application before making any decisions about data storage (even though these decisions might change at a later stage). You don't have to repeat this layout work when you start adding functionality to your screen designs—everything evolves dynamically with your requirements.

▓ Unlike code written in C or Java, Rails applications don't need to go through a compilation step in order to be executable. Ruby code is interpreted on the fly, so it doesn't need any form of binary compilation to make it executable. Changing code during development provides developers with immediate feedback, which can significantly boost the speed of application development.

▓ Rails provides a comprehensive framework for the automated testing of application code. Developers who make use of this testing framework can be confident that they're not causing functionality to break when they change existing code, even if they weren't the ones who originally developed it.

▓ Refactoring (rewriting code with an emphasis on optimization) existing Rails application code to better cope with changed priorities, or to implement new features for a development project, can be done much more easily when developers adhere to the DRY principles we discussed above. This is because far fewer changes are required when a certain functionality is implemented just once, and is then reused elsewhere as required.

If your head is spinning from trying to digest these principles, don't worry—they'll be reinforced continually throughout this book, as we step through building our very own web application in Ruby on Rails!

Building the Example Web Application

As you read on, I expect you'll be itching to put the techniques we discuss into practice. For this reason, I've planned a fully functional web application that we'll build together through the ensuing chapters. The key concepts, approaches, and methodologies we'll discuss will have a role to play in the sample application, and we'll implement them progressively as your skills improve over the course of this book.

The application we'll build will be a functional clone of the popular story-sharing web site, Digg.[6] I've included all necessary files for this application in this book's code archive.

---

[6] http://www.digg.com/

What Is Digg?

Digg describes itself as follows:[7]

> Digg is a place for people to discover and share content from any-where on the web. From the biggest online destinations to the most obscure blog, Digg surfaces the best stuff as voted on by our users. You won't find editors at Digg—we're here to provide a place where people can collectively determine the value of content and we're changing the way people consume information online.

> How do we do this? Everything on Digg—from news to videos to images to podcasts—is submitted by our community (that would be you). Once something is submitted, other people see it and Digg what they like best. If your submission rocks and receives enough Diggs, it is promoted to the front page for the millions of our visitors to see.

Basically, if you want to tell the world about that interesting article you found on the Internet—be it a weblog post that's right up your street, or a news story from a major publication—you can submit its URL to Digg, along with a short summary of the item. Your story sits in a queue, waiting for other users to **digg** it (give your item a positive vote). As well as voting for a story, users can comment on the story to create often lively discussions within Digg.

As soon as the number of diggs for a story crosses a certain threshold, it's automatically promoted to the Digg homepage, where it attracts a far greater number of readers than the story-queuing area receives. Figure 1.1 shows a snapshot of the Digg homepage.

---

[7] http://digg.com/about/

Figure 1.1. The original digg.com

The Digg Effect

Due to the huge number of visitors that Digg receives, web sites that are listed on the front page may suffer from what is known as the **Digg effect**: the servers of many sites cannot cope with the sudden surge in traffic, and become inaccessible until the number of simultaneous visitors dies down or the hosting company boosts the site's capacity to deal with the increase in traffic.

Digg was launched in December 2004, and has since been listed in the Alexa traffic rankings as one of the Internet's top 200 web sites.[8]

I didn't decide to show you how to develop your own Digg clone just because the site is popular with Internet users, though; Digg's feature set is not particularly complicated, but it's sufficient to allow us to gain firsthand experience with the most important and useful facets of the Ruby on Rails framework.

And while your application might not be able to compete with the original site, reusing this sample project to share links within your family, company, or college

---

[8] http://www.alexa.com/data/details/traffic_details/digg.com

class is perfectly conceivable. Also, with any luck you'll learn enough along the way to branch out and build other types of applications as well.

Features of the Example Application

As I mentioned, we want our application to accept user-submitted links to stories on the Web. We also want to allow other users to vote on the submitted items. In order to meet these objectives, we'll implement the following features as we work through this book:

- We'll build a database back end that permanently stores every story, user, vote, and so on. This way, nothing is lost when you close your browser and shut the application down.

- We'll build a story submission interface, which is a form that's available only to users who have registered and logged in.

- We'll develop a simplistic layout, as is typical for Web 2.0 applications. We'll style it with Cascading Style Sheets (CSS) and enhance it with visual effects.

- We'll create clean URLs for all the pages on our site. **Clean URLs** (also known as search engine-friendly URLs) are usually brief and easily read when they appear in the browser status bar. An example of a clean URL is http://del.icio.us/popular/software, which I'm sure you'll agree is a lot nicer than http://www.amazon.com/gp/homepage.html/103-0615814-1415024/.

- We'll create a user registration system that allows users to log in with their usernames and passwords.

- We'll create two different views for stories: the homepage of our application, and the story queue containing stories that haven't yet received enough votes to appear on the homepage.

- We'll give users the ability to check voting history on per-user and per-story bases.

- We'll facilitate the tagging of stories, and give users the ability to view only those stories that relate to **programming** or **food**, for example. For a definition of tagging, see the note below.

It's quite a list, and the result will be one slick web application! Some of the features rely upon others being in place, and we'll implement each feature as a practical example when we look at successive aspects of Rails.

What is Tagging?

Tagging can be thought of as a free-form categorization method. Instead of the site's owners creating a fixed content categorization scheme (often represented as a tree), users are allowed to enter one or more keywords to describe a content item. Resources that share one or more identical tags can be linked together easily—the more overlap between tags, the more characteristics the resources are likely to have in common.

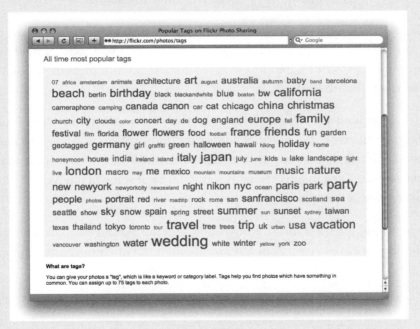

Figure 1.2. Tags on flickr.com

Instead of displaying a hierarchical category tree, the tags used in an application are commonly displayed as a **tag cloud** in which each of the tags is represented in a font size that corresponds to how often that tag has been applied to content items within the system.

Tags are used extensively on sites such as the Flickr photo-sharing web site[9] shown in Figure 1.2, the del.icio.us bookmark-sharing site,[10] and the Technorati weblog search engine.[11]

Summary

We've explored a bit of history in this chapter. Along the way, we learned where both the Ruby language and the Rails framework have come from, and looked in some detail at the niche that followers of the Ruby on Rails philosophy have carved out for themselves in the web development world. I also explained the philosophy behind the Ruby programming language and showed you a snippet of Ruby code. We'll cover much more of Ruby's inner workings in Chapter 3.

We also talked briefly about some of the basic principles that drive Rails development, and saw how Rails supports Agile development methods. Now that you're aware of the possibilities, perhaps some of these ideas and principles will influence your own work with Rails.

Finally, we created a brief specification for the web application we're going to build throughout this book. We described what our application will do, and identified the list of features that we're going to implement. We'll develop a clone of the story-sharing web site Digg iteratively, taking advantage of some of the Agile development practices that Rails supports.

In the next chapter, we'll install Ruby, Rails, and the SQLite database server software in order to set up a development environment for the upcoming development tasks.

Are you ready to join in the fun? If so, turn the page …

---

[9] http://flickr.com/
[10] http://del.icio.us/
[11] http://www.technorati.com/

Getting Started

To get started with Ruby on Rails, we first need to install some development software on our systems. The packages we'll be installing are:

the Ruby language interpreter

The Ruby interpreter translates our Ruby code (or any Ruby code, for that matter, including Rails itself) into a form the computer can understand and execute. At the time of writing, Ruby 1.8.6 is recommended for use with Rails, so that's what I've used here.

the Ruby on Rails framework

Once we've downloaded Ruby, we can install the Rails framework itself. As I mentioned in Chapter 1, Rails is written in Ruby. At the time of writing, version 2.0.2 was the most recent stable version of the framework.

the SQLite database engine

The SQLite database engine is a self-contained software library which provides an SQL database without actually running a separate server process. While Rails supports plenty of other database servers (MySQL, PostgreSQL, Microsoft SQL Server, and Oracle, to name a few), SQLite is easy to install and does not require any configuration, and is the default database for which a new Rails application is configured straight out of the box. Oh, and it's free!

At the time of writing, the most recent stable release of the SQLite database was version 3.5.4.

Instructions for installing Rails differ ever so slightly between operating systems. You may also need to install some additional tools as part of the process, depending on the platform you use. Here, I'll provide installation instructions for Windows, Mac OS X, and Linux.

 Watch Your Version Numbers!

It's possible that by the time you read this, a more recent version of Ruby, SQLite, or one of the other packages mentioned here will have been released. Beware! Don't just assume that because a package is newer, it can reliably be used for Rails development. While, in theory, every version should be compatible and these instructions should still apply, sometimes the latest is *not* the greatest.

In fact, the Rails framework itself also has a reputation for experiencing large changes between releases, such as specific methods or attributes being deprecated. While every effort has been made to ensure the code in this book is future-proof, there's no guarantee that changes included in future major releases of Rails won't require this code to be modified in some way for it to work. Such is the fast-paced world of web development!

Feel free to skip the sections relevant to operating systems other than yours, and to focus on those that address your specific needs.

What Does All This Cost?

Everything we need is available for download from the Web, and is licensed under free software licenses. This basically means that everything you'll be installing is free for you to use in both personal and commercial applications. If you're curious about the differences between each license, you can check out each package's individual license file, which is included in its download.

Installing on Windows

For some reason, Windows has the easiest install procedure. A very helpful programmer by the name of Curt Hibbs sat down and packaged everything required to develop Rails applications on a Windows machine. He constructed the package as an easy-to-install, easy-to-run, single file download called Instant Rails and released version 1.0 in early 2006. When Rails 2.0 was released in late 2007, maintenance of Instant Rails was taken over by Rob Bazinet, and nowadays consists of the following components:

- the Ruby interpreter
- the SQLite and MySQL database engines
- the Apache web server (although we won't be using it in this book)
- Ruby on Rails

That's everything we need in one handy package. How convenient!

To install Instant Rails, download the latest Instant Rails zip archive from the Instant Rails project file list[1] on RubyForge and extract its contents to a folder of your choice.

 Time Flies

> The version of Instant Rails used to test the code in this book was 2.0. As discussed earlier in the chapter, due to the fast-changing nature of the framework, I can't guarantee that later versions will work.

Be careful, though; Instant Rails doesn't support folders with names that contain spaces; unfortunately, this means that the obvious choice of **C:\Program Files** is not a good one. I recommend choosing **C:\InstantRails** instead.

After you've extracted the **.zip** file (it has approximately 18,000 items in packaged documentation, so if you're using the Windows built-in file compression tool, it could take quite some time to unzip them all), navigate to the **InstantRails** folder and double-click the **InstantRails.exe** file. You'll be prompted with a dialog like the one shown in Figure 2.1; click **OK** to continue.

---

[1] http://rubyforge.org/frs/?group_id=904

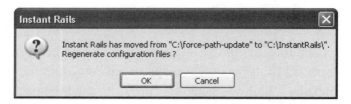

Figure 2.1. Configuring Instant Rails doesn't get much easier ...

If you're on Windows XP Service Pack 2 or later, you'll also be greeted with the alert message in Figure 2.2 from the Windows internal firewall (or any additional personal firewall software that you might have installed). Of course, the Apache web server isn't trying to do anything malicious—Instant Rails just fires it up as part of its initialization process. Go ahead and click **Unblock** to allow it to start.

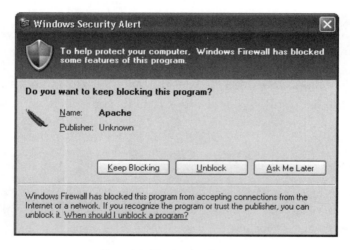

Figure 2.2. Allowing Apache to run

You should now see the Instant Rails control panel, which, as Figure 2.3 illustrates, should report that everything has started up successfully.

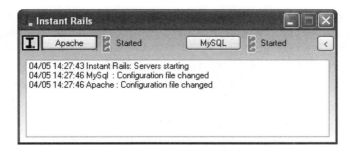

Figure 2.3. The Instant Rails control panel

Next, you'll need to update the version of RubyGems that comes with Instant Rails. Click on the **I** button in the top-left of the control panel. From the menu that appears, select **Rails Applications > Open Ruby Console Window**. Once the console opens, enter the following command:

```
C:\InstantRails\rails_apps> gem update --system
```

The final step is to update Rails. The following command, entered in the Ruby Console you opened previously, should do the trick:

```
C:\InstantRail\rails_apps> gem update
```

That's it! Everything you need is installed and configured. Feel free to skip the instructions for Mac and Linux, and start building your application!

Installing on Mac OS X

Okay, so the Windows guys had it easy. Unfortunately, life isn't quite so simple for the rest of us, at least as far as Rails installation is concerned. While Mac OS X isn't usually a platform that makes things tricky, installing Rails is just a tad harder than installing a regular Mac application.

Lose the Locomotive

There was an all-in-one installer available for Mac OS X 10.4 and earlier, called Locomotive (http://locomotive.raaum.org/). Unfortunately, it's no longer maintained by its creator, Ryan Raaum. For this reason, I don't recommend that you use Locomotive to work through this book.

Mac OS X 10.5 (Leopard)

If your Mac is a relatively recent purchase, you may be running OS X version 10.5 (Leopard) or later. If this is the case, you've got much less to do, because your machine comes preinstalled with both Ruby *and* Rails—congratulations! All you'll need to do is update your Rails installation, but we'll worry about that when we reach that step in the Rails installation instructions for Mac OS X 10.4—you'll see that it's very easy.

Of course, it wouldn't do you any harm to read through all of the steps below anyway, just to make sure that you're familiar with the software components and concepts that are introduced; for example, the Mac OS X Terminal, the command line interface, and RubyGems.

Mac OS X 10.4 (Tiger) and Earlier

"But wait!" I hear you cry. "My slightly older Mac comes with Ruby preinstalled!" Yes, that may indeed be true. However, the version of Ruby that shipped with OS X prior to version 10.5 is a slimmed-down version that's incompatible with Rails, and is therefore unsuited to our needs. While there are packages out there that make the installation of Ruby easier, such as MacPorts,[2] for the sake of completeness, I'll show you how to build Ruby on your machine from scratch.[3] Don't worry. It may sound intimidating, but it's actually relatively painless—and you'll only need to do it once!

Let's start installing then, shall we?

Installing Xcode

The first step in the process is to make sure we have everything we need for the installation to go smoothly. The only prerequisite for this process is Xcode, the Apple Developer Tools that come on a separate CD with Mac OS X. If you haven't

---

[2] http://www.macports.org/

[3] A tip of the hat is in order for Dan Benjamin, who did a lot of the heavy lifting in the early days of documenting the installation of Rails on OS X. Parts of these installation instructions are heavily influenced by his article "Building Ruby, Rails, Subversion, Mongrel, and MySQL on Mac OS X". [http://hivelogic.com/articles/ruby-rails-mongrel-mysql-osx/]

installed the tools yet, and don't have your installation CD handy, you can download the Xcode package for free[4] (although at more than 900MB, it's a hefty download!).

To install Xcode, run the packaged installer by clicking on the **XcodeTools.mpkg** icon and following the on-screen instructions illustrated in Figure 2.4. The installation tool is a simple wizard that will require you to click **Continue** a few times, agree to some fairly standard terms and conditions, and hit the **Install** button.

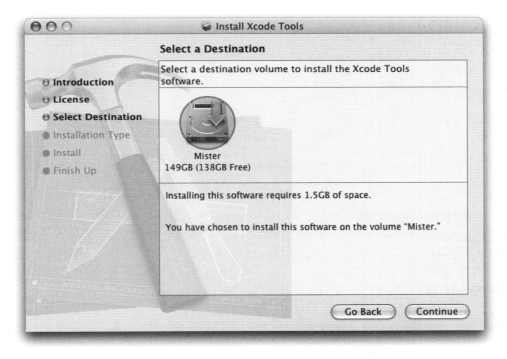

Figure 2.4. Installing the Xcode developer tools

Introducing the Command Line

For the next few steps, we're going to leave the comfort and security of our pretty graphical user interface and tackle the much geekier UNIX command line. If this is the first time you've used the command line on your Mac, don't worry—we'll be using it often as we work through this book, so you'll have plenty of practice! Let's dive in.

---

[4] http://developer.apple.com/

First, open up a UNIX session in OS X using the Terminal utility. Launch Terminal by selecting **Go** > **Utilities** from the Finder menu bar, and double-clicking the **Terminal** icon. Your Terminal window should look a lot like Figure 2.5.

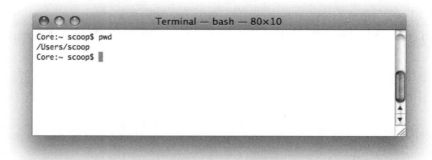

Figure 2.5. A Terminal window on Mac OS X

Let's dissect these crazy command line shenanigans. The collection of characters to the left of the cursor is called the **prompt**. By default, it displays:

- the name of your Mac
- the current directory
- the name of the user who's currently logged in

In my case, this is:

```
Core:~ scoop$
```

So, what's what here?

- `Core` is the name of my Mac.
- `scoop` is the name of the user who's currently logged in.

But what on earth is *this* character: ~? It's called a **tilde**, and it's shorthand notation for the path to the current user's home directory. Take another look at Figure 2.5, and you'll see I've used the pwd command to *p*rint the *w*orking *d*irectory. The result is **/Users/scoop**, which just happens to be my home directory. For future command line instructions, though, I'll simply display the prompt as: $, to avoid occupying valuable real estate on the page.

Setting the Path

Next, we need to make sure that Mac OS X can locate all the command line tools that we'll be using during this installation. The PATH environment variable stores the list of folders to which OS X has access; we'll store the changes we make to this variable in a file in our home directory.

The name of the file we'll use is **.profile**. (On UNIX-based systems such as Mac OS X, files that start with a period are usually hidden files.) If you type out the following command exactly, your PATH environment variable will be set correctly every time you open a new Terminal window:

```
$ echo 'export PATH="/usr/local/bin:/usr/local/sbin:$PATH"' >>
    ~/.profile
```

To activate this change (without having to open and close the Terminal window), type the following command:

```
$ . ~/.profile
```

Yes, that's a single period at the beginning of the line. Note that these commands don't produce any feedback, as Figure 2.6 shows, but they're still taking effect.

Figure 2.6. Setting the correct path

It would be a shame to clutter up this home directory—or our desktop—with a huge number of files, so let's go about this installation business in an organized fashion.

Staying Organized

The process of extracting, configuring, and compiling the source code for all the packages that we'll be downloading will take up a reasonable amount of space on your hard drive. Let's keep things organized and operate within a single folder rather than making a mess of the desktop.

The desktop on your Mac is actually a subfolder of your home directory. Change to the **Desktop** folder using the cd command (short for *change directory*). Once you're there, you can use mkdir to *make* a *directory* in which to store our downloads and other assorted files. Let's call this directory **build**:

```
$ cd Desktop
$ mkdir build
$ cd build
```

The result is that we have on the desktop a new directory, which is now our current working directory. This is also reflected by our prompt. As Figure 2.7 shows, mine now reads:

```
Core:build scoop$
```

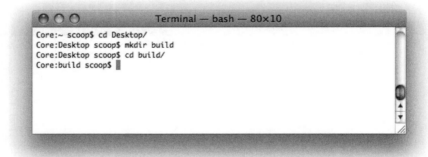

Figure 2.7. Creating a temporary working directory

Now the fun begins!

Installing Ruby on a Mac

Before installing Ruby itself, we need to install another library on which Ruby depends: Readline.

Here's the sequence of slightly convoluted commands for installing the Readline library. It's a fairly small library, so the installation shouldn't take long:

```
$ curl ftp://ftp.gnu.org/gnu/readline/readline-5.2.tar.gz
➥ | tar xz
$ cd readline-5.2
$ ./configure --prefix=/usr/local
$ make
$ sudo make install
$ cd ..
```

With Readline in place, we're now able to install Ruby itself. This step may test your patience a bit, as the configuration step could take half an hour or more to complete, depending on the speed of your system and your network connection. Type out the following series of commands, *exactly* as you see them here (it's not important that you understand every line, but it is important that you don't make any typos):

```
$ curl ftp://ftp.ruby-lang.org/pub/ruby/1.8/
➥ruby-1.8.6.tar.gz | tar xz
$ cd ruby-1.8.6
$ ./configure --prefix=/usr/local --enable-pthread
➥ --with-readline-dir=/usr/local
$ make
$ sudo make install
$ sudo make install-doc
$ cd ..
```

How did you do? It's wise to run some checks at this point, to determine whether our installation is on track so far. The simplest and safest way to ascertain whether our Ruby installation is working is to type the following command into the Terminal window:

```
$ ruby -v
```

The version displayed should match that which you downloaded—in my case, `ruby 1.8.6 (2007-09-24 patchlevel 111)`, as shown in Figure 2.8. If anything else is displayed here (such as `ruby 1.8.2 (2004-12-25)`), something's gone wrong. You should carefully repeat the instructions up to this point.

A Friend in Need's a Friend Indeed

Remember—if you get really stuck, you can always try asking for help on Site-Point's Ruby forum.[5]

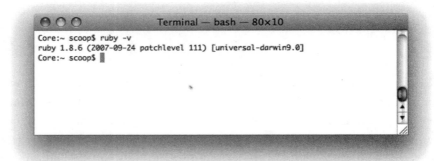

Figure 2.8. Checking the Ruby version

Be a Super User for a Day

`sudo` is a way for "regular" computer users to perform system-wide installations that are normally reserved for system administrators. You'll need to enter your account password before you'll be allowed to execute this command. To use `sudo`, the user account must have the **Allow user to administer this computer** setting checked. This can be changed in the **Accounts** section of the Apple **System Preferences** window.

Next up, we have the installation of RubyGems.

Installing RubyGems on a Mac

"What is this RubyGems?" I hear you ask. RubyGems is a utility for managing the additions to the Ruby programming language that other people have developed and

---

[5] http://www.sitepoint.com/launch/rubyforum/

made available as free downloads. Think of it as prepackaged functionality that you can install on your machine so you don't have to reinvent the wheel over and over again while you're working on your own projects.[6] Rails is released and published through the RubyGems system.

The following sequence of commands will download and install RubyGems on your Mac. It should be a relatively quick procedure:

```
$ curl -L http://rubyforge.org/frs/download.php/29548/
➥rubygems-1.0.1.tgz | tar xz
$ cd rubygems-1.0.1
$ sudo ruby setup.rb
$ cd ..
```

Are you getting the hang of this command line thing? Good! We now have *another* new command at our fingertips: gem. The gem command is used to install and manage Ruby packages on your machine—enter the following to check that Ruby-Gems is working properly:

```
$ gem -v
```

The output should identify the version of RubyGems that you installed, as Figure 2.9 shows. We'll use the gem command to install Rails.

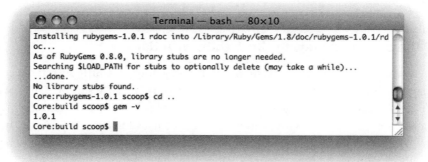

Figure 2.9. Confirmation of a successful RubyGems installation

---

[6] The RubyGems web site [http://gems.rubyforge.org/] has additional documentation for the gem command that we'll use in this section.

Updating RubyGems

RubyGems is constantly being developed and improved, and new versions are released frequently. If you ever need to update RubyGems—for compatibility reasons, for example—simply enter the following command into a terminal window:

```
$ sudo gem update --system
```

Installing Rails on a Mac

Whew! After several pages of installation instructions, we're finally here: the installation of the Rails framework. Don't underestimate the importance of the work you've already done, though. Plus, you'll now have an easy upgrade path the next time a new version of Ruby or Rails is released (which I'll explain later).

Without further ado, enter this command to install Rails:

```
$ sudo gem install rails
```

This command prompts the RubyGems system to download Rails and the packages on which it depends, before installing the necessary files and documentation. This process may take ten minutes or more to complete, so it's a good time to grab yourself a coffee.

The Secret of Staying Up to Date with Rails

While you're waiting for Rails to install, I'll let you in on a little secret: the command we just entered is the very same one that you can use to stay up to date with future Rails releases. Whenever you want to upgrade Rails, just enter that command again, and your system will be updated. Very cool, as I'm sure you'll agree. In fact, if you're running the above command on Mac OS X 10.5, that's exactly what you'll be doing: upgrading your existing Rails installation.

Once the installation has finished, you can verify the version of Rails you just installed by running the following command in your Terminal window:

```
$ rails -v
```

Taking this small step should reward you with the version number of Rails, as illustrated in Figure 2.10.

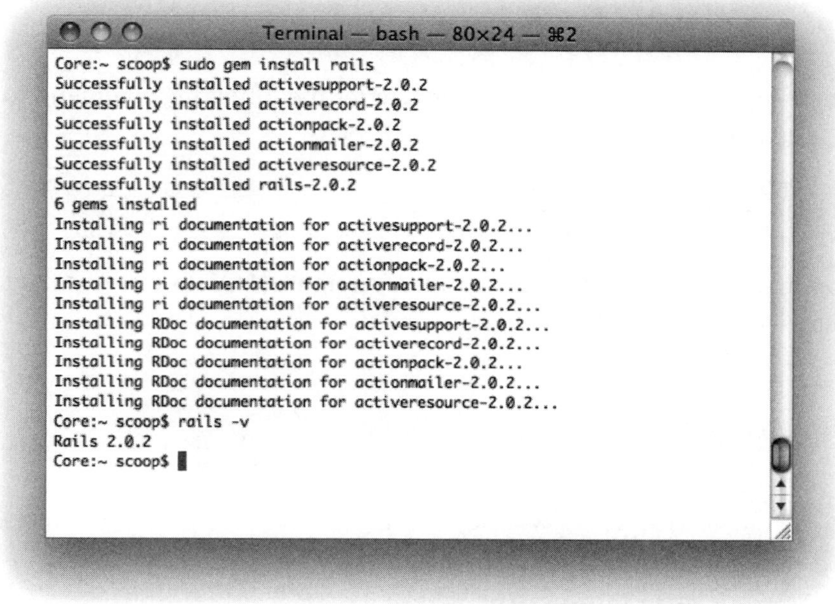

```
Core:~ scoop$ sudo gem install rails
Successfully installed activesupport-2.0.2
Successfully installed activerecord-2.0.2
Successfully installed actionpack-2.0.2
Successfully installed actionmailer-2.0.2
Successfully installed activeresource-2.0.2
Successfully installed rails-2.0.2
6 gems installed
Installing ri documentation for activesupport-2.0.2...
Installing ri documentation for activerecord-2.0.2...
Installing ri documentation for actionpack-2.0.2...
Installing ri documentation for actionmailer-2.0.2...
Installing ri documentation for activeresource-2.0.2...
Installing RDoc documentation for activesupport-2.0.2...
Installing RDoc documentation for activerecord-2.0.2...
Installing RDoc documentation for actionpack-2.0.2...
Installing RDoc documentation for actionmailer-2.0.2...
Installing RDoc documentation for activeresource-2.0.2...
Core:~ scoop$ rails -v
Rails 2.0.2
Core:~ scoop$
```

Figure 2.10. Installing Rails on Mac OS X via RubyGems

I told you we'd get there in the end. Don't break out the champagne just yet, though—we still need a database!

Installing SQLite on a Mac

The last thing we need to do is install the storage container that's going to house the data we (or our users) enter through our application's web interface, the SQLite database engine.

As mentioned in the introductory paragraph, SQLite is a self-contained, serverless database engine. As such, there's not much more to it than the actual download and compilation steps. You don't need to mess with startup scripts or configuration files. It all just works!

```
$ curl http://www.sqlite.org/sqlite-3.5.4.tar.gz | tar zx
$ cd sqlite-3.5.4
$ ./configure --prefix=/usr/local
$ make
$ sudo make install
```

After the installation has been completed, enter the following command to make sure SQLite has been properly installed:

```
$ sqlite3 --version
```

This command should come back with the version of SQLite you installed—3.5.4 in my case—as shown in Figure 2.11.

Figure 2.11. Installing SQLite on Mac OS X

Installing the SQLite Database Interface for Ruby

Lastly, we need to install a tiny little module which will allow Ruby to talk to SQLite databases. We'll use the RubyGems system we prepared earlier, which means that the installation boils down to just a single command:

```
$ sudo gem install sqlite3-ruby
```

Running this command should yield the result shown in Figure 2.12.

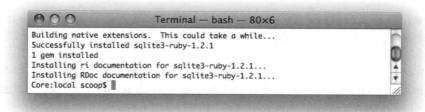

Figure 2.12. Installing the SQLite database interface for Ruby

Congratulations, Mac users, you're all done!

Installing on Linux

I bet you Linux people smirked when the Mac OS X guys had to use the command line (possibly for the first time), didn't you?

Well, if you're running Linux, I'll assume that you're used to the command line, so I won't feel bad throwing you an archaic series of commands to install all the software you need to be up and running with Rails.

One Size Fits All?

There are literally thousands of different distributions of Linux—more than any other operating system. Each distribution has its own quirks and pitfalls, its own package manager, and different permissions settings, and installations are often tweaked and customized over time. So while I've put every effort into ensuring that these instructions are sound, it would be impossible to offer an absolute guarantee that they'll work on any possible installation of Linux without individual tweaking.

If you do run into any problems installing Rails or its constituents on your machine, I recommend you ask for assistance on the friendly SitePoint Ruby forum.[7] Chances are that someone else has experienced the same problem, and will be happy to help you out.

---

[7] http://www.sitepoint.com/launch/rubyforum/

Using a Package Manager

As I mentioned, many Linux distributions come with their own package managers, including `apt-get` , `yum`, and `rpm`, among others.

Of course, you're free to use the package manager that's bundled with your Linux distribution to install Ruby, and if you become stuck with the instructions given here for whatever reason, that may be a good option for you.

Rather than attempt to cover all the different package managers available, I'll show you how to install Ruby the manual way.

Prerequisites

The only prerequisite for installing Ruby on Linux is that you have the `gcc` compiler installed on your machine. `gcc` ships with most Linux distributions by default, but if it's not on your system, you'll either need to use your system's package management system to install it (look for "build essential" or "basic compiler"), or to download a native binary for your system.[8]

Enter the following instructions at the command line to confirm that your compiler is in place:

```
$ gcc -v
```

If the version number for the compiler is displayed, as shown in Figure 2.13, you're ready to install Ruby.

---

[8] http://gcc.gnu.org/install/binaries.html

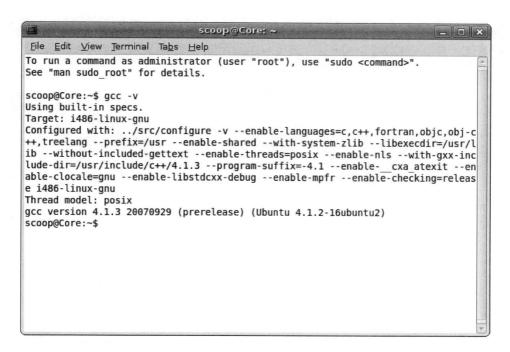

Figure 2.13. Confirming the gcc compiler is installed

Installing Ruby on Linux

Ruby is available for download from the Ruby ftp site.[9] As mentioned at the outset of this chapter, I recommend the use of version 1.8.6 of the Ruby interpreter.

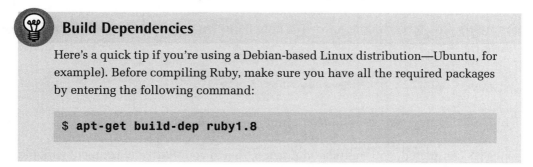

Build Dependencies

Here's a quick tip if you're using a Debian-based Linux distribution—Ubuntu, for example). Before compiling Ruby, make sure you have all the required packages by entering the following command:

```
$ apt-get build-dep ruby1.8
```

Download the appropriate **tar** file for Ruby (this will be named something like **ruby-1.8.6.tar.gz**), and extract the archive using the gunzip and tar commands:

---

[9] ftp://ftp.ruby-lang.org/pub/ruby/1.8/ruby-1.8.6.tar.gz

```
$ gunzip ruby-1.8.6.tar.gz
$ tar xvf ruby-1.8.6.tar
$ cd ruby-1.8.6
```

Then change into the new directory that was created, as illustrated in Figure 2.14.

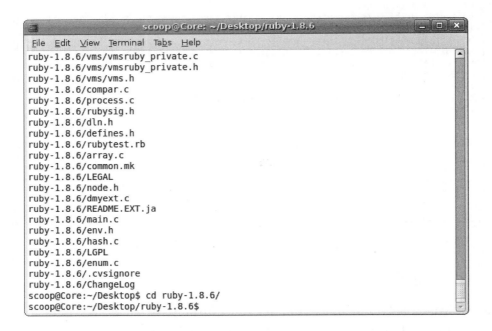

Figure 2.14. Extracting the Ruby archive on Linux

From this directory, run the following command to compile and install Ruby in **/usr/local**:

```
$ ./configure && make && sudo make install
```

This process may take 20 minutes or more, so be patient.

Once it's completed, you should add **/usr/local/bin** to your PATH environment variable. I'll assume that, being a Linux user, you know how to do that. Once that environment variable is set, you can enter the following command to check which version of Ruby you installed:

```
$ ruby -v
```

The message displayed should confirm that you're running version 1.8.6, as Figure 2.15 illustrates.

```
scoop@Core: ~/Desktop/ruby-1.8.6                              _ □ ×

File  Edit  View  Terminal  Tabs  Help
hread.so thread.o  -ldl -lcrypt -lm   -lc
cp ../.././ext/thread/lib/thread.rb ../.././ext/common
make[1]: Leaving directory `/home/scoop/Desktop/ruby-1.8.6/ext/thread'
compiling tk
compiling tk/tkutil
compiling win32ole
compiling zlib
making ruby
make[1]: Entering directory `/home/scoop/Desktop/ruby-1.8.6'
gcc -g -O2  -DRUBY_EXPORT   -rdynamic -Wl,-export-dynamic -L.   main.o  -lruby-s
tatic -ldl -lcrypt -lm   -o ruby
make[1]: Leaving directory `/home/scoop/Desktop/ruby-1.8.6'
./miniruby  ./instruby.rb --dest-dir="" --extout=".ext" --make="make" --mflags="
" --make-flags="" --installed-list .installed.list --mantype="doc"
installing binary commands
installing command scripts
installing library scripts
installing headers
installing manpages
installing extension objects
installing extension scripts
scoop@Core:~/Desktop/ruby-1.8.6$ ruby -v
ruby 1.8.6 (2007-03-13 patchlevel 0) [i686-linux]
scoop@Core:~/Desktop/ruby-1.8.6$ █
```

Figure 2.15. Installing Ruby on Linux

Now, on to the next step: installing RubyGems.

Installing RubyGems on Linux

Next up is the installation of RubyGems, the package manager for Ruby-related software. RubyGems works much like the package manager that your operating system uses to manage the various Linux utilities installed on your machine. RubyGems makes it easy to install all sorts of additional software and extensions for Ruby.

RubyGems is available for download from http://rubyforge.org/projects/rubygems/. Once you've downloaded and extracted it, change to the **rubygems** directory and run the following command:

```
$ sudo ruby setup.rb
```

This will set up and install RubyGems for use on your system, and also make the gem command available for you to use—the gem command is what we'll use to install Rails itself. It shouldn't take long, and once it completes, you can execute the gem command to confirm that your installation was successful. The output should look like that shown in Figure 2.16.

```
scoop@Core: ~/Desktop/rubygems-1.0.1

File  Edit  View  Terminal  Tabs  Help
install -c -m 0644 rubygems/package.rb /usr/local/lib/ruby/site_ruby/1.8/rubygem
s/package.rb
install -c -m 0644 rubygems/source_index.rb /usr/local/lib/ruby/site_ruby/1.8/ru
bygems/source_index.rb
install -c -m 0644 rubygems/open-uri.rb /usr/local/lib/ruby/site_ruby/1.8/rubyge
ms/open-uri.rb
cp gem /tmp/gem
install -c -m 0755 /tmp/gem /usr/local/bin/gem
rm /tmp/gem
cp update_rubygems /tmp/update_rubygems
install -c -m 0755 /tmp/update_rubygems /usr/local/bin/update_rubygems
rm /tmp/update_rubygems
Removing old RubyGems RDoc and ri...
Installing rubygems-1.0.1 ri into /usr/local/lib/ruby/gems/1.8/doc/rubygems-1.0.
1/ri...
Installing rubygems-1.0.1 rdoc into /usr/local/lib/ruby/gems/1.8/doc/rubygems-1.
0.1/rdoc...
As of RubyGems 0.8.0, library stubs are no longer needed.
Searching $LOAD_PATH for stubs to optionally delete (may take a while)...
...done.
No library stubs found.
scoop@Core:~/Desktop/rubygems-1.0.1$ gem -v
1.0.1
scoop@Core:~/Desktop/rubygems-1.0.1$ 
```

Figure 2.16. Installing RubyGems on Linux

We have successfully installed RubyGems. Now we can finally install the Rails framework!

 Updating RubyGems

RubyGems is constantly being developed and improved, and new versions are released frequently. If you ever need to update RubyGems—for compatibility reasons, for example—simply enter the following at the command line:

```
$ sudo gem update --system
```

Installing Rails on Linux

Using RubyGems, the installation of Rails itself is a breeze. To install Rails, type the following input at the command prompt as the `root` user (or using `sudo` if it's installed on your system):

```
$ sudo gem install rails
```

The process may take ten minutes or so, depending on the speed of your Internet connection, but that's all you need to do! And as an added bonus, RubyGems gives us an easy way to stay up to date with future Rails releases—whenever we want to upgrade Rails, we just need to type this command!

To confirm that your Rails installation was successful, type the following command to display the version of Rails that was installed:

```
$ rails -v
```

The result that you see should be the same as that shown in Figure 2.17.

```
scoop@Core: ~
File  Edit  View  Terminal  Tabs  Help
Bulk updating Gem source index for: http://gems.rubyforge.org
Successfully installed rake-0.8.1
Successfully installed activesupport-2.0.2
Successfully installed activerecord-2.0.2
Successfully installed actionpack-2.0.2
Successfully installed actionmailer-2.0.2
Successfully installed activeresource-2.0.2
Successfully installed rails-2.0.2
7 gems installed
Installing ri documentation for rake-0.8.1...
Installing ri documentation for activesupport-2.0.2...
Installing ri documentation for activerecord-2.0.2...
Installing ri documentation for actionpack-2.0.2...
Installing ri documentation for actionmailer-2.0.2...
Installing ri documentation for activeresource-2.0.2...
Installing RDoc documentation for rake-0.8.1...
Installing RDoc documentation for activesupport-2.0.2...
Installing RDoc documentation for activerecord-2.0.2...
Installing RDoc documentation for actionpack-2.0.2...
Installing RDoc documentation for actionmailer-2.0.2...
Installing RDoc documentation for activeresource-2.0.2...
scoop@Core:~$ rails -v
Rails 2.0.2
scoop@Core:~$ █
```

Figure 2.17. Installing Rails via RubyGems on Linux

All that's left now is to install a database—then we can get to work!

Installing SQLite on Linux

Most modern Linux distributions may or may not come packaged with a (more or less) recent version of SQLite and you're free to use that. It is crucial, however, that you're installing SQLite 3.x (as opposed to SQLite 2.x).

In case your Linux distribution doesn't ship with a prepackaged version of SQLite, follow the simple installation instructions found below.

SQLite is available for download from http://www.sqlite.org/download.html. The rest of these instructions assume you download the source tarball. As of this writing, the most recent version of SQLite available was 3.5.4.

Once you have the file, it's time to extract and compile it using the following batch of commands:

```
$ tar zxvf sqlite-3.5.4.tar.gz
$ cd sqlite-3.5.4
$ ./configure --prefix=/usr/local
$ make
$ sudo make install
```

At this point you have successfully installed SQLite on your Linux system. To confirm that, the following command will print out the version of SQLite that you downloaded and installed:

```
$ sqlite3 --version
```

Assuming that you have the directory /usr/local/bin in your operating system PATH, Figure 2.18 shows the desired output.

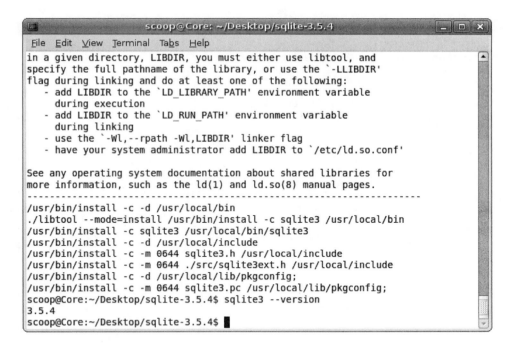

Figure 2.18. Confirming the successful installation of SQLite

Installing the SQLite Database Interface for Ruby

Lastly, we need to install a tiny little module that allows Ruby to talk to SQLite databases. To do so, we'll use the RubyGems system we've installed earlier. Because of that, the installation boils down to a single command only:

```
$ sudo gem install sqlite3-ruby
```

Figure 2.19 shows the desired result.

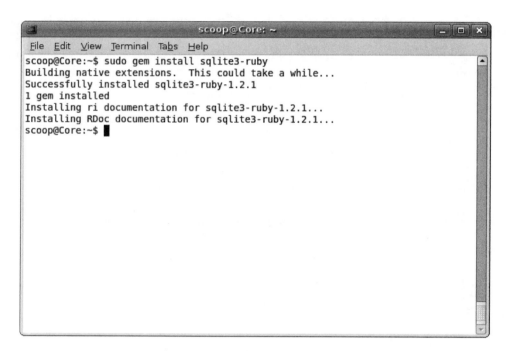

Figure 2.19. Installing the SQLite Ruby interface

Congratulations, now you're all done!

Building a Foundation

Is everyone prepared? Good! Now that you've put your workstation on Rails, let's do something with it. In this section, we'll build the foundations of the application that we'll develop throughout the rest of this book.

One Directory Structure to Rule Them All

In Chapter 1, I mentioned that Rails applications follow certain conventions. One of these conventions is that an application written in Rails always has the same directory structure—one in which every file has its designated place. By gently forcing this directory structure upon developers, Rails ensures that your work is semi-automatically organized the Rails way.

Figure 2.20 shows what the structure looks like. We'll create this directory structure for our application in just a moment.

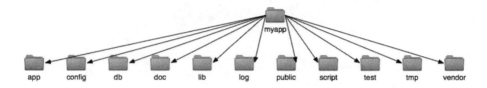

Figure 2.20. The default directory structure for a Rails application

As you can see, this standard directory structure consists of quite a few subdirectories (and I'm not even showing *their* subdirectories yet!). This wealth of subdirectories can be overwhelming at first, but we'll explore them one by one. A lot of thought has gone into establishing and naming the folders, and the result is an application with a well structured file system.

Before you go and manually create all these directories yourself, let me show you how to set up that pretty directory structure using just one command—I told you that Rails allows us to do *less* typing!

Creating the Standard Directory Structure

It's easy to generate the default directory structure shown in Figure 2.20 for a new Rails application using the `rails` command.

Before we start, I'd like to introduce you to the secret, under-the-hood project name we'll give to our digg clone: *Shovell*. Yes, it's cheeky, but it'll work.

Now, let's go ahead and create the directory structure to hold our application.

 A Regular Console Window Just Won't Do!

If you're a Windows user, you might be tempted to fire up a regular DOS console for your command line work. This won't work at all, I'm afraid.

Instead, launch a Ruby console by starting Instant Rails, then clicking on the I button at the top-left corner of the control panel. From the menu that appears, select **Rails Applications > Open Ruby Console Window**, as pictured in Figure 2.21.

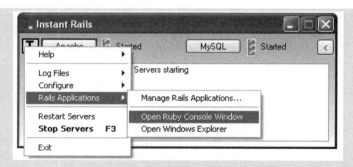

Figure 2.21. Launching a console window from Instant Rails

The Ruby console must be used, because Instant Rails doesn't modify anything in your regular Windows environment when it installs. Launching a console from the Instant Rails control panel ensures that your console will be loaded with all the environment settings that Rails needs. The Windows Ruby console is depicted in Figure 2.22.

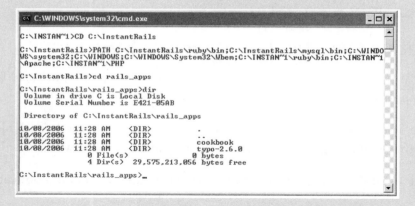

Figure 2.22. The Ruby Console under Windows

The `rails` command takes a single parameter: the directory where you'd like to store your application. You can, and are encouraged to, execute it from the parent directory in which you want your new Rails application to live. I'll do this right in my home directory:

```
$ rails shovell
create
create app/controllers
create app/helpers
```

```
create app/models
create app/views/layouts
create config/environments
create config/initializers
create db
create doc
create lib
create lib/tasks
create log
: log entries...
```

Congratulations, your directory structure has been created!

Starting Our Application

Even before we write any code, it's possible to start up our application environment to check that our setup is working correctly. This exercise should give us a nice boost of confidence before we progress any further.

What we'll do is launch **Mongrel**, a fast, stand-alone HTTP library and web server for Ruby. Mongrel is included with the Ruby installation that we stepped through earlier in this chapter, so it's installed on our machine and ready to use.

In previous versions of Rails the default built-in web server was WEBrick. WEBrick is still included with Rails and can be used instead of Mongrel if desired (the Mongrel output below tells you how). For our purposes, however, Mongrel will do just fine.

WEBrick or Mongrel?

If you installed Rails on Mac OS X 10.4 or Linux, you may find WEBrick is still your default web server. This is fine; there's no pressing reason to use Mongrel. If you'd like to install it anyway, you can do so via the command: `sudo gem install mongrel`.

To start up Mongrel—and the rest of the Rails environment for our application—we return once again to the command line. Change into the **Shovell** subdirectory that was created when we executed the `rails` command in the previous section. From the **shovell** directory, enter the command `ruby script/server`.

This command will fire up the Mongrel web server, which will then begin to listen for requests on TCP port 3000 of your local machine:

```
$ cd shovell
$ ruby script/server
ruby script/server
=> Booting Mongrel (use 'script/server webrick' to force WEBrick)
=> Rails application starting on http://0.0.0.0:3000
=> Call with -d to detach
=> Ctrl-C to shutdown server
** Ruby version is up-to-date; cgi_multipart_eof_fix was not loaded
** Starting Mongrel listening at 0.0.0.0:3000
** Starting Rails with development environment...
** Rails loaded.
** Loading any Rails specific GemPlugins
** Signals ready.  TERM => stop.  USR2 => restart.  INT => stop (no
 restart).
** Rails signals registered.  HUP => reload (without restart).  It
might not work well.
** Mongrel available at 0.0.0.0:3000
** Use CTRL-C to stop.
```

Well done: you just started up your application for the first time! Okay, so it's not going to be doing a whole lot—we haven't written any lines of code yet, after all—but you can now connect to your application by entering http://localhost:3000/ into your web browser's address bar; you should see something similar to Figure 2.23.

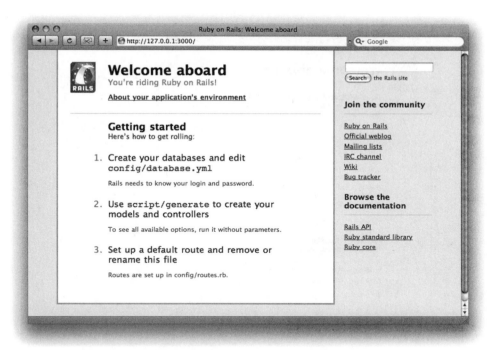

Figure 2.23. Welcome aboard: the Rails welcome screen

This welcome screen provides us with quite a few items, including some steps for getting started with Rails application development. Don't investigate these just yet; we'll deal with that soon enough. You'll also notice in the sidebar some links to sites such as the Rails wiki and the mailing list archives, which you can browse through at your leisure. And there are some links to documentation for Rails and for Ruby; you'll find these resources useful once you've progressed further with Rails development.

If you're interested to see the version numbers of each of the components we've installed, click on the link labeled **About your application's environment**. You'll see a nicely animated information box, like the one in Figure 2.24. This dialog contains all the version information you'll ever likely to need. If you've followed the installation instructions in this book, you should have the latest versions of everything.

Figure 2.24. Viewing version information

Okay, so you're finally ready to write some code. But wait! Which text editor will you be using?

Which Text Editor?

The question of which text editor is best for web development has spawned arguments that border on religious fanaticism. However, while it's certainly possible to develop Rails applications using the default text editor that comes bundled with your operating system, I don't recommend it—the benefits provided by a specifically designed programmer's editor can prevent typing errors and increase your productivity immeasurably.

In this section, I've suggested a couple of alternatives for each operating system, and I'll let you make a choice that suits your personal preferences and budget.

Windows Text Editors

UltraEdit

The most popular option for editing Rails code on Windows seems to be UltraEdit, which is shown in Figure 2.25. UltraEdit is available for download as a free trial, and may be purchased online for US$49.95.[10] It offers syntax highlighting, code completion, and proper Unicode support (for international characters), as well as providing the facility to jump quickly between several files. This last is a huge plus for Rails applications, which usually consist of several dozen files!

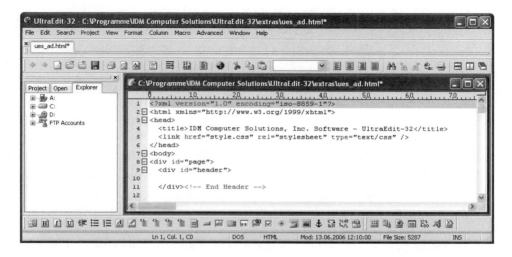

Figure 2.25. UltraEdit: a powerful Windows editor

ConTEXT

A free text editor alternative is ConTEXT,[11] shown in Figure 2.26, which holds its own in the features department. ConTEXT also supports syntax highlighting for Ruby (which is available as a separate download),[12] the ability to open multiple documents in tabs, and a host of other features to make your development experience more enjoyable. I especially like the fact that ConTEXT is quite lightweight, so it loads very quickly. Oh, and that lack of a price tag is rather attractive, too!

---

[10] http://www.ultraedit.com/

[11] http://context.cx/

[12] http://www.context.cx/component/option,com_docman/task,cat_view/gid,76/Itemid,48/

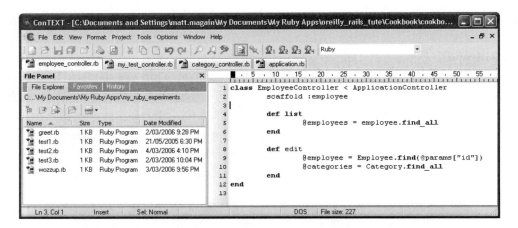

Figure 2.26. ConTEXT: a free, feature-rich text editor for Windows

Mac OS X Text Editors

TextMate

For Mac OS X users, the hands-down winner in the Rails code editor popularity contest is TextMate,[13] which is shown in Figure 2.27. TextMate is the editor you can see in action in numerous screencasts[14] available from the Rails web site. It's available for download as a free, 30-day trial, and the full version of the product costs €39.

TextMate boasts terrific project management support, amazing macro recording/code completion functionality, and one of the most complete syntax highlighting implementations for Rails code. As you can probably tell, I'm a big fan, and recommend it heartily. But this is beginning to sound like a television commercial, so I'll leave it at that.

---

[13] http://www.macromates.com/
[14] http://www.rubyonrails.org/screencasts/

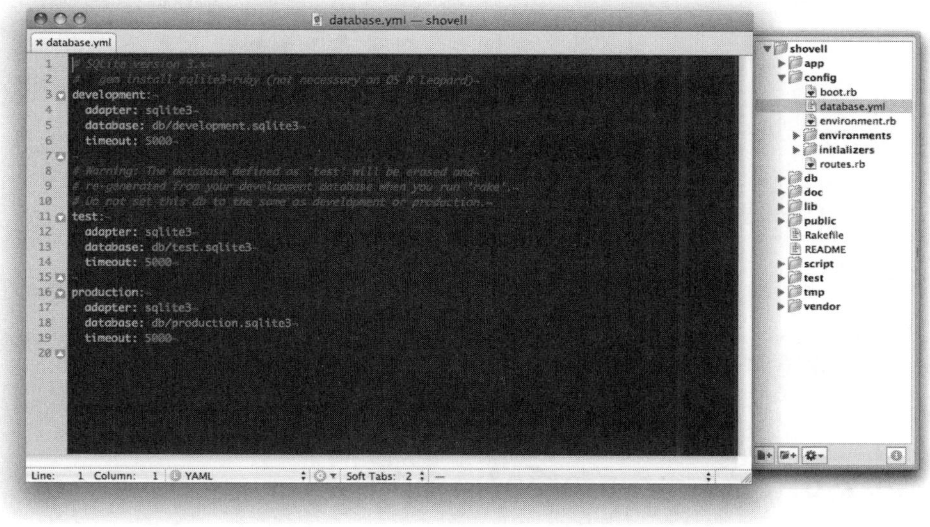

Figure 2.27. TextMate running under Mac OS X

TextWrangler

TextWrangler is a free, simple text editor made by BareBones Software. As with the other editors listed here, TextWrangler tidies up your workspace by allowing you to have several files open at the same time. The documents are listed in a pull-out "drawer" to one side of the interface, rather than as tabs.

You can download TextWrangler from the BareBones Software web site.[15] Figure 2.28 shows TextWrangler in action.

---

[15] http://barebones.com/products/textwrangler/

Figure 2.28. TextWrangler, a free text editor for Mac OS X

Linux and Cross-platform Editors

A number of development-centric text editors that run on a variety of platforms are available for free download. The following editors have loyal followings, and all run equally well on Linux as on Microsoft Windows and Mac OS X:

- Emacs, http://www.emacswiki.org/
- jEdit, http://www.jedit.org/
- RadRails, http://www.radrails.org/
- Vim, http://www.vim.org/

A more comprehensive list of text editors can be found in the Rails Wiki.[16] This page also covers potential enhancement modules for other editors.

Summary

In this chapter, I showed you how to install all the software you need to develop a web application in Ruby on Rails.

We installed Ruby, Rails, and SQLite, and set up the standard directory structure for our application, which we've named "Shovell." We even launched the application for the first time, which enabled us to check which versions we were running of the components involved. And finally, I gave you some options for text editors you can use to build the application.

---

[16] http://wiki.rubyonrails.org/rails/pages/Editors/

All this work has been completed in preparation for Chapter 4, where we'll begin to write our first lines of application code. But first, there's some theory we have to tackle. Hold on tight, we'll start coding soon enough!

Chapter 3

Introducing Ruby

While this chapter certainly makes no attempt to constitute a complete guide to the Ruby language, it will introduce you to some of the basics of Ruby. We'll power through a crash course in object oriented programming that covers the more common features of the language, and leave the more obscure aspects of Ruby for a dedicated reference guide.[1] I'll also point out some of the advantages that Ruby has over other languages when it comes to developing applications for the Web.

Some Rails developers suggest that it's possible to learn and use Rails without learning the Ruby basics first, but as far as I'm concerned, it's extremely beneficial to know even a *little* Ruby before diving into the guts of Rails. In fact, you'll automatically become a better Rails programmer.

Ruby Is a Scripting Language

In general, programming languages fall into one of two categories: they're either compiled languages or scripting languages. Let's explore what each of those terms means, and understand the differences between them.

---

[1] http://www.ruby-doc.org/stdlib/

Compiled Languages

The language in which you write an application is not actually something that your computer understands. Your code needs to be translated into bits and bytes that can be executed by your computer. This process of translation is called **compilation**, and any language that requires compilation is referred to as a **compiled language**. Examples of compiled languages include C, C#, and Java.

For a compiled language, the actual compilation is the final step in the development process. You invoke a **compiler**—the software program that translates your final handwritten, human-readable code into machine-readable code—and the compiler creates an executable file. This final product is then able to execute independently of the original source code.

Thus, if you make changes to your code, and you want those changes to be incorporated into the application, you must stop the running application, recompile it, then start the application again.

Scripting Languages

On the other hand, a scripting language such as Ruby, PHP, or Python relies upon an application's source code all the time. **Scripting languages** don't have a compiler or a compilation phase per se; instead, they use an **interpreter**—a program that runs on the web server—to translate handwritten code into machine-executable code on the fly. The link between the running application and your handcrafted code is never severed, because that scripting code is translated every time it is invoked; in other words, for every web page that your application renders.

As you might have gathered from the name, the use of an interpreter rather than a compiler is the major difference between a scripting language and a compiled language.

The Great Performance Debate

If you've come from a compiled-language background, you might be concerned by all this talk of translating code on the fly—how does it affect the application's performance?

These concerns are valid. Translating code on the web server every time it's needed is certainly more expensive, performance-wise, than executing precompiled code, as it requires more effort on the part of your machine's processor. The good news is that there are ways to speed up scripted languages, including techniques such as code caching—caching the output of a script for reuse rather than executing the script every time—and persistent interpreters—loading the interpreter once and keeping it running instead of having to load it for every request. However, performance topics are beyond the scope of this book.

There's also an upside to scripted languages in terms of performance—namely, *your* performance while developing an application.

Imagine that you've just compiled a shiny new Java application, and launched it for the first time … and then you notice an embarrassing typo on the welcome screen. To fix it, you have to stop your application, go back to the source code, fix the typo, wait for the code to recompile, and restart your application to confirm that it is fixed. And if you find another typo, you'll need to repeat that process *again*. Lather, rinse, repeat.

In a scripting language, you can fix the typo and just reload the page in your browser—no restart, no recompile, no nothing. It's as simple as that.

Ruby Is an Object Oriented Language

Ruby, from its very beginnings, was built as a programming language that adheres to the principles of **object oriented programming** (OOP). Before getting into Ruby specifics, let's unpack some fundamental concepts of OOP. The theory can be a bit dry when you're itching to start coding, but we'll cover a lot of ground in this short section. It will hold you in good stead, so don't skip it.

OOP is a programming paradigm that first surfaced in the 1960s, but didn't gain traction until the 1980s with C++. Its core idea is that programs should be composed of individual entities, or **objects**, each of which has the ability to communicate with other objects around it. Additionally, each object may have the facility to store data internally, as depicted in Figure 3.1.

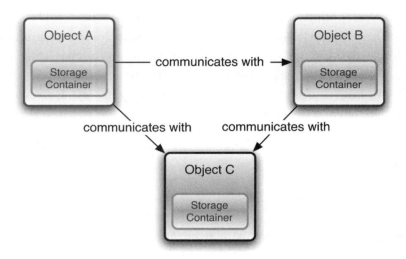

Figure 3.1. Communication between objects

Objects in an OOP application are often modeled on real-world objects, so even non-programmers can usually recognize the basic role that an object plays.

And, just like the real world, OOP defines objects with similar characteristics as belonging to the same **class**. A class is a construct for defining properties for objects that are alike, and equipping them with functionality. For example, a class named Car might define the attributes color and mileage for its objects, and assign them functionality: actions such as open the trunk, start the engine, and change gears. These different actions are known as **methods**, although you'll often see Rails enthusiasts refer to the methods of a controller (a kind of object used in Rails, which you'll become very familiar with) as "actions"; you can safely consider the two terms to be interchangeable.

Understanding the relationship between a class and its objects is integral to understanding how OOP works. For instance, one object can invoke functionality on another object, and can do so without affecting other objects of the same class. So, if one car object was instructed to open its trunk, its trunk would open, but the trunk of other cars would remain closed—think of KITT, the talking car from the television show *Knight Rider*, if it helps with the metaphor.[2] Similarly, if our high-tech talking car were instructed to change color to red, it would do so, but other cars would not.

---

[2] *Knight Rider* [http://en.wikipedia.org/wiki/Knight_Rider] was a popular 1980s series which featured modern-day cowboy Michael Knight (played by David Hasselhoff) and his opinionated, talking, black

When we create a new object in OOP, we base it on an existing class. The process of creating new objects from a class is called **instantiation**. Figure 3.2 illustrates this concept.

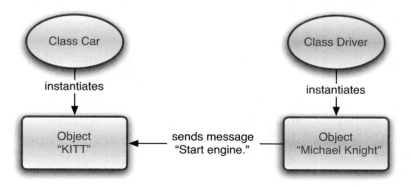

Figure 3.2. Classes and objects

As I mentioned, objects can communicate with each other and invoke functionality (methods) on other objects. Invoking an object's methods can be thought of as asking the object a question, and getting an answer in return.

Consider the example of our famous talking car again. Let's say we ask the talking car object to report its current mileage. This question is not ambiguous: the answer that the object gives is called a **return value**, and is shown in Figure 3.3.

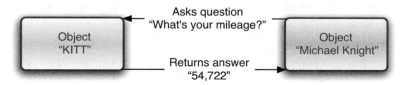

Figure 3.3. Asking a simple question

In some cases, the question-and-answer analogy doesn't quite fit. In these situations, we might rephrase the analogy to consider the question to be an instruction, and the answer a status report indicating whether or not the instruction was executed successfully. This process might look something like the diagram in Figure 3.4.

Pontiac Firebird named KITT. If you missed it in the '80s, you may be more familiar with the Val Kilmer-voiced Ford Mustang in the 2008 remake. Don't worry, having seen the show isn't a prerequisite to understanding object oriented programming!

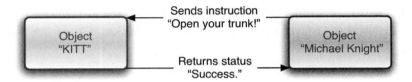

Figure 3.4. Sending instructions

Sometimes we need a bit more flexibility with our instructions. For example, if we wanted to tell our car to change gear, we need to tell it not only to change gear, but also which gear to change to. The process of asking these kinds of questions is referred to as passing an argument to the method.

An **argument** is an input value that's provided to a method. An argument can be used in two ways:

- to influence how a method operates
- to influence which object a method operates on

An example is shown in Figure 3.5, where the method is "change gear," and the number of the gear to which the car must change (two) is the argument.

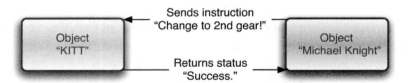

Figure 3.5. Passing arguments

A more general view of all of these different types of communication between objects is this: invoking an object's methods is accomplished by sending messages to it. As one might expect, the object sending the message is called the **sender**, and the object receiving the message is called the **receiver**.

Armed with this basic knowledge about object oriented programming, let's look at some Ruby specifics.

Reading and Writing Ruby Code

Learning the syntax of a new language has the potential to induce the occasional yawn. So, to make things more interesting, I'll present it to you in a practical way that lets you play along at home: we'll use the **interactive Ruby shell**.

The Interactive Ruby Shell (`irb`)

You can fire up the interactive Ruby shell by entering `irb` into a terminal window.

 Not the Standard DOS Box!

Windows users, don't forget to use the **Open Ruby Console Window** option from the Instant Rails control panel, to make sure the environment you're using contains the right settings.

`irb` allows you to issue Ruby commands interactively, one line at a time. This ability is great for playing with the language, and it's also handy for debugging, as we'll see in Chapter 11.

A couple of points about the `irb` output you'll see in this chapter:

▥ Lines beginning with the Ruby shell prompt (`irb>`) are typed in by the user.

▥ Lines beginning with => show the return value of the command that has been entered.

We'll start with a *really* brief example:

```
irb> 1
=> 1
```

In this example, I've simply thrown the number 1 at the Ruby shell, and received back what appears to be the very same number.

Looks can be deceiving, though. It's actually *not* the very same number. What has been handed back is in fact a fully featured Ruby object.

Remember our discussion about object oriented programming in the previous section? Well, in Ruby, absolutely everything is treated as an object with which we can interact; each object belongs to a certain class, therefore each object is able to store data and functionality in the form of methods.

To find the class to which our number belongs, we call the number's `class` method:

```
irb> 1.class
=> Fixnum
```

We touched on senders and receivers earlier. In this example, we've sent the `class` message to the 1 object, so the 1 object is the receiver (there's no sender, as we're sending the message from the interactive command line rather than from another object). The value that's returned by the method we've invoked is `Fixnum`, which is the Ruby class that represents integer values.

Since everything in Ruby (*including* a class) is an object, we can actually send the very same message to the `Fixnum` class. The result is different, as we'd expect:

```
irb> Fixnum.class
=> Class
```

This time, the return value is `Class`, which is reassuring—we did invoke it on a classname, after all.

Note that the method `class` is all lowercase, yet the return value `Class` begins with a capital letter. A method in Ruby is always written in lowercase, whereas the first letter of a class is always capitalized.

Interacting with Ruby Objects

Becoming accustomed to thinking in terms of objects can take some time. Let's look at a few different types of objects, and see how we can interact with them.

Literal Objects

Literal objects are character strings or numbers that appear directly in the code, as did the number 1 that was returned in the previous section. We've seen numbers in action; next, let's look at a string literal.

A **string literal** is an object that contains a string of characters, such as a name, an address, or an especially witty phrase. In the same way that we created the 1 literal object in the previous example, we can easily create a new string literal object, then send it a message. A string literal is created by enclosing the characters that make up the string in single or double quotes, like this:

```
irb> "The quick brown fox"
=> "The quick brown fox"
```

First, we'll confirm that our string literal indeed belongs to class `String`:

```
irb> "The quick brown fox".class
=> String
```

This `String` object has a wealth of embedded functionality. For example, we can ascertain the number of characters that our string literal comprises by sending it the `length` message:

```
irb> "The quick brown fox".length
=> 19
```

Easy stuff, eh?

Variables and Constants

Every application needs a way to store information. Enter our variables and constants! As their names imply, these two data containers have their own unique roles to play.

A **constant** is an object that's assigned a value once, and once only (usually when the application starts up). Constants are therefore used to store information that doesn't need to change within a running application. As an example, a constant might be used to store the version number for an application. Constants in Ruby are always written using uppercase letters, as shown below:

```
irb> CONSTANT = "The quick brown fox in a constant"
=> "The quick brown fox in a constant"
irb> APP_VERSION = 5.04
=> 5.04
```

Variables, in contrast, are objects that are able to change at any time. They can even be reset to nothing, which frees up the memory space that they previously occupied. Variables in Ruby always start with a lowercase character:

```
irb> variable = "The quick brown fox in a variable"
=> "The quick brown fox in a variable"
```

There's one more special (and, you might say, *evil*) side to a variable: its **scope**. The scope of a variable is the part of the program to which a variable is visible. If you try to access a variable from outside its scope (for example, from a part of an application to which that variable is not visible), your attempts will generally fail.

The notable exception to the rules defining a variable's scope are global variables. As the name implies, a **global variable** is accessible from any part of the program. While this might sound convenient at first, usage of global variables is discouraged—the fact that they can be written to and read from any part of the program introduces security concerns.

Let's return to the string literal example we just saw. Assigning a String to a variable allows us to invoke on that variable the same methods we invoked on the string literal earlier:

```
irb> fox = "The quick brown fox"
=> "The quick brown fox"
irb> fox.class
=> String
irb> fox.length
=> 19
```

Punctuation in Ruby

The use of punctuation in Ruby code differs greatly from other languages such as Perl and PHP, so it can seem confusing at first if you're used to programming in those languages. However, once you have a few basics under your belt, punctuation in Ruby begins to feel quite intuitive and can greatly enhance the readability of your code.

Dot Notation

One of the most common punctuation characters in Ruby is the period (.). As we've seen, Ruby uses the period to separate the receiver from the message that's being sent to it, in the form *Object.receiver*.

If you need to comment a line, either for documentation purposes or to temporarily take a line of code out of the program flow, use a hash mark (#). Comments may start at the beginning of a line, or they may appear further along, after some Ruby code:

```
irb> # This is a comment. It doesn't actually do anything.
irb> 1 # So is this, but this one comes after a statement.
=> 1
irb> fox = "The quick brown fox"     # Assign to a variable
=> "The quick brown fox"
irb> fox.class                       # Display a variable's class
=> String
irb> fox.length                      # Display a variable's length
=> 19
```

Chaining Statements Together

Ruby doesn't require us to use any character to separate commands, unless we want to chain multiple statements together on a single line. In this case, a semicolon (;) is used as the separator. However, if you put every statement on its own line (as we've been doing until now), the semicolon is completely optional.

If you chain multiple statements together in the interactive shell, only the output of the last command that was executed will be displayed to the screen:

```
irb> fox.class; fox.length; fox.upcase
=> "THE QUICK BROWN FOX"
```

Use of Parentheses

If you ever delved into the source code of one of the many JavaScript libraries out there, you might have run screaming from your computer when you saw all the parentheses that are involved in the passing of arguments to methods.[3]

---

[3] http://www.sitepoint.com/article/javascript-library/

In Ruby, the use of parentheses for method calls is optional in cases in which no arguments are passed to the method. The following statements are therefore equal:

```
irb> fox.class()
=> String
irb> fox.class
=> String
```

It's common practice to include parentheses for method calls with multiple arguments, such as the insert method of the String class:

```
irb> "jumps over the lazy dog".insert(0, 'The quick brown fox ')
=> "The quick brown fox jumps over the lazy dog"
```

This call inserts the second argument passed to the insert object ("The quick brown fox ") at position 0 of the receiving String object ("jumps over the lazy dog"). Position 0 refers to the very beginning of the string.

Method Notation

Until now, we've looked at cases where Ruby uses *less* punctuation than its competitors. In fact, Ruby makes heavy use of expressive punctuation when it comes to the naming of methods.

A regular method name, as we've seen, is a simple, alphanumeric string of characters. If a method has a potentially destructive nature (for example, it directly modifies the receiving object rather than changing a copy of it), it's commonly suffixed with an exclamation mark (!).

The following example uses the upcase method to illustrate this point:

```
irb> fox.upcase
=> "THE QUICK BROWN FOX"
irb> fox
=> "The quick brown fox"
irb> fox.upcase!
=> "THE QUICK BROWN FOX"
irb> fox
=> "THE QUICK BROWN FOX"
```

Here, the contents of the fox variable have been modified by the upcase! method.

Punctuation is also used in the names of methods that return **boolean values**. A boolean value is a value that's either `true` or `false`; these values are commonly used as return values for methods that ask yes/no questions. Such methods end in a question mark, which nicely reflects the fact that they have yes/no answers:

```
irb> fox.empty?
=> false
irb> fox.is_a? String
=> true
```

These naming conventions make it easy to recognize methods that are destructive, and those that return boolean values, making your Ruby code more readable.

Object Oriented Programming in Ruby

Let's build on the theory that we covered at the start of this chapter as we take a look at Ruby's implementation of OOP.

As we already know, the structure of an application based on OOP principles is focused on interaction with objects. These objects are often representations of real-world objects, like a `Car`. Interaction with an object occurs when we send it a message or ask it a question. If we really did have a `Car` object called `kitt` (no, we don't—yet), starting the car might be as simple as doing this:

```
irb> kitt.start
```

This short line of Ruby code sends the message `start` to the object `kitt`. Using OOP terminology, we would say that this code statement calls the `start` method of the `kitt` object.

As I mentioned before, in contrast to other object oriented programming languages such as Python and PHP, in Ruby, *everything* is an object. Especially when compared with PHP, Ruby's OOP doesn't feel like a tacked-on afterthought—it was clearly intended to be a core feature of the language from the beginning, which makes using the OOP features in Ruby a real pleasure.

As we saw in the previous section, even the simplest of elements in Ruby (like literal strings and numbers) are objects to which you can send messages.

Classes and Objects

As in any other OOP language, in Ruby, each object belongs to a certain class (for example, `pontiac_firebird` might be an object of class `Car`). As we saw in the discussion at the beginning of this chapter, a class can group objects of a certain kind, and equip those objects with common functionality. This functionality comes in the form of methods, and in the object's ability to store information. For example, a `pontiac_firebird` object might need to store its mileage, as might any other object of the class `Car`.

In Ruby, the instantiation of a new object that's based on an existing class is accomplished by sending that class the `new` message. The result is a new object of that class. The following few lines of code show an extremely basic class definition in Ruby; the third line is where we create an instance of the class that we just defined:

```
irb> class Car
irb> end
=> nil
irb> kitt = Car.new
=> #<Car:0x75e54>
```

Another basic principle in OOP is **encapsulation**. According to this principle, objects should be treated as independent entities, each taking care of its own internal data and functionality. If we need to access an object's information—its internal variables, for instance—we make use of the object's **interface**, which is the subset of the object's methods that are made available for other objects to call.

Ruby provides objects with functionality at two levels—the object level, and class level—and adheres to the principle of encapsulation while it's at it! Let's dig deeper.

Object-level Functionality

At the object level, data storage is handled by **instance variables** (a name that's derived from the instantiation process mentioned above). Think of instance variables as storage containers that are attached to the object, but to which other objects do not have direct access.

To store or retrieve data from these variables, another object must call an **accessor method** on the object. An accessor method has the ability to set (and get) the value of the object's instance variables.

Let's look at how instance variables and accessor methods relate to each other, and how they're implemented in Ruby.

Instance Variables

Instance variables are bound to an object, and contain values for that object only.

Revisiting our car example, the mileage values for a number of different `Car` objects are likely to differ, as each car will have a different mileage. Therefore, `mileage` is held in an instance variable.

An instance variable can be recognized by its prefix: a single "at" sign (@). And what's more, instance variables don't even need to be declared! There's only one problem: we don't have any way to retrieve or change them from outside the object once they do exist. This is where instance methods come into play.

Instance Methods

Data storage and retrieval is not the only capability that can be bound to a specific object—functionality, too, can be bound to objects. We achieve this binding through the use of **instance methods**, which are specific to an object. Invoking an instance method (in other words, sending a message that contains the method name to an object) will invoke that functionality on the receiving object only.

Instance methods are defined using the `def` keyword, and end with the `end` keyword. Enter the following example into a new Ruby shell:

```
$ irb
irb> class Car
irb>   def open_trunk
irb>     # code to open trunk goes here
irb>   end
irb> end
=> nil
irb> kitt = Car.new
=> #<Car:0x75e54>
```

What you've done is define a class called `Car`, which has an instance method with the name `open_trunk`. A `Car` object instantiated from this class will—possibly using some fancy robotics connected to our Ruby program—open its trunk when its `open_trunk` method is called. Ignore that `nil` return value for the moment; we'll look at `nil` values in the next section.

Indenting Your Code

While the indentation of code is a key element of the syntax of languages such as Python, in Ruby, indentation is purely cosmetic—it aids readability, but does not affect the code in any way. In fact, while we're experimenting with the Ruby shell, you needn't be too worried about indenting any of the code. However, when we're saving files that will be edited later, you'll want the readability benefits that come from indenting nested lines.

The Ruby community has agreed upon two spaces as being optimum for indenting blocks of code such as class or method definitions. We'll adhere to this indentation scheme throughout this book.

With our class in place, we can make use of this method:

```
irb> kitt.open_trunk
=> nil
```

Since we don't want the trunks of all our cars to open at once, we've made this functionality available as an instance method.

I know, I know: we *still* haven't modified any data. We use accessor methods for this task.

Accessor Methods

An accessor method is a special type of instance method, and is used to read or write to an instance variable. There are two types: **readers** (sometimes called "getters") and **writers** (or "setters").

A reader method will look inside the object, fetch the value of an instance variable, and hand this value back to us. A writer method, on the other hand, will look inside the object, find an instance variable, and assign the variable the value that it was passed.

Let's add some methods for getting and setting the `@mileage` attribute of our `Car` objects. Once again, exit from the Ruby shell so that we can create an entirely new `Car` class definition. Our class definition is getting a bit longer now, so enter each line carefully. If you make a typing mistake, exit the shell and start over.

```
$ irb
irb> class Car
irb>    def set_mileage(x)
irb>       @mileage = x
irb>    end
irb>    def get_mileage
irb>       @mileage
irb>    end
irb> end
=> nil
irb> kitt = Car.new
=> #<Car:0x75e54>
```

Now, we can finally modify and retrieve the mileage of our `Car` objects!

```
irb> kitt.set_mileage(5667)
=> 5667
irb> kitt.get_mileage
=> 5667
```

This is still a bit awkward. Wouldn't it be nice if we could give our accessor methods exactly the same names as the attributes that they read from or write to? Luckily, Ruby contains shorthand notation for this very task. We can rewrite our class definition as follows:

```
$ irb
irb> class Car
irb>    def mileage=(x)
irb>       @mileage = x
irb>    end
irb>    def mileage
irb>       @mileage
irb>    end
irb> end
=> nil
irb> kitt = Car.new
=> #<Car:0x75e54>
```

With these accessor methods in place, we can read to and write from our instance variable as if it were available from outside the object:

```
irb> kitt.mileage = 6032
=> 6032
irb> kitt.mileage
=> 6032
```

These accessor methods form part of the object's interface.

Class-level Functionality

At the class level, **class variables** handle data storage. They're commonly used to store state information, or as a means of configuring default values for new objects. Class variables are typically set in the body of a class, and can be recognized by their prefix: a double "at" sign (@@).

First, enter the following class definition into a new Ruby shell:

```
$ irb
irb> class Car
irb>    @@number_of_cars = 0
irb>    def initialize
irb>       @@number_of_cars = @@number_of_cars + 1
irb>    end
irb> end
=> nil
```

The class definition for the class Car above has an internal counter for the total number of Car objects that have been created. Using the special instance method initialize, which is invoked automatically every time an object is instantiated, this counter is incremented for each new Car object.

By the way, we have actually already used a class method; I snuck it in there. The new method is an example of a class method that ships with Ruby and is available to all classes, whether they're defined by you or form part of the Ruby Standard Library.[4]

---

[4] The Ruby Standard Library is a large collection of classes that's included with every Ruby installation. The classes facilitate a wide range of common functionality, such as accessing web sites, date calculations, file operations, and more.

Custom class methods are commonly used to create objects with special properties (such as a default color for our `Car` objects), or to gather statistics about the class's usage.

Extending the earlier example, we could use a class method called `count` to return the value of the `@@number_of_cars` class variable. Remember that this is a variable that's incremented for every new `Car` object that's created. Class methods are defined identically to instance methods: using the `def` and `end` keywords. The only difference is that class method names are prefixed with `self`. Enter this code into a new Ruby shell:

```
$ irb
irb> class Car
irb>    @@number_of_cars = 0
irb>    def self.count
irb>       @@number_of_cars
irb>    end
irb>    def initialize
irb>       @@number_of_cars += 1
irb>    end
irb> end
=> nil
```

The following code instantiates some new `Car` objects, then makes use of our new class method:

```
irb> kitt = Car.new         # Michael Knight's talking car
=> #<0xba8c>
irb> herbie = Car.new       # The famous VolksWagen love bug!
=> #<0x8cd20>
irb> batmobile = Car.new    # Batman's sleek automobile
=> #<0x872e4>
irb> Car.count
=> 3
```

The method tells us that three instances of the `Car` class have been created. Note that we can't call a class method on an object.[5]

---

[5] Ruby actually does provide a way to invoke *some* class methods on an object, using the `::` operator, but we won't worry about that for now. We'll see the `::` operator in use in Chapter 4.

```
irb> kitt.count
NoMethodError: undefined method 'count' for #<Car:0x89da0>
```

As implied by the name, the count class method is available only to the Car class, not to any objects instantiated from that class.

I sneakily introduced something else in there. In many languages, including PHP and Java, the ++ and - - operators are used to increment a variable by one. Ruby doesn't support this notation; instead, when working with Ruby, we need to use the += operator. Therefore, the shorthand notation for incrementing our counter in the class definition is:

```
irb>      @@number_of_cars += 1
```

This code is identical to the following:

```
irb>      @@number_of_cars = @@number of cars + 1
```

Both of these lines can be read as "my_variable becomes equal to my_variable plus one."

Inheritance

If your application deals with more than the flat hierarchy we've explored so far, you may want to construct a scenario whereby some classes inherit from other classes. Continuing with the car analogy, let's suppose that we have a green limousine named Larry (this assignment of names to cars may seem a little strange, but it's important for this example, so bear with me). In Ruby, the larry object would probably descend from a StretchLimo class, which could in turn descend from the class Car. Let's implement that class relationship, to see how it works:

```
$ irb
irb> class Car
irb>    WHEELS = 4
irb> end
=> nil
irb> class StretchLimo < Car
irb>    WHEELS = 6
irb>    def turn_on_television
```

```
irb>       # Invoke code for switching on on-board TV here
irb>     end
irb> end
=> nil
```

Now, if we were to instantiate an object of class StretchLimo, we'd end up with a different kind of car. Instead of the regular four wheels that standard Car objects have, this one would have six wheels (stored in the class constant WHEELS). It would also have extra functionality, made possible by the presence of the extra method—turn_on_television—which would be available to be called by other objects.

However, if we were to instantiate a regular Car object, the car would have only four wheels, and there would be no instance method for turning on an on-board television. Think of inheritance as a way for the functionality of a class to become more specialized the further we move down the inheritance path.

Don't worry if you're struggling to wrap your head around all the aspects of OOP. You'll automatically become accustomed to them as you work through this book. You may find it useful to come back to this section, though, especially if you need a reminder about a certain term later on.

Return Values

It's always great to receive feedback. Remember our talk about passing arguments to methods? Well, regardless of whether or not a method accepts arguments, invoking a method in Ruby *always* results in feedback—it comes in the form of a return value, which is returned either explicitly or implicitly.

To return a value explicitly, use the return statement in the body of a method:

```
irb> def toot_horn
irb>    return "toooot!"
irb> end
=> nil
```

Calling the toot_horn method in this case would produce the following:

```
irb> toot_horn
=> "toooot!"
```

However, if no return statement is used, the result of the last statement that was executed is used as the return value. This behavior is quite unique to Ruby:

```
irb> def toot_loud_horn
irb>    "toooot!".upcase
irb> end
=> nil
```

Calling the toot_loud_horn method in this case would produce:

```
irb> toot_loud_horn
=> "TOOOOT!"
```

Standard Output

When you need to show output to the users of your application, use the print and puts ("put string") statements. Both methods will display the arguments passed to them as Strings; puts also inserts a carriage return at the end of its output. Therefore, in a Ruby program the following lines:

```
print "The quick "
print "brown fox"
```

... would produce this output:

```
The quick brown fox
```

However, using puts like so:

```
puts "jumps over"
puts "the lazy dog"
```

... would produce this output:

```
jumps over
the lazy dog
```

At this stage, you might be wondering why *all* of the trial-and-error code snippets that we've typed into the Ruby shell actually produced output, given that we haven't been making use of the `print` or `puts` methods. The reason is that `irb` automatically writes the return value of the last statement it executes to the screen before displaying the `irb` prompt. This means that using a `print` or `puts` from within the Ruby shell might in fact produce two lines of output: the output that you specify should be displayed, and the return value of the last command that was executed, as in the following example:

```
irb> puts "The quick brown fox"
"The quick brown fox"
=> nil
```

Here, `nil` is actually the return value of the `puts` statement. Looking back at previous examples, you will have encountered `nil` as the return value for class and method definitions, and you'll have received a hexadecimal address, such as `#<Car:0x89da0>`, as the return value for object definitions. This hexadecimal value showed the location in memory that the object we instantiated occupied, but luckily we won't need to bother with such geeky details any further.

Having met the `print` and `puts` statements, you should be aware that a Rails application actually has a completely different approach to displaying output, called templates. We'll look at templates in Chapter 4.

Ruby Core Classes

We've already talked briefly about the `String` and `Fixnum` classes in the previous sections, but Ruby has a lot more under its hood. Let's explore!

Arrays

We use Ruby's `Arrays` to store collections of objects. Each individual object that's stored in an `Array` has a unique numeric key, which we can use to reference it. As with many languages, the first element in an `Array` is stored at position 0 (zero).

To create a new `Array`, simply instantiate a new object of class `Array` (using the `Array.new` construct). You can also use a shortcut approach, which is to enclose the objects you want to place inside the `Array` in square brackets.

For example, an `Array` containing the mileage at which a car is due for its regular service might look something like this:

```
irb> service_mileage = [5000, 15000, 30000, 60000, 100000]
=> [5000, 15000, 30000, 60000, 100000]
```

To retrieve individual elements from an Array, we specify the numeric key in square brackets:

```
irb> service_mileage[0]
=> 5000
irb> service_mileage[2]
=> 30000
```

Ruby has another shortcut, which allows us to create an Array from a list of Strings: the %w( ) syntax. Using this shortcut saves us from having to type a lot of double-quote characters:

```
irb> available_colors = %w( red green blue black )
=> ["red", "green", "blue", "black"]
irb> available_colors[0]
=> "red"
irb> available_colors[3]
=> "black"
```

In addition to facilitating simple element retrieval, Arrays come with an extensive set of class methods and instance methods that ease data management tasks tremendously.

■ empty? returns true if the receiving Array doesn't contain any elements:

```
irb> available_colors.empty?
=> false
```

■ size returns the number of elements in an Array:

```
irb> available_colors.size
=> 4
```

- `first` and `last` return an Array's first and last elements, respectively:

```
irb> available_colors.first
=> "red"
irb> available_colors.last
=> "black"
```

- `delete` removes the named element from the Array and returns it:

```
irb> available_colors.delete "red"
=> "red"
irb> available_colors
=> ["green", "blue", "black"]
```

The complete list of class methods and instance methods provided by the Array class is available via the Ruby reference documentation, which you can access by entering the `ri` command into the terminal window (for your operating system, *not* the Ruby shell), followed by the class name you'd like to look up:

```
$ ri Array
```

Oh, and `ri` stands for **r**uby **i**nteractive, in case you're wondering. Don't confuse it with `irb`.

Hashes

A `Hash` is another kind of data storage container. `Hash`es are similar, conceptually, to dictionaries: they map one object (the `key`: a word, for example) to another object (the `value`: a word's definition, for example) in a one-to-one relationship.

New `Hash`es can be created either by instantiating a new object of class `Hash` (using the `Hash.new` construct) or by using the curly brace shortcut shown below. When we define a `Hash`, we must specify each entry using the `key => value` syntax.

For example, the following `Hash` maps car names to a color:

```
irb> car_colors = {
irb>    'kitt' => 'black',
irb>    'herbie' => 'white',
irb>    'batmobile' => 'black',
irb>    'larry' => 'green'
irb> }
=> {"kitt"=>"black", "herbie"=>"white", "batmobile"=>"black",
    "larry"=>"green"}
```

To query this newly built Hash, we pass the key of the entry we want to look up in square brackets, like so:

```
irb> car_colors['kitt']
=> "black"
```

All sorts of useful functionality is built into Hashes, including the following methods:

■ empty? returns true if the receiving Hash doesn't contain any elements:

```
irb> car_colors.empty?
=> false
```

■ size returns the number of elements in a Hash:

```
irb> car_colors.size
=> 4
```

■ keys returns all keys of a Hash as an Array:

```
irb> car_colors.keys
=> ["kitt", "herbie", "batmobile", "larry"]
```

■ values returns all values of a Hash as an Array, although care should be taken with regards to the order of the elements (keys in a Hash are ordered for optimal storage and retrieval; this order does not necessarily reflect the order in which they were entered):

```
irb> car_colors.values
=> ["black", "white", "black", "green"]
```

There are lots more class methods and instance methods provided by the Hash class. For a complete list, consult the Ruby reference documentation.

Strings

The typical Ruby String object—yep, that very same object we've been using in the past few sections—holds and manipulates sequences of characters. Most of the time, new String objects are created using string literals that are enclosed in single or double quotes. The literal can then be stored in a variable for later use:

```
irb> a_phrase = "The quick brown fox"
=> "The quick brown fox"
irb> a_phrase.class
=> String
```

If the string literal includes the quote character used to enclose the string itself, it must be escaped with a backslash character (\):

```
irb> 'I\'m a quick brown fox'
=> "I'm a quick brown fox"
irb> "Arnie said, \"I'm back!\""
=> "Arnie said, \"I'm back!\""
```

An easier way to specify string literals that contain quotes is to use the %Q shortcut, like this:

```
irb> %Q(Arnie said, "I'm back!")
=> "Arnie said, \"I'm back!\""
```

String objects also support the substitution of Ruby code into a string literal via the Ruby expression #{}:

```
irb> "The current time is: #{Time.now}"
=> "The current time is: Wed Aug 02 21:15:19 CEST 2006"
```

The String class also has rich embedded functionality for modifying String objects. Here are some of the most useful methods:

- gsub substitutes a given pattern within a String:

```
irb> "The quick brown fox".gsub('fox', 'dog')
=> "The quick brown dog"
```

- include? returns true if a String contains another specific String:

```
irb> "The quick brown fox".include?('fox')
=> true
```

- length returns the length of a String in characters:

```
irb> "The quick brown fox".length
=> 19
```

- slice returns a portion of a String:

```
irb> "The quick brown fox".slice(0, 3)
=> "The"
```

The complete method reference is available using the ri command line tool:

```
$ ri String
```

Numerics

Since there are so many different types of numbers, Ruby has a separate class for each, the popular Float, Fixnum, and Bignum classes among them. In fact, they're all subclasses of Numeric, which provides the basic functionality.

Just like Strings, numbers are usually created from literals:

```
irb> 123.class
=> Fixnum
irb> 12.5.class
=> Float
```

Each of the specific `Numeric` subclasses comes with features that are relevant to the type of number it's designed to deal with. However, the following functionality is shared between all `Numeric` subclasses:

▨ `integer?` returns `true` if the object is a whole integer:

```
irb> 123.integer?
=> true
irb> 12.5.integer?
=> false
```

▨ `round` rounds a number to the nearest integer:

```
irb> 12.3.round
=> 12
irb> 38.8.round
=> 39
```

▨ `zero?` returns `true` if the number is equal to zero:

```
irb> 0.zero?
=> true
irb> 8.zero?
=> false
```

Additionally, there are ways to convert numbers between the `Numeric` subclasses. `to_f` converts a value to a `Float`, and `to_i` converts a value to an `Integer`:

```
irb> 12.to_f
=> 12.0
irb> 11.3.to_i
=> 11
```

Symbols

In Ruby, a `Symbol` is a simple textual identifier. Like a `String`, a `Symbol` is created using literals; the difference is that a `Symbol` is prefixed with a colon:

```
irb> :fox
=> :fox
irb> :fox.class
=> Symbol
```

The main benefit of using a `Symbol` instead of a `String` is that a `Symbol` contains less functionality. This can be an advantage in certain situations. For example, the `car_colors` Hash that we looked at earlier could be rewritten as follows:

```
car_colors = {
  :kitt => 'black',
  :herbie => 'white',
  :batmobile => 'black',
  :larry => 'green'
}
```

Objects of class `String` can be converted to `Symbols`, and vice versa:

```
irb> "fox".to_sym
=> :fox
irb> :fox.to_s
=> "fox"
```

We'll use `Symbols` frequently as we deal with Rails functionality in successive chapters of this book.

nil

I promised earlier that I'd explain `nil` values—now's the time!

All programming languages have a value that they can use when they actually mean *nothing*. Some use `undef`; others use `NULL`. Ruby uses `nil`. A `nil` value, like everything in Ruby, is also an object. It therefore has its own class: `NilClass`.

Basically, if a method doesn't return anything, it is, in fact, returning the value `nil`. And if you assign `nil` to a variable, you effectively make it empty. `nil` shows up in a couple of additional places, but we'll cross those bridges when we come to them.

Running Ruby Files

For the simple Ruby basics that we've experimented with so far, the interactive Ruby shell (`irb`) has been our tool of choice. I'm sure you'll agree that experimenting in a shell-like environment, where we can see immediate results, is a great way to learn the language.

However, we're going to be talking about control structures next, and for tasks of such complexity, you'll want to work in a text editor. This environment will allow you to run a chunk of code many times without having to retype it.

In general, Ruby scripts are simple text files containing Ruby code and have a **.rb** extension. These files are passed to the Ruby interpreter, which executes your code, like this:

```
$ ruby myscript.rb
```

To work with the examples that follow, I'd recommend that you open a new text file in your favorite text editor (which might be one of those I recommended back in Chapter 2) and type the code out as you go—this really is the best way to learn. However, I acknowledge that some people aren't interested in typing everything out, and just want to cut to the chase. For access to all of these examples, these more impatient readers can download the code archive for this book.[6] You can execute this code in the Ruby interpreter straight away.

As demonstrated above, to run the files from the command line, you simply need to type **ruby**, followed by the filename.

Control Structures

Ruby has a rich set of features for controlling the flow of your application. **Conditionals** are keywords that are used to decide whether or not certain statements are executed based on the evaluation of one or more conditions; **loops** are constructs

---

[6] http://www.sitepoint.com/books/rails2/code.php

that execute statements more than once; **blocks** are a means of encapsulating functionality (for example, to be executed in a loop).

To demonstrate these control structures, let's utilize some of the Car classes that we defined earlier. Type out the following class definition and save the file (or load it from the code archive); we'll build on it in this section as we explore some control structures:

01-car-classes.rb

```ruby
class Car
  WHEELS = 4                # class constant
  @@number_of_cars = 0      # class variable
  def initialize
    @@number_of_cars = @@number_of_cars + 1
  end
  def self.count
    @@number_of_cars
  end
  def mileage=(x)           # instance variable writer
    @mileage = x
  end
  def mileage               # instance variable reader
    @mileage
  end
end

class StretchLimo < Car
  WHEELS = 6                # class constant
  @@televisions = 1         # class variable
  def turn_on_television
    # Invoke code for switching on on-board TV here
  end
end

class PontiacFirebird < Car
end

class VolksWagen < Car
end
```

Conditionals

There are two basic conditional constructs in Ruby: `if` and `unless`. Each of these constructs can be used to execute a group of statements on the basis of a given condition.

The `if` Construct

An `if` construct wraps statements that are to be executed only if a certain condition is met. The keyword `end` defines the end of the `if` construct. The statements that are contained between the condition and the `end` keyword are executed only if the condition is met.

02-if-construct.rb *(excerpt)*

```
if Car.count.zero?
  puts "No cars have been produced yet."
end
```

You can provide a second condition by adding an `else` block: when the condition is met, the first block is executed; otherwise, the `else` block is executed. This kind of control flow will probably be familiar to you. Here it is in action:

03-if-else-construct.rb *(excerpt)*

```
if Car.count.zero?
  puts "No cars have been produced yet."
else
  puts "New cars can still be produced."
end
```

The most complicated example involves an alternative condition. If the first condition is not met, a second condition is evaluated. If neither conditions are met, the `else` block is executed:

04-if-elsif-else.rb *(excerpt)*

```
if Car.count.zero?
  puts "No cars have been produced yet."
elsif Car.count >= 10
  puts "Production capacity has been reached."
```

```
else
  puts "New cars can still be produced."
end
```

If the `count` method returned 5, the code above would produce the following output:

```
New cars can still be produced.
```

An alternative to the traditional `if` condition is the `if` **statement modifier**. A statement modifier does just that: it modifies the statement of which it is part. The `if` statement modifier works exactly like a regular `if` condition, but it sits at the *end* of the line that's affected, rather than before a block of code:

05-if-statement-modifier.rb *(excerpt)*

```
puts "No cars have been produced yet." if Car.count.zero?
```

This version of the `if` condition is often used when the code that's to be executed conditionally comprises just a single line. Having the ability to create conditions like this results in code that's a lot more like English than other programming languages with more rigid structures.

The `unless` Construct

The `unless` condition is a negative version of the `if` condition. It's useful for situations in which you want to execute a group of statements when a certain condition is *not* met.

Let's create a few instances to work with:[7]

06-unless-construct.rb *(excerpt)*

```
kitt = PontiacFirebird.new
kitt.mileage = 5667
```

---

[7] Aficionados of comics will notice that I've visualized the BatMobile as a Pontiac Firebird—in fact, the caped crusader's choice of transport has varied over the years, taking in many of the automobile industry's less common innovations, and including everything from a 1966 Lincoln Futura to an amphibious tank. But we'll stick with a Pontiac for this example.

```
herbie = VolksWagen.new
herbie.mileage = 33014

batmobile = PontiacFirebird.new
batmobile.mileage = 4623

larry = StretchLimo.new
larry.mileage = 20140
```

Now if we wanted to find out how many Knight Rider fans KITT could take for a joyride, we could check which class the kitt object was. As with the if expression, the end keyword defines the end of the statement:

06-unless-construct.rb *(excerpt)*

```
unless kitt.is_a?(StretchLimo)
  puts "This car is only licensed to seat two people."
end
```

Like the if condition, the unless condition may have an optional else block of statements, which is executed when the condition is met:

07-unless-else.rb *(excerpt)*

```
unless kitt.is_a?(StretchLimo)
  puts "This car only has room for two people."
else
  puts "This car is licensed to carry up to 10 passengers."
end
```

Since KITT is definitely *not* a stretch limousine, this code would return:

```
This car only has room for two people.
```

Unlike if conditions, unless conditions do *not* support a second condition. However, like the if condition, the unless condition is also available as a statement modifier. The following code shows an example of this. Here, the message will not display if KITT's mileage is less than 25,000:

```
08-unless-statement-modifier.rb (excerpt)

puts "Service due!" unless kitt.mileage < 25000
```

Loops

Ruby provides the `while` and `for` constructs for looping through code (that is, executing a group of statements a specified number of times, or until a certain condition is met). Also, a number of instance methods are available for looping over the elements of an `Array` or `Hash`; we'll cover these in the next section.

`while` and `until` Loops

A `while` loop executes the statements it encloses repeatedly, as long as the specified condition is met:

```
09-while-loop.rb (excerpt)

while Car.count < 10
  Car.new
  puts "A new car instance was created."
end
```

This simple `while` loop executes the `Car.new` statement repeatedly, as long as the total number of cars is below 10. It exits the loop when the number reaches 10.

Like the relationship between `if` and `unless`, the `while` loop also has a complement: the `until` construct. If we use `until`, the code within the loop is executed *until* the condition is met. We could rewrite the loop above using `until` like so:

```
10-until-loop.rb (excerpt)

until Car.count == 10
  Car.new
  puts "A new car instance was created."
end
```

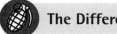 **The Difference Between = and ==**

It's important to note the difference between the **assignment operator** (a single equal sign) and the **equation operator** (a double equal sign) when using them within a condition.

If you're comparing two values, use the equation operator:

```
if Car.count == 10
  ⋮
end
```

If you're assigning a value to a variable, use the assignment operator:

```
my_new_car = Car.new
```

If you confuse the two, you might modify a value that you were hoping only to inspect, with potentially disastrous consequences!

for Loops

for loops allow us to iterate over the elements of a collection, such as an Array, and execute a group of statements once for each element. Here's an example:

11-for-loop.rb *(excerpt)*

```
for car in [ kitt, herbie, batmobile, larry ]
  puts car.mileage
end
```

The code above would produce the following output:

```
5667
33014
4623
20140
```

This simple for loop iterates over an Array of Car objects and outputs the mileage for each car. For each iteration, the car variable is set to the current element of the Array. The first iteration has car set to the equivalent of kitt, the second iteration has it set to herbie, and so forth.

In practice, the traditional `while` and `for` loops covered here are little used. Instead, most people tend to use the instance methods provided by the `Array` and `Hash` classes, which we'll cover next.

Blocks

Blocks are probably the single most attractive feature of Ruby. However, they're also one of those things that take a while to drop into place for Ruby newcomers. Before we dig deeper into creating blocks, let's take a look at some of the core features of Ruby that use blocks.

We looked at some loop constructs in the previous section, and this was a useful way to explore the tools that are available to us. However, you'll probably never actually come across many of these constructs in your work with other Ruby scripts, simply because it's almost always much easier to use a block to perform the same task. A block, in conjunction with the `each` method that is provided by the `Array` and `Hash` classes, is a very powerful way to loop through your data.

Let me illustrate this point with an example. Consider the `for` loop we used a moment ago. We could rewrite that code to use the `each` method, which is an instance method of the `Array` class, like so:

12-simple-block.rb *(excerpt)*

```
[ kitt, herbie, batmobile, larry ].each do |car_name|
  puts car_name.mileage
end
```

Let's analyze this: the block comprises the code between the `do` and `end` keywords. A block is able to receive parameters, which are placed between vertical bars (|) at the beginning of the block. Multiple parameters are separated by commas. Therefore, this code performs an identical operation to the `for` loop we saw before, but in a much more succinct manner.

Let's take another example. To loop through the elements of a `Hash`, we use the `each` method, and pass two parameters to the block: the key (`car_name`) and the value (`color`):

```
                                          13-block-with-params.rb (excerpt)
car_colors = {
  'kitt' => 'black',
  'herbie' => 'white',
  'batmobile' => 'black',
  'larry' => 'green'
}
car_colors.each do |car_name, color|
  puts "#{car_name} is #{color}"
end
```

This code produces the following output:

```
kitt is black
herbie is white
batmobile is black
larry is green
```

The `Integer` class also sports a number of methods that use blocks. The `times` method of an `Integer` object, for example, executes a block exactly *n* times, where *n* is the value of the object:

```
                                               14-block-integer.rb (excerpt)
10.times { Car.new }
puts "#{Car.count} cars have been produced."
```

The code above produces this output:

```
10 cars have been produced.
```

One final point to note here is the alternative block syntax of curly braces. Instead of the do…end keywords that we used in previous examples, curly braces are the preferred syntax for blocks that are very short, as in the previous example.

Here's another method of the `Integer` class; in the spirit of `times`, the `upto` method counts from the value of the object up to the argument passed to the method:

```
                                                               15-block-upto.rb
5.upto(7) { |i| puts i }
```

This code produces the output shown here:

```
5
6
7
```

In Ruby parlance, the object i is a parameter of the block. Parameters for blocks are enclosed in vertical bars, and are usually available only from within the block. If we have more than one parameter, we separate them using commas, like so: |parameter1, parameter2|. In the example above, we would no longer have access to i once the block had finished executing.

As we work through this book, we'll explore many more uses of blocks in combination with the Rails core classes.

Summary

Wow, we covered a lot in this chapter! First, we swept through a stack of object oriented programming theory—probably the equivalent of an introductory computer science course! This gave us a good grounding for exploring the basics of the Ruby programming language, and the Interactive Ruby Shell (irb) was a fun way to do this exploration.

We also investigated many of the Ruby core classes, such as String, Array, and Hash, from within the Ruby shell. We then moved from the shell to create and save proper Ruby files, and using these files, we experimented with control structures such as conditionals, loops, and blocks.

In the next chapter, we'll look at the major cornerstones that make up the Rails framework—the integrated testing facilities—as well as the roles played by the development, testing, and production environments.

Rails Revealed

As you'll have gathered from Chapter 1, quite a bit of thought has been put into the code base that makes up the Rails framework. Over time, many of the internals have been rewritten, which has improved their speed and efficiency and allowed the implementation of additional features, but the original architecture remains largely unchanged. This chapter will shed some light on the inner workings of Rails.

Three Environments

Rails encourages the use of a different environment for each of the stages in an application's life cycle—development, testing, and production. If you've been developing web applications for a while, this is probably how you operate anyway; Rails just formalizes these environments.

development

In the development environment, changes to an application's source code are immediately visible; all we need to do is reload the corresponding page in a web browser. Speed is not a critical factor in this environment. Instead, the focus is on providing the developer with as much insight as possible into the components responsible for displaying each page. When an error occurs in the development environment, we are able to tell at a glance which line of code is responsible for the error, and how that particular line was invoked. This capability is provided by the **stack trace** (a comprehensive list of all the method calls leading up to the error), which is displayed when an unexpected error occurs.

test

In testing, we usually refresh the database with a baseline of dummy data each time a test is repeated: this step ensures that the results of the tests are consistent, and that behavior is reproducible. Unit and functional testing procedures are fully automated in Rails.

When we test a Rails application, we don't view it using a traditional web browser. Instead, tests are invoked from the command line, and can be run as background processes. The testing environment provides a dedicated space in which these processes can operate.

production

By the time your application finally goes live, it should be sufficiently tested that all—or at least most—of the bugs have been eliminated. As a result, updates to the code base should be infrequent, which means that the production environments can be optimized to focus on performance. Tasks such as writing extensive logs for debugging purposes should be unnecessary at this stage. Besides, if an error does occur, you don't want to scare your visitors away with a cryptic stack trace; that's best kept for the development environment.

As the requirements of each of the three environments are quite different, Rails stores the data for each environment in entirely separate databases. So at any given time, you might have:

- live data with which real users are interacting in the production environment

- a partial copy of this live data that you're using to debug an error or develop new features in the development environment

- a set of testing data that's constantly being reloaded into the testing environment

Let's look at how we can configure our database for each of these environments.

Database Configuration

Configuring the database for a Rails application is incredibly easy. All of the critical information is contained in just one file. We'll take a close look at this database configuration file, then create some databases for our application to use.

The Database Configuration File

The separation of environments is reflected in the Rails database configuration file **database.yml**. We saw a sample of this file back in Chapter 1, and in fact we created our very own configuration file in Chapter 2, when we used the `rails` command. Go take a look—it lives in the **config** subdirectory of our Shovell application.

With the comments removed, the file should look like this:

```
                                                               01-database.yml
development:
  adapter: sqlite3
  database: db/development.sqlite3
  timeout: 5000

test:
  adapter: sqlite3
  database: db/test.sqlite3
  timeout: 5000

production:
  adapter: sqlite3
  database: db/production.sqlite3
  timeout: 5000
```

This file lists the minimum amount of information we need in order to connect to the database server for each of our environments (development, test, and production). With the default setup of SQLite that we installed in Chapter 2, every environment is allocated its own physically separate database file, which calls the **db** subdirectory home.

The parameter `database` sets the name of the database that is to be used in each environment. As the configuration file suggests, Rails can support multiple databases (and even different types of database engines, such as MySQL for production and

SQLite for development) in parallel. Note that we're actually talking about different *databases* here, not just different tables—each database can host an arbitrary number of different tables in parallel.

Figure 4.1 shows a graphical representation of this architecture.

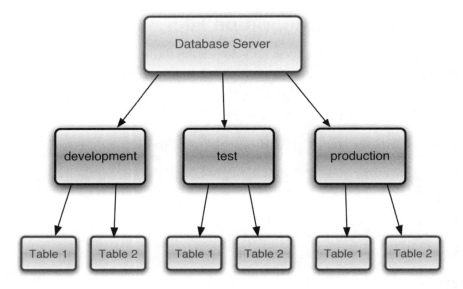

Figure 4.1. The database architecture of a Rails application

However, there's one startling aspect missing from our current configuration: looking at the **db** subdirectory, the databases referenced in our configuration file don't exist yet! Fear not, Rails will auto-create them as soon as they're needed. There's nothing we need to do as far as they are concerned.

The Model–View–Controller Architecture

The model-view-controller (MVC) architecture that we first encountered in Chapter 1 is not unique to Rails. In fact, it predates both Rails and the Ruby language by many years. However, Rails really takes the idea of separating an application's data, user interface, and control logic to a whole new level.

Let's take a look at the concepts behind building an application using the MVC architecture. Once we have the theory in place, we'll see how it translates to our Rails code.

MVC in Theory

MVC is a pattern for the architecture of a software application. It separates an application into the following three components:

models

for handling data and business logic

controllers

for handling the user interface and application logic

views

for handling graphical user interface objects and presentation logic

This separation results in user requests being processed as follows:

1. The browser, on the client, sends a request for a page to the controller on the server.

2. The controller retrieves the data it needs from the model in order to respond to the request.

3. The controller hands the retrieved data to the view.

4. The view is rendered and sent back to the client for the browser to display.

This process is illustrated in Figure 4.2.

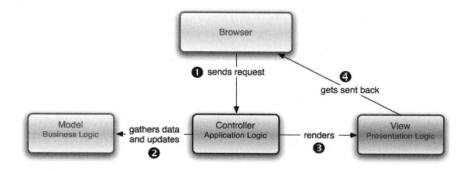

Figure 4.2. Processing a page request in an MVC architecture

Separating a software application into these three distinct components is a good idea for a number of reasons, including the following:

It improves scalability (the ability for an application to grow).

For example, if your application begins experiencing performance issues because database access is slow, you can upgrade the hardware running the database without other components being affected.

It makes maintenance easier.

As the components have a low dependency on each other, making changes to one (to fix bugs or change functionality) does not affect another.

It promotes reuse.

A model may be reused by multiple views, and vice versa.

If you haven't quite got your head around the concept of MVC yet, don't worry. For now, the important thing is to remember that your Rails application is separated into three distinct components. Jump back to Figure 4.2 if you need to refer to it later on.

MVC the Rails Way

Rails promotes the concept that models, views, and controllers should be kept quite separate by storing the code for each of these elements as separate files in separate directories.

This is where the Rails directory structure that we created back in Chapter 2 comes into play. The time has come for us to poke around a bit within that structure. If you take a look inside the **app** directory, which is depicted in Figure 4.3, you'll see some folders whose names might be starting to sound familiar.

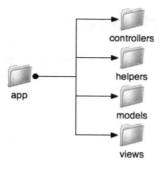

Figure 4.3. The app subdirectory

As you can see, each component of the model-view-controller architecture has its place within the **app** subdirectory—the **models**, **views**, and **controllers** subdirectories, respectively. (We'll talk about that **helpers** directory in Chapter 6.)

This separation continues within the code that comprises the framework itself. The classes that form the core functionality of Rails reside within the following modules:

`ActiveRecord`

`ActiveRecord` is the module for handling business logic and database communication. It plays the role of model in our MVC architecture.[1]

`ActionController`

`ActionController` is the component that handles browser requests and facilitates communication between the model and the view. Your controllers will inherit from this class. It forms part of the `ActionPack` library, a collection of Rails components that we'll explore in depth in Chapter 5.

`ActionView`

`ActionView` is the component that handles the presentation of pages returned to the client. Views inherit from this class, which is also part of the `ActionPack` library.

---

[1] While it might seem odd that `ActiveRecord` doesn't have the word "model" in its name, there is a reason for this: Active Record is also the name of a famous design pattern—one that this component implements in order to perform its role in the MVC world. Besides, if it had been called `ActionModel` then it would have sounded more like an overpaid Hollywood star than a software component …

Let's take a closer look at each of these components in turn.

ActiveRecord (the Model)

ActiveRecord is designed to handle all of an application's tasks that relate to the database, including:

- establishing a connection to the database server
- retrieving data from a table
- storing new data in the database

ActiveRecord also has a few other neat tricks up its sleeve. Let's look at some of them now.

Database Abstraction

ActiveRecord ships with database adapters to connect to SQLite, MySQL, and PostgreSQL. A large number of adapters are also available for other popular database server packages, such as Oracle, DB2, and Microsoft SQL Server, via the RubyGems system.

The ActiveRecord module is based on the concept of database abstraction. As we mentioned in Chapter 1, database abstraction is a way of coding an application so that it isn't dependent upon any one database. Code that's specific to a particular database server is hidden safely in ActiveRecord, and invoked as needed. The result is that a Rails application is not bound to any specific database server software. Should you need to change the underlying database server at a later time, no changes to your application code should be required.

Examples of code that differs greatly between vendors, and which ActiveRecord abstracts, include:

- the process of logging into the database server
- date calculations
- handling of boolean (true/false) data
- evolution of your database structure

Before I can show you the magic of ActiveRecord in action, though, we need to do a little housekeeping.

Database Tables

Tables are the containers within a database that store our data in a structured manner, and they're made up of rows and columns. The rows map to individual objects, and the columns map to the attributes of those objects. The collection of all the tables in a database, and the relationships between those tables, is called the database **schema**.

An example of a table is shown in Figure 4.4.

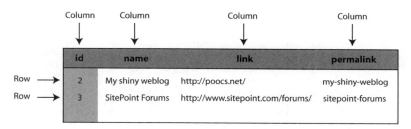

Figure 4.4. The structure of a typical database table, including rows and columns

In Rails, the naming of Ruby classes and database tables follows an intuitive pattern: if we have a table called `stories` which consists of five rows, this table will store the data for five `Story` objects. The nicest thing about the mapping between classes and tables is that you don't need to write code to achieve it—the mapping just happens, because `ActiveRecord` infers the name of the table from the name of the class.

Note that the name of our class in Ruby is a singular noun (`Story`), but the name of the table is plural (`stories`). This relationship makes sense if you think about it: when we refer to a `Story` object in Ruby, we're dealing with a single story. But the SQL table holds a multitude of stories, so its name should be plural. While you can override these conventions—as is sometimes necessary when dealing with legacy databases—it's much easier to adhere to them.

The close relationship between tables and objects extends even further: if our `stories` table were to have a `link` column, as our example in Figure 4.4 does, the data in this column would automatically be mapped to the `link` attribute in a `Story` object. And adding a new column to a table would cause an attribute of the same name to become available in all of that table's corresponding objects.

So, let's create some tables to hold the stories we create.

For the time being, we'll create a table using the old-fashioned approach of entering SQL into the SQLite console. You could type out the following SQL commands, although typing out SQL isn't much fun. Instead, I encourage you to download the following script from the code archive, and copy and paste it straight into your SQLite console that you invoked via the following command in the application directory:

```
$ sqlite3 db/development.sqlite3
```

Once your SQLite console is up, paste in the following:

02-create-stories-table.sql

```
CREATE TABLE stories (
  "id" INTEGER PRIMARY KEY AUTOINCREMENT NOT NULL,
  "name" varchar(255) DEFAULT NULL,
  "link" varchar(255) DEFAULT NULL,
  "created_at" datetime DEFAULT NULL,
  "updated_at" datetime DEFAULT NULL
);
```

You needn't worry about remembering these SQL commands to use in your own projects; instead, take heart in knowing that in Chapter 5 we'll look at **migrations**. Migrations are special Ruby classes that we can write to create database tables for our application without using any SQL at all.

Using the Rails Console

Now that we have our `stories` table in place, let's exit the SQLite console (simply type `.quit`) and open up a Rails console. A Rails console is just like the interactive Ruby console (`irb`) that we used in Chapter 3, but with one key difference. In a Rails console, you have access to all the environment variables and classes that are available to your application while it's running. These are not available from within a standard `irb` console.

To enter a Rails console, change to your **shovell** folder, and enter the command `ruby script/console`, as shown below. The >> prompt is ready to accept your commands:

```
$ cd shovell
$ ruby script/console
Loading development environment (Rails 2.0.2)
>>
```

Saving an Object

To start using `ActiveRecord`, simply define a class that inherits from the `ActiveRecord::Base` class. (We touched on the `::` operator very briefly in Chapter 3, where we mentioned that it was a way to invoke class methods on an object. It can also be used to refer to classes that exist within a module, which is what we're doing here.) Flip back to the section on object oriented programming (OOP) in Chapter 3 if you need a refresher on inheritance.

Consider the following code snippet:

```
class Story < ActiveRecord::Base
end
```

These two lines of code define a seemingly empty class called `Story`. However, this class is far from empty, as we'll soon see.

From the Rails console, let's create this `Story` class, and an instance of the class called `story`, by entering these commands:

```
>> class Story < ActiveRecord::Base; end
=> nil
>> story = Story.new
=> #<Story id: nil, name: nil, url: nil, created_at: nil,
       updated_at: nil>
>> story.class
=> Story(id: integer, name: string, link: string,
       created_at: datetime, updated_at: datetime)
```

As you can see, the syntax for creating a new `ActiveRecord` object is identical to the syntax we used to create other Ruby objects in Chapter 3. At this point, we've created a new `Story` object. However, this object exists in memory only—we haven't stored it in our database yet.

We can confirm the fact that our `Story` object hasn't been saved yet by checking the return value of the `new_record?` method:

```
>> story.new_record?
=> true
```

Since the object has not been saved yet, it will be lost when we exit the Rails console. To save it to the database, we need to invoke the object's `save` method:

```
>> story.save
=> true
```

Now that we've saved our object (a return value of `true` indicates that the `save` method was successful) our story is no longer a new record. It's even been assigned a unique ID, as shown below:

```
>> story.new_record?
=> false
>> story.id
=> 1
```

Defining Relationships Between Objects

As well as the basic functionality that we've just seen, `ActiveRecord` makes the process of defining relationships (or associations) between objects as easy as it can be. Of course, it's possible with some database servers to define such relationships entirely within the database schema. However, in order to put `ActiveRecord` through its paces, let's look at the way it defines these relationships within Rails.

Object relationships can be defined in a variety of ways; the main difference between these relationships is the number of records that are specified in the relationship. The primary types of database associations are:

- one-to-one associations
- one-to-many associations
- many-to-many associations

Let's look at some examples of each of these associations. Feel free to type them into the Rails console if you like, for the sake of practice. Remember that your class definitions won't be saved, though—I'll show you how to define associations in a file later.

Suppose our application has the following associations:

■ An `Author` can have one `Weblog`:

```ruby
class Author < ActiveRecord::Base
  has_one :weblog
end
```

■ An `Author` can submit many `Stories`:

```ruby
class Author < ActiveRecord::Base
  has_many :stories
end
```

■ A `Story` belongs to an `Author`:

```ruby
class Story < ActiveRecord::Base
  belongs_to :author
end
```

■ A `Story` has, and belongs to, many different `Topics`:

```ruby
class Story < ActiveRecord::Base
  has_and_belongs_to_many :topics
end
class Topic < ActiveRecord::Base
  has_and_belongs_to_many :stories
end
```

You're no doubt growing tired of typing class definitions into a console, only to have them disappear the moment you exit the console. For this reason, we won't go any further with the associations between our objects—we'll delve into the Rails `ActiveRecord` module in more detail in Chapter 5.

The `ActionPack` Module

`ActionPack` is the name of the library that contains the view and controller parts of the MVC architecture. Unlike the `ActiveRecord` module, these modules are a little more intuitively named: `ActionController` and `ActionView`.

Exploring application logic and presentation logic on the command line doesn't make a whole lot of sense; views and controllers *are* designed to interact with a web browser, after all! Instead, I'll just give you a brief overview of the `ActionPack` components, and we'll cover the hands-on stuff in Chapter 5.

ActionController (the Controller)

The controller handles the application logic of your program, acting as glue between the application's data, the presentation layer, and the web browser. In this role, a controller performs a number of tasks, including:

- deciding how to handle a particular request (for example, whether to render a full page or just one part of it)

- retrieving data from the model to be passed to the view

- gathering information from a browser request, and using it to create or update data in the model

When we introduced the MVC diagram in Figure 4.2 earlier in this chapter, it might not have occurred to you that a Rails application can consist of a number of different controllers. Well, it can! Each controller is responsible for a specific part of the application.

For our Shovell application, we'll create:

- one controller for displaying story links, which we'll name `StoriesController`
- another controller for handling user authentication, called `SessionsController`
- a controller to display user pages, named `UsersController`
- and finally a fourth controller to handle story voting, called `VotesController`

All controllers will inherit from the `ActionController::Base` class,[2] but they'll have different functionality, implemented as instance methods. Here's a sample class definition for the `StoriesController` class:

---

[2] There will actually be an intermediate class between this class and the `ActionController::Base` class; we'll cover the creation of the `StoriesController` class in more detail in Chapter 5. However, this doesn't change the fact that `ActionController::Base` is the base class from which every controller inherits.

```
class StoriesController < ActionController::Base
  def index
  end

  def show
  end
end
```

This simple class definition sets up our `StoriesController` with two empty methods: the `index` method, and the `show` method. We'll expand upon both of these methods in later chapters.

Each controller resides in its own Ruby file (with a **.rb** extension), which lives within the **app/controllers** directory. The `StoriesController` class that we just defined, for example, would inhabit the file **app/controllers/stories_controller.rb**.

 Naming Classes and Files

You'll have noticed by now that the names of classes and files follow different conventions:

- Class names are written in **CamelCase** (each word beginning with a capital letter, with no spaces between words).[3]

- Filenames are written in lowercase, with underscores separating each word.

This is an important detail! If this convention is *not* followed, Rails will have a hard time locating your files. Luckily, you won't need to name your files manually very often, if ever, as you'll see when we look at generated code in Chapter 5.

ActionView (the View)

As we discussed earlier, one of the principles of MVC is that a view should contain **presentation logic** only. This principle holds that the code in a view should only perform actions that relate to displaying pages in the application—none of the code in a view should perform any complicated application logic, nor should it store or

---

[3] There are actually two variations of CamelCase: one with an uppercase first letter (also known as PascalCase), and one with a lowercase first letter. The Ruby convention for class names requires an uppercase first letter.

retrieve any data from the database. In Rails, everything that is sent to the web browser is handled by a view.

Predictably, views are stored in the **app/views** folder of our application.

A view need not actually contain any Ruby code at all—it may be the case that one of your views is a simple HTML file. However, it's more likely that your views will contain a combination of HTML and Ruby code, making the page more dynamic. The Ruby code is embedded in HTML using **embedded Ruby** (ERb) syntax.

ERb is similar to PHP or JSP in that it allows server-side code to be scattered throughout an HTML file by wrapping that code in special tags. For example, in PHP you may write code like this:

```
<strong><?php echo 'Hello World from PHP!' ?></strong>
```

The equivalent code in ERb would be the following:

```
<strong><%= 'Hello World from Ruby!' %></strong>
```

There are two forms of the ERb tag pair: one that includes the equal sign, and one that doesn't:

<%= … %>

> This tag pair is for regular output. The output of a Ruby expression between these tags will be displayed in the browser.

<% … %>

> This tag pair is for code that is not intended to be displayed, such as calculations, loops, or variable assignments.

An example of each ERb tag is shown below:

```
<%= 'This line is displayed in the browser' %>
<% 'This line executes silently, without displaying any output' %>
```

You can place any Ruby code—be it simple or complex—between these tags.

Creating an instance of a view is a little different to that of a model or a controller. While `ActionView::Base` (the parent class for all views) is one of the base classes for views in Rails, the instantiation of a view is handled completely by the `Action-View` module. The only file a Rails developer needs to modify is the **template**, which is the file that contains the presentation code for the view. As you might have guessed, these templates are stored in the **app/views** folder.

As with everything else Rails, a strict convention applies to the naming and storage of template files:

▪ A template has a one-to-one mapping to the action (method) of a controller. The name of the template file matches the name of the action to which it maps.

▪ The folder that stores the template is named after the controller.

▪ The extension of the template file is twofold and varies depending on the template's type and the actual language in which a template is written. By default there are three types of extensions in Rails:

html.erb

This is the extension for standard HTML templates that are sprinkled with ERb tags.

xml.builder

This extension is used for templates that output XML (for example, to generate RSS feeds for your application).

js.rjs

This extension is used for templates that return JavaScript instructions. This type of template might be used, for example, to modify an existing page (via Ajax) to update the contents of a `<div>` tag.

This convention may sound complicated, but it's actually quite intuitive. For example, consider the `StoriesController` class defined earlier. Invoking the `show` method for this controller would, by default, attempt to display the `ActionView` template that lived in the **app/views/stories** directory. Assuming the page was a standard HTML page (containing some ERb code), the name of this template would be **show.html.erb**.

Rails also comes with special templates such as **layouts** and **partials**. Layouts are templates that control the global layout of an application, such as structures that remain unchanged between pages (the primary navigation menu, for instance).

Partials are special subtemplates (the result of a template being split into separate files, such as a secondary navigation menu or a form) that can be used multiple times within the application. We'll cover both layouts and partials in Chapter 7.

Communication between controllers and views occurs via instance variables that are populated from within the controller's action. Let's expand upon our sample `StoriesController` class to illustrate this point (there's no need to type any of this out just yet):

```
class StoriesController < ActionController::Base
  def index
    @variable = 'Value being passed to a view'
  end
end
```

As you can see, the instance variable `@variable` is being assigned a string value within the controller's action. Through the magic of `ActionView`, this variable can now be referenced directly from the corresponding view, as shown in the code below:

```
<p>The instance variable @variable contains: <%= @variable %></p>
```

This approach allows more complex computations to be performed outside the view—remember, it should only contain presentational logic—and allow the view to display just the end result of the computation.

Rails also provides access to special containers, such as the `params` and `session` hashes. These contain such information as the current page request and the user's session. We'll make use of these hashes in the chapters that follow.

The REST

When I introduced Rails in Chapter 1 I mentioned quite a few common development principles and best practices that the Rails team advises you to adopt in your own projects. One that I kept under my hat until now was RESTful-style development, or resource-centric development. REST will make much more sense with your fresh knowledge about models and controllers as the principal building blocks of a Rails application.

In Theory

REST stands for *R*epresentational *S*tate *T*ransfer and originates from the doctoral dissertation of Roy Fielding,[4] one of the co-founders of The Apache Software Foundation and one of the authors of the HTTP specification.

REST, according to the theory, is not restricted to the World Wide Web. The basis of the resource-centric approach is derived from the fact that most of the time spent using network-based applications can be characterized as a client or user interacting with distinct resources. For example, in an ecommerce application, a book and a shopping cart are separate resources with which the customer interacts.

Every resource in an application needs to be addressed by a unique and uniform identifier. In the world of web applications, the unique identifier would be the URL by which a resource can be accessed. In our Shovell application, each submitted story will be able to be viewed at a unique URL.

The potential interactions within an application are defined as a set of operations (or verbs) that can be performed with a given resource. The most common verbs are *c*reate, *r*ead, *u*pdate, and *d*elete, which are often collectively referred to as "*CRUD* operations." If you relate this to our Shovell application you'll see that it covers most of the interactions possible with the Shovell stories: a user will create a story, another user will read the story, the story can also be updated or deleted.

The client and server have to communicate via the same language (or protocol) in order to implement the REST architecture style successfully. This protocol is also required to be **stateless**, **cacheable**, and **layered**.

Here, stateless means that each request for information from the client to the server needs to be completely independent of prior or future requests. Each request needs to contain everything necessary for the server to understand the request and provide an appropriate answer.

Cacheable and layered are architectural attributes that improve the communication between client and server without affecting the communication protocol.

---

[4] http://www.ics.uci.edu/~fielding/pubs/dissertation/top.htm

REST and the Web

As mentioned in the previous section, REST as a design pattern can be used in any application domain. But the Web is probably the domain that implements REST most often. Since this is a book that deals with building web applications, we'd better take a look at the implementation details of RESTful style development in web applications in particular.

HTTP (Hypertext Transfer Protocol: the communication protocol used on the Web), as the astute reader will know, also makes heavy use of verbs in its day-to-day operations. When your browser requests a web page from any given web server, it will issue a so-called GET-request. If you submit a web page form, your browser will do so using a POST-request (not always, to be honest, but 99% of the time).

In addition to GET and POST, HTTP defines two additional verbs that are less commonly used by web browsers. (In fact, none of the browsers in widespread use actually implement them.) These verbs are PUT and DELETE. If you compare the list of HTTP verbs with the verbs of CRUD from the previous section, they line up fairly nicely, as you can see in Table 4.1.

Table 4.1. HTTP Verbs Versus CRUD Verbs

CRUD	HTTP
CREATE	POST
READ	GET
UPDATE	PUT
DELETE	DELETE

The language in which client (the browser) and server (the web server) talk to each other is obviously HTTP. HTTP is, by definition, stateless. This means that as soon as a browser has downloaded all of the information the server offered as a reply to the browser's request, the connection is closed and the two might never ever talk again. Or the browser could send another request just milliseconds later, asking for additional information. Each request contains all the necessary information for the server to respond appropriately, including potential cookies, the format, and the language in which the browser expects the server to reply.

HTTP is also layered and cacheable, both of which are attributes the REST definition expects of the spoken protocol. Routers, proxy servers, and firewalls are only three (very common) examples of architectural components that implement layering and caching on top of HTTP.

REST in Rails

REST and Rails not only both start with the letter R, they have a fairly deep relationship. Rails comes with a generator for resources (see the section called "Code Generation" for a primer on this topic) and provides all sorts of assistance for easy construction of the uniform addresses by which resources can be accessed.

Rails's focus on the MVC architecture (which we'll be getting our hands on shortly, in Chapter 5) is also a perfect companion for RESTful style development. Models resemble the resources themselves, while controllers provide access to the resource and allow interaction based on the interaction verbs listed above.

I mentioned in the previous section that two verbs aren't implemented in the majority of browsers on the market. To support the verbs PUT and DELETE, Rails uses POST requests with a little tacked-on magic to simulate the PUT and DELETE verbs transparently for both the user and the Rails application developer. Nifty, isn't it?

We will gradually start implementing and interacting with resources for our Shovell application over the course of the next hands-on chapters, so let's now move on and talk about yet another batch of components that make up the Rails framework.

Code Generation

Rather than having us create all of our application code from scratch, Rails gives us the facility to generate an application's basic structure with considerable ease. In the same way that we created our application's entire directory structure, we can create new models, controllers, and views using a single command.

To generate code in Rails, we use the **generate** script, which lives in the **script** folder. Give it a try now: type `ruby script/generate` without any command parameters. Rails displays an overview of the available parameters for the command, and lists the generators from which we can choose, as Figure 4.5 illustrates.

Figure 4.5. Sample output from `script/generate`

Rails can generate code of varying complexity. At its simplest, creating a new controller causes a template file to be placed in the appropriate subdirectory of your application. The template itself consists of a mainly empty class definition, similar to the Story and Author classes that we looked at earlier in this chapter.

However, code generation can also be a very powerful tool for automating complex, repetitive tasks; for instance, you might generate a foundation for handling user authentication. We'll launch straight into generating code in Chapter 5, when we begin to generate our models and controllers.

Another example is the generation of a basic web-based interface to a model, referred to as **scaffolding**. We'll also look at scaffolding in Chapter 5, as we make a start on building our views.

ActionMailer

While not strictly part of the Web, email is a big part of our online experience, and Rails's integrated support for email is worth a mention. Web applications frequently make use of email for tasks like sending sign-up confirmations to new users and resetting a user's password.

`ActionMailer` is the Rails component that makes it easy to incorporate the sending and receiving of email into your application. `ActionMailer` is structured in a similar way to `ActionPack` in that it consists of controllers and actions with templates.

While the creation of emails, and the processing of incoming email, are complex tasks, `ActionMailer` hides these complexities and handles the tasks for you. This means that creating an outgoing email is simply a matter of supplying the subject, body, and recipients of the email using templates and a little Ruby code. Likewise, `ActionMailer` processes incoming email for you, providing you with a Ruby object that encapsulates the entire message in a way that's easy to access.

Adding email functionality to a web application is beyond the scope of this book, but you can read more about `ActionMailer` on the Ruby on Rails wiki.[5]

Testing and Debugging

As mentioned in Chapter 1, an automated testing framework is already built into Ruby on Rails. It also, rather helpfully, supplies a full stack trace for errors to assist with debugging.

Testing

A number of different types of testing are supported by Rails, including automated and integration testing.

---

[5] http://wiki.rubyonrails.com/rails/pages/ActionMailer/

Automated Testing

The concept of automated testing isn't new to the world of traditional software development, but it's fairly uncommon in web application development. While most Java-based web applications make use of comprehensive testing facilities, a large number of PHP and Perl web applications go live after only some manual tests have been performed (and sometimes without any testing at all!). Although performing automated tests is optional, developers may decide against this option for reasons ranging from the complexity of the task to time constraints.

We touched on this briefly in Chapter 1, but it's worth stressing again: the fact that comprehensive automated testing is built into Rails, and is dead easy to implement, means there's no longer a question about whether or not you should test your apps. *Just do it!*

The `generate` command that we introduced a moment ago can automatically create testing templates that you can use with your controllers, views, and models. (Note that Rails just assists you in doing your job, it's not replacing you—yet!)

The extent to which you want to implement automated testing is up to you. It may suit your needs to wait until something breaks, then write a test that proves the problem exists. Once you've fixed the problem so that the test no longer fails, you'll never again get a bug report for that particular problem.

If, on the other hand, you'd like to embrace automated testing completely, you can even write tests to ensure that a specific HTML tag exists at a precise position within a page's hierarchy.[6] Yes, automated tests *can* be that exact.

Integration Testing

Rails's testing capabilities also include **integration testing**.

Integration testing refers to the testing of several web site components in succession—typically, the order of the components resembles the path that a user would follow when using the application. You could, for example, construct an integration test that reconstructs the actions of a user clicking on a link, registering for a user

---

[6] The hierarchy referred to here is the Document Object Model (DOM), a W3C standard for describing the hierarchy of an (X)HTML page.

account, confirming the registration email you send, and visiting a page that's restricted to registered users.

We'll look at both automated testing and integration testing in more detail as we progress through the development of our application.

Debugging

When you're fixing problems, the first step is to identify the source of the problem. Like many languages, Rails assists this process by providing the developer (that's you!) with a full stack trace of the code. We mentioned earlier in the section called "Three Environments" that a stack trace is a list of all of the methods that were called up to the point at which an exception was raised. The list includes not only the name of each method, but also the classes those methods belong to, and the names of the files they reside within.

Using the information contained in the stack trace, you can go back to your code to determine the problem. There are several ways to tackle this, depending on the nature of the problem itself:

- If you have a rough idea of what the problem may be, and are able to isolate it to your application's model (either a particular class or aspect of your data), your best bet is to use the Rails console that we looked at earlier in this chapter. Type **console** from the **script** directory to launch the console. Once inside, you can load the particular model that you're interested in, and poke at it to reproduce and fix the problem.

- If the problem leans more towards something related to the user's browser or session, you can add a `debugger` statement around the spot at which the problem occurs. With this in place, you can reload the browser and step through your application's code using the ruby-debug tool to explore variable content or to execute Ruby statements manually.

We'll be covering all the gory details of debugging in Chapter 11.

Summary

In this chapter, we peeled back some of the layers that comprise the Ruby on Rails framework. By now you should have a good understanding of which parts of Rails perform particular roles in the context of an MVC architecture. We also discussed how a request that's made by a web browser is processed by a Rails application.

We looked at the different environments that Rails provides to address the different stages in the life cycle of an application, and we configured databases to support these environments. We also provided Rails with the necessary details to connect to our database.

We also had our first contact with real code, as we looked at the `ActiveRecord` models, `ActionController` controllers, and `ActionView` templates for our Shovell application. We explored the topics of the REST style of application architecture, code generation, testing, as well as debugging.

In the next chapter, we'll build on all this knowledge as we use the code generation tools to create actual models, controllers, and views for our Shovell application. It's going to be a big one!

Chapter 5

Models, Views, and Controllers

In Chapter 4, we introduced the principles behind the model-view-controller architectural pattern, and saw how each of the components is implemented within the Rails framework. Now we'll put this knowledge to good use as we use Rails's code generation techniques to create these components for our own Shovell application.

Generating a Model

As our application will be used to share links to **stories** on the Web, a Story is the fundamental object around which our application will evolve. Here, we'll use the Rails model generator to create a Story model, then build everything else around it.

The Model Generator

The model generator is actually driven by a command line script that we encountered back in the section called "Code Generation" in Chapter 4: the **generate** script. This lives in the **script** directory, and makes our generation of a Story model very simple.

Running the generate Script

generate can be called from the command line and takes several parameters. The first parameter is the type of component that's to be generated. You can probably guess which value I'm going to suggest you use for this parameter: we're creating a model, so the parameter to pass is simply `model`. Let's take a look at what happens when we pass that to the script:

```
$ cd shovell
$ ruby script/generate model
```

Figure 5.1 shows the resulting output.

We can deduce from this output that using **generate** to create a new model for our application in its simple form won't actually do very much—some **stubs** (empty files) will be created in the appropriate directories, but that's about all.

The second example in Figure 5.1 shows the slightly more advanced version. To give our model a jump-start by adding everything necessary to start playing with it right away, we tell **generate** the names and types of the attributes the model is going to have. So let's go ahead and create the `Story` model with its attributes (and their respective types), then examine each of the generated files in turn.

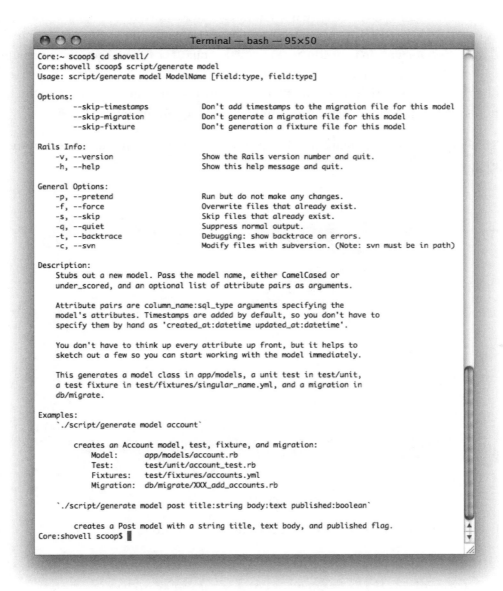

```
Core:~ scoop$ cd shovell/
Core:shovell scoop$ script/generate model
Usage: script/generate model ModelName [field:type, field:type]

Options:
        --skip-timestamps              Don't add timestamps to the migration file for this model
        --skip-migration               Don't generate a migration file for this model
        --skip-fixture                 Don't generation a fixture file for this model

Rails Info:
    -v, --version                      Show the Rails version number and quit.
    -h, --help                         Show this help message and quit.

General Options:
    -p, --pretend                      Run but do not make any changes.
    -f, --force                        Overwrite files that already exist.
    -s, --skip                         Skip files that already exist.
    -q, --quiet                        Suppress normal output.
    -t, --backtrace                    Debugging: show backtrace on errors.
    -c, --svn                          Modify files with subversion. (Note: svn must be in path)

Description:
    Stubs out a new model. Pass the model name, either CamelCased or
    under_scored, and an optional list of attribute pairs as arguments.

    Attribute pairs are column_name:sql_type arguments specifying the
    model's attributes. Timestamps are added by default, so you don't have to
    specify them by hand as 'created_at:datetime updated_at:datetime'.

    You don't have to think up every attribute up front, but it helps to
    sketch out a few so you can start working with the model immediately.

    This generates a model class in app/models, a unit test in test/unit,
    a test fixture in test/fixtures/singular_name.yml, and a migration in
    db/migrate.

Examples:
    `./script/generate model account`

        creates an Account model, test, fixture, and migration:
            Model:      app/models/account.rb
            Test:       test/unit/account_test.rb
            Fixtures:   test/fixtures/accounts.yml
            Migration:  db/migrate/XXX_add_accounts.rb

    `./script/generate model post title:string body:text published:boolean`

        creates a Post model with a string title, text body, and published flag.
Core:shovell scoop$ ▮
```

Figure 5.1. Sample output from the model generator

From the **shovell** folder, enter the following:

```
$ ruby script/generate model Story name:string link:string
```

As you can see, the attributes we want our Story model to have are specified simply as space-separated arguments to the **generate** script using the notation *attribute name:attribute type*. In this case, we specify that our Story model gets two attributes of type string (Rails defines the string type as up to 255 alphanumeric characters): one named name which holds the title of our stories, and one named link which holds, as you might have guessed, a link to the story on the Internet.

The output of this command will list exactly what has been done; it's shown in Figure 5.2.

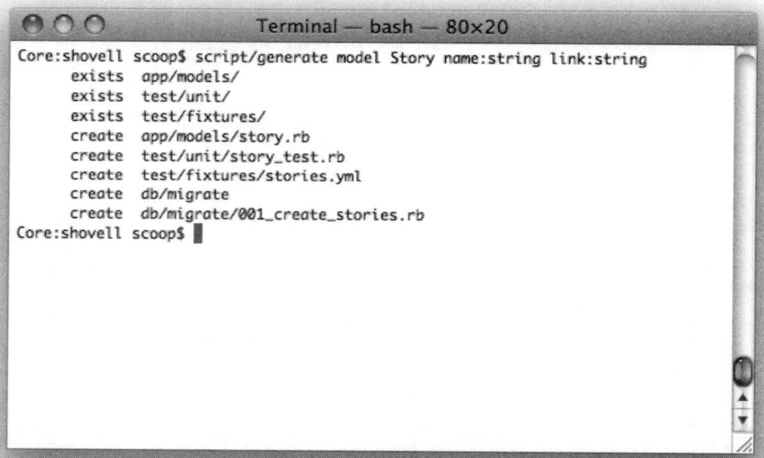

```
Core:shovell scoop$ script/generate model Story name:string link:string
      exists  app/models/
      exists  test/unit/
      exists  test/fixtures/
      create  app/models/story.rb
      create  test/unit/story_test.rb
      create  test/fixtures/stories.yml
      create  db/migrate
      create  db/migrate/001_create_stories.rb
Core:shovell scoop$ 
```

Figure 5.2. Generating a Story model

Let's take a closer look at what the **generate** script has done here.

Understanding the Output

To begin with, generate skipped over three folders that already exist. The script indicates that it's skipping a folder by displaying the word **exists**, followed by the name of the folder. The folders that were skipped in Figure 5.2 were those that were generated when we ran the rails command back in the section called "Creating the Standard Directory Structure" in Chapter 2.

Next, **generate** actually created some files (indicated by the word **create**, followed by the name of the file that was created) and a folder. Let's look at each of the files in turn:

story.rb

This file contains the actual class definition for the `Story` model. Locate the file in the **app/models** folder and examine its contents in your text editor—the class definition is absolutely identical to the one that we typed out in the section called "Saving an Object" in Chapter 4:

```
01-story.rb

class Story < ActiveRecord::Base
end
```

What happened to the attributes we specified? They're nowhere to be found! Don't panic—Rails has used the information we provided to create the database table. It turns out Rails doesn't need you to declare each attribute of a model explicitly in the model's class definition. Rails determines a model's attribute by reading the columns of the database table that the model is mapped to. This technique is called **introspection**, which we'll meet again later on.

Okay, being able to generate these two lines of code isn't exactly groundbreaking. But stay with me here!

test/unit/story_test.rb

This file is much more exciting; it's an automatically generated unit test for our model. We'll look at it in detail in Chapter 6, but, briefly, building up the contents of this file allows us to ensure that all of the code in our model is covered by a unit test. As we mentioned back in Chapter 1, once we have all our unit tests in place, we can automate the process of checking that our code behaves as intended.

test/fixtures/stories.yml

To help with our unit test, a file called **stories.yml** is created. This file is referred to as a **fixture**. Fixtures are files that contain sample data for unit testing purposes—when we run the test suite, Rails will wipe the database belonging to the testing environment and populate our tables using the fixtures. In this way, fixtures allow us to ensure that every unit test of a given application is run against a consistent baseline.

The **stories.yml** fixture file will come prepared with two sample story records for our `stories` table, prepopulated with values for each of the attributes we defined. The **.yml** extension for that file indicates that it is a YAML file. We'll look at what this means next up.

db/migrate/001_create_stories.rb

This file is what's known as a migration file; we'll be exploring migrations shortly.

Understanding YAML

YAML (a tongue-in-cheek recursive acronym that stands for YAML Ain't a Markup Language) is a lightweight format for representing data. YAML files have the extension **.yml**. As they employ none of the confusing tags that XML uses, YAML files are much easier for humans to read, and are just as efficiently read by computers.

Rails uses YAML files extensively to specify fixtures. We've seen a couple of examples of YAML files so far: the **database.yml** file that we used to configure our database connection was one; the **stories.yml** file that we just created with the **generate** script is another.

Let's dissect the **stories.yml** file—open it up in a text editor (you'll find it in the **test/fixtures** directory), and you'll see the following code:

```
                                                          02-stories.yml
one:
  name: MyString
  link: MyString

two:
  name: MyString
  link: MyString
```

This YAML file represents two separate records (one, and two). Each record contains values for the two attributes we defined. These values are obviously made up and are not exactly descriptive.

Let's expand on each of these records by filling in meaningful values for the `name` and `link` fields. Edit the file so that it looks like this:

```
                                                          03-stories.yml
one:
  name: My shiny weblog
  link: http://poocs.net/

two:
  name: SitePoint Forums
  link: http://www.sitepoint.com/forums/
```

As you can see, each record in a YAML file begins with a unique name, which is *not* indented. This name is not the name of the record, or of any of the fields in the database; it's simply used to identify the record within the file. (It's also utilized in testing, as we'll see in Chapter 11.) In our expanded **stories.yml** file, `one` and `two` are these identifying names.

After the unique name, we see a series of key/value pairs, each of which is indented by one or more spaces (we'll use two spaces, to keep consistent with our convention for Rails code). In each case, the key is separated from its value by a colon.

Now, let's take a look at the last file that was generated—the migration file. If your experience with modifying databases has been limited to writing SQL, this next section is sure to be an eye-opener, so buckle up! This is going to be an exciting ride.

Modifying the Schema Using Migrations

As we mentioned earlier, the last of the four files that our **generate** script created—**001_create_stories.rb**—is a **migration file**. A migration file is a special file that can be used to adjust the database schema in a variety of ways (each change that's defined in the file is referred to as a **migration**).

Migrations can be a handy way to make alterations to your database as your application evolves. Not only do they provide you with a means to change your database schema in an iterative manner, but they let you do so using Ruby code, rather than SQL. As you may have gathered by now, I'm not a big fan of writing lots of SQL, and migrations are a great way to avoid it.

Migration files are numbered so that they can be executed sequentially. In our case, the file for creating stories is the first migration file, so our migration file has the number 001 in its name.

Like SQL scripts, migrations can be built on top of each other, which reinforces the need for these files to be executed in order. Sequential execution removes the possibility of, for example, any attempt to add a new column to a table that doesn't yet exist.

Let's examine the migration file that was generated for us.

Creating a Skeleton Migration File

Open the file **001_create_stories.rb** in your text editor—it lives in **db/migrate**. It should look like this:

```
                                                    04-001_create_stories.rb
class CreateStories < ActiveRecord::Migration
  def self.up
    create_table :stories do |t|
      t.string :name
      t.string :link

      t.timestamps
    end
  end

  def self.down
    drop_table :stories
  end
end
```

As you can see, a migration file contains a class definition that inherits from the `ActiveRecord::Migration` class. The class that's defined in the migration file is assigned a name by the **generate** script, based on the parameters that are passed to it. In this case, our migration has been given the name `CreateStories`, which is a fairly accurate description of the task that it will perform—we're generating a new model (a `Story`), so the code in the migration file creates a `stories` table in which to store our stories.

The class contains two class methods:

- `self.up` is called when the migration is applied—when we're setting *up* our schema.

- `self.down` is called when the migration is reversed—when we're tearing it *down*.

These methods are complementary: the task performed by the down method in a migration file should be the exact opposite of that performed by the up method.

Luckily, our down method is complete and needs no tweaking. Its purpose is to undo the changes that are applied in the up method; all it needs to do to achieve this is to drop the database table.

What may come as a surprise is that the up method looks mostly complete, too. Since we took the time to tell the generate script on the command line which columns the generated model should have, the generator auto-filled the migration with instructions to create a table including (but not limited to, as we'll see shortly) the two attributes to hold the name and the link of a story. But let's take a few minutes to walk through the generated code line by line.

Creating the stories Table

In the generated migration code in the `self.up` method, the first line includes a call to the `create_table` method, into which we pass the name of the table we'd like to create (which is `stories`) as a symbol (`:stories`). The method is also being passed a block (jump back to the section called "Blocks" in Chapter 3 if you need a refresher), used to define the individual columns in the table:

```
create_table :stories do |t|
  : block body...
end
```

Within the block, we have two lines to define the attributes we specified on the **generate** command line as columns in our SQL table. Like an SQL script, each column in our migration file should have a name and a type of data storage (such as a string, number, or date):

```
create_table :stories do |t|
  t.string :name
  t.string :link
  : block body…
end
```

Here, the first line defines the column `name` as type `string` and the second line defines the column `link`, also of type `string`. This could even be rewritten, in shorthand syntax, as you see here:

```
create_table :stories do |t|
  t.string :name, :link
  : block body…
end
```

The third line in the block is a little special. Instead of creating a `timestamps` column of questionable value, the `timestamps` method automatically creates two "magic" columns in the `stories` table named `created_at` and `updated_at`:

```
create_table :stories do |t|
  : block body…
  t.timestamps
end
```

We'll take an in-depth look at this functionality in Chapter 9.

In addition to creating completely new tables, migrations can be used to alter existing tables. If you were to decide tomorrow that your `stories` table needed to store a description for each story, it would be a painful task to have to recreate the whole table just to add the extra column. Once again, good old SQL can be used to perform this job efficiently, but to use it, you'd have to learn yet *another* awkward SQL command. The migrations option, on the other hand, allows you to add this column to an existing table without losing any of the data that the table contains.

We'll use migrations to alter the `stories` table when we get to Chapter 9. For now, let's just add one minor parameter to the `self.up` method, like so:

```
                                    05-001_create_stories.rb (excerpt)
def self.up
  create_table :stories, :force => true do |t|
    t.string :name
    t.string :link

    t.timestamps
  end
end
```

The :force => true at the beginning of the block isn't usually required—we've included it in this case to counter the fact that we created a table for this model back in Chapter 4, using raw SQL. Without it, our create_table call would fail, because the table already exists. However, leaving :force => true in this migration will mean that Story records will be wiped with each future migration, so set it back to false after you've performed the migration to prevent this from happening.

In addition to the explicitly named columns we've talked about in this section, this code will also create a column named id which will serve as the primary identifier for each row in the table.

This approach to schema definitions reflects the "pure" Rails method of creating and altering database tables that we talked about earlier in this section.

Now that we have a migration file complete with methods for setting up and tearing down our schema, we just need to make the migration happen. We use the rake tool to achieve this task.

Using rake to Migrate Our Data

rake is a tool for executing a set of tasks that are specific to your project.

If you've ever written or compiled a C program, you'll have come across the make tool. Well, rake is to Ruby code as make is to C code. Written by Jim Weirich, the rake package borrows its naming conventions and basic functionality from make, but that's where the similarities end.[1]

---

[1] Jim maintains a blog about Ruby and Rails at http://onestepback.org/.

You can define the tasks that you want `rake` to execute in a file named **Rakefile**, which is written purely in Ruby code. In fact, Rails itself uses its own **Rakefile** to supply you with a number of handy tasks; you'll find it in your **shovell** folder. Alternatively, you can access the entire list of tasks available to a Rails application by typing `rake -T` from the application's root folder—in our case, the **shovell** directory. Some of those tasks are shown in Figure 5.3.

Figure 5.3. Some of the tasks available using `rake`

A `rake` task can also accept a **namespace**, which is a conceptual container that allows us to group related tasks together.

One example is the db namespace, which groups all tasks that are related to the database. Namespaces are designated by the use of a colon, so tasks within the db namespace are addressed using the prefix db:.

Common rake tasks that you might use in your day-to-day Rails work include:

- db:migrate, for applying new migrations

- db:test:clone_structure, for recreating your test database using the structure in your development environment

- test, for running your test suite

As the last of these examples demonstrates, not every task belongs to a namespace—some tasks stand alone.

As we saw in Figure 5.3, the default Rakefile for our application comes with a boatload of predefined tasks, each of which offers unique functionality. For now, we're only interested in the db:migrate task (that is, the migrate task from the db namespace). We'll explore some other rake tasks as we progress through later chapters.

The rake command accepts a number of options: type rake --help to see them all. At its simplest, rake uses the following format:

```
$ rake namespace:task
```

For example, to apply the migrations in the migration file that we created earlier, we'd type the following:

```
$ rake db:migrate
```

When executed without any other arguments, this command achieves the following tasks:

1. It checks the database for the unique number of the migration that was most recently applied.

2. It steps through the migrations that have not yet been applied, one by one.

3. For each migration, it executes the up method for that migration class, to bring the database in line with the structure specified in the migration files.

Go ahead and execute our database migration task from the **shovell** folder now. Figure 5.4 shows the output you should receive.

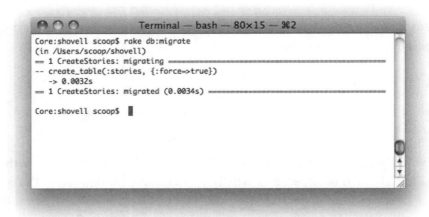

```
Core:shovell scoop$ rake db:migrate
(in /Users/scoop/shovell)
== 1 CreateStories: migrating =================================================
-- create_table(:stories, {:force=>true})
   -> 0.0032s
== 1 CreateStories: migrated (0.0034s) ========================================

Core:shovell scoop$ ▊
```

Figure 5.4. Database migration using rake

As the output indicates, running this task has caused the CreateStories migration that we created to be applied to our database. Assuming it was applied successfully, you should now (once again) have a stories table within your shovell_development database.

With this table in place, we can create some data about stories!

Rolling Back Is Easy, Too!

As our database schema evolves, so do the migration files that represent it. Rolling back to a previous version of the schema is incredibly easy with migrations. Simply type the following to revert to a previous version of the database (*n* represents the version number that you want to restore):

```
$ rake db:migrate VERSION=n
```

For example, the following command would undo the `stories` table that we just created, resulting in the blank database that we began with:

```
$ rake db:migrate VERSION=0
```

Managing Data Using the Rails Console

While we've developed a solid architecture for our application, and created a table to store data, we don't yet have a nice front-end interface for managing that data. We'll start to build that interface in Chapter 6, but in the meantime, we need to find a way to add stories to our table.

That's right—it's the Rails console to the rescue once again!

Creating Records

We can use two approaches to create records from the console. Let's look at the long-winded approach first. We create the object, then populate each of its attributes one by one, as follows:

```
$ ruby script/console
Loading development environment (Rails 2.0.2)
>> s = Story.new
=> #<Story id: nil, name: nil, link: nil, created_at: nil,
   updated_at: nil>
>> s.name = 'My shiny weblog'
=> "My shiny weblog"
>> s.link = 'http://poocs.net/'
=> "http://poocs.net/"
>> s.save
=> true
```

Now let's step through what we've done here.

After loading the Rails console, we created a new `Story` object. We assigned this object to a variable named `s` (the `s` is for `Story`—I know, it won't win any awards for creativity). We then assigned values to each of the columns that exist on a `Story` object. Finally, we called the `save` method, and our `Story` was stored in the database.

How can we be sure that the data was written successfully? We could look at the raw data using a trusty SQL database console, but we're trying to keep our distance from SQL. Instead, we can confirm that our story saved correctly by checking its id (the unique identifier that the database generates automatically when an object is saved). We can do this from within the Rails console:

```
>> s.id
=> 1
```

Our object's id is not nil, so we know that the save was successful. Of course, there's another way to ensure that the data was written successfully, and that is to use the new_record? method, which you may remember from the section called "Saving an Object" in Chapter 4:

```
>> s.new_record?
=> false
```

Hooray! As this method returns false, we know for certain that the object was written to the database. Just in case you need even more reassurance, there's one more check that we can use: the count class method of the Story class. This method allows us to query the database for the number of stories it currently contains:

```
>> Story.count
=> 1
```

Okay, that makes sense.

Let's create another Story now, this time using the second technique: this one's a shortcut!

```
>> Story.create(
➡      :name => 'SitePoint Forums',
➡      :link => 'http://www.sitepoint.com/forums/')
=> #<Story id: 2, name: "SitePoint Forums", link:
   "http://www.sitepoint.com/forums/", created_at:
   "2008-01-22 18:28:11", updated_at: "2008-01-22 18:28:11">
```

The create class method achieves the same task as the long-winded approach we just saw, but it only uses one line (not counting word wrapping). This method also—very conveniently—saves the record to the database once the object has been created. And it allows us to assign values to the columns of the record (in this case, in the columns `name` and `link`) at the same time as the record is created.

Hang on—we forgot to assign the object to a variable! How can we query it for additional information?

Retrieving Records

It's all very well to be able to create and save new information, but what good is that information if we can't retrieve it? One approach to retrieving a story from our database would be to guess its `id`; the `id`s are auto-incremented, so we could anticipate the number of the record that we're after. We could then use the `find` class method to retrieve a row based on its `id`:

```
>> Story.find(2)
=> #<Story id: 2, name: "SitePoint Forums",
     link: "http://www.sitepoint.com/forums/",
     created_at: "2008-01-22 18:28:11",
     updated_at: "2008-01-22 18:28:11">
```

This approach might be fine for our testing setup, but once our application has deleted and created more than a handful of records, it won't work.

Another approach is to retrieve every row in the table. We can do this by passing `:all` as the argument to the `find` method:

```
>> Story.find(:all)
=> [#<Story id: 1, name: "My shiny weblog", link:
     "http://poocs.net/", created_at: "2008-01-22 18:26:02",
     updated_at: "2008-01-22 18:26:02">, #<Story id: 2, name:
     "SitePoint Forums", link: "http://www.sitepoint.com/forums/",
     created_at: "2008-01-22 18:28:11", updated_at:
     "2008-01-22 18:28:11">]
```

This process returns an object of class `Array` containing all rows of the `stories` table.

Arrays also have `first` and `last` methods to retrieve (surprise!) the first and last elements of the array:

```
>> Story.find(:all).last
=> #<Story id: 2, name: "SitePoint Forums", …>
```

Making use of the :all argument and the first and last methods gives us some additional flexibility, but this approach isn't exactly resource-friendly—especially if we're working with larger sets of data. As its name suggests, using :all has the effect of transferring *all* database records from the database into Ruby's memory. This may not be the most efficient solution, particularly if your application is only looking for a single record.

A better approach would be to let the record selection process be handled by the database itself. To facilitate this goal, we pass two arguments to the find method:

:first

>   This argument retrieves the first element from the set of retrieved records.

:order

>   This argument allows us to specify the sort order of the returned objects.

The :order argument should contain a tiny bit of SQL that tells the database how the records should be ordered. To get the last element, for example, we would assign :order a value of id DESC, which specifies that the records should be sorted by the id column in descending order:

```
>> Story.find(:first, :order => 'id DESC')
=> #<Story id: 2, name: "SitePoint Forums", …>
```

The object that's returned is identical to the one we retrieved using :all in conjunction with our object's last attribute, but this approach is much more resource-friendly.

Now, while all of these retrieval techniques have worked for us so far, any approach that retrieves an object on the basis of its id is fundamentally flawed. It assumes that no one else is using the database, which certainly will not be a valid assumption when our social news application goes live!

What we need is a more reliable method of retrieving records—one that retrieves objects based on a column other than the id. What if we were to retrieve a Story by its name? Easy:

```
>> Story.find_by_name('My shiny weblog')
=> #<Story id: 1, name: "My shiny weblog", …>
```

In fact, we can even query the database using the link column, or any other column in our stories table! Rails automatically creates these **dynamic finder** methods by prefixing the column name in question with find_by_. In this case, the Story class has the dynamic finders find_by_name and find_by_link (find_by_id would be redundant, as a simple find does the same thing). Cool, huh?

Updating Records

We know how to add stories to our database, but what happens when someone submits a story riddled with typos or (gasp!) factual errors to our Shovell application? We need to be able to update existing stories, to ensure the integrity and quality of the information on Shovell, and the continuation of our site's glowing reputation.

Before we can update an object, we need to retrieve it. Any of the techniques outlined in the previous section would suffice, but for this example, we'll retrieve a Story from the database using its name:

```
>> s = Story.find_by_name('My shiny weblog')
=> #<Story id: 1, name: "My shiny weblog", …>
>> s.name
=> "My shiny weblog"
>> s.name = 'A weblog about Ruby on Rails'
=> "A weblog about Ruby on Rails"
```

As you can see, the task of changing the value of an attribute (name, in this case) is as straightforward as assigning a new value to it. Of course, this change is not yet permanent—we've simply changed the attribute of an object in memory. To save the change to the database, we need to call the save method, just as we did when we learned how to create new objects earlier in this chapter:

```
>> s.save
=> true
```

Once again, there's a shortcut—update_attribute—which allows us to update the attribute and save the object to the database in one fell swoop:

```
>> s.update_attribute :name, 'A weblog about Ruby on Rails'
=> true
```

This is straightforward stuff. Just one more command, then we'll leave the console for good. (Well, for this chapter, anyway!)

Deleting Records

To destroy a database record, simply call the `destroy` method of the `ActiveRecord` object:

```
>> s.destroy
=> #<Story id: 1, name: "My shiny weblog", …>
```

This will remove the record from the database *immediately*.

If you try to use the `find` method to locate an object that has been destroyed (or didn't exist in the first place), Rails will throw an error:

```
>> Story.find(1)
=> ActiveRecord::RecordNotFound: Couldn't find Story with ID=1
```

As you can see, deleting records is a cinch—at least, for Rails developers! In fact, SQL is doing a good deal of work behind the scenes. Let's exit the Rails console and pull back the curtain for a closer look at the SQL statements that result from our commands.

Where's the SQL?

In all of the creating, updating, and deleting of records that we've done in this section, we haven't seen a lot of SQL.

If you'd like to peek at the SQL statements that Rails has saved you from having to type, take a look at the log files located in the `log` folder. In it, you'll find files named after each of the environments. We've been working in the development environment, so have a look at **development.log**. Figure 5.5 shows the contents of the log file on my computer.

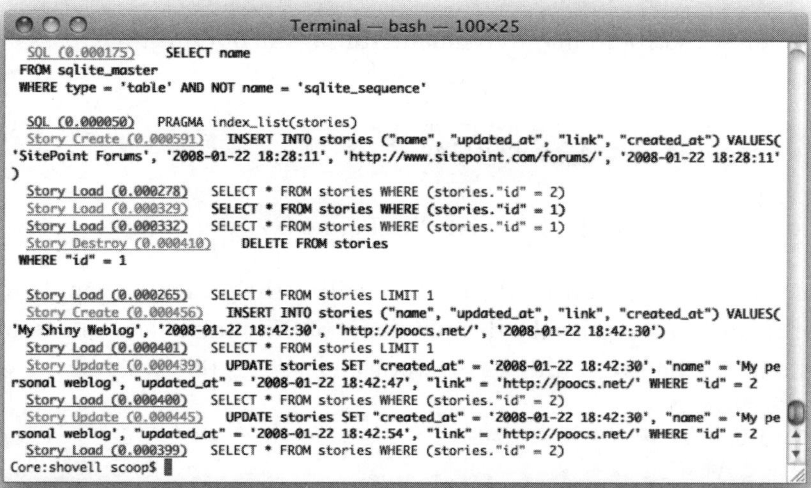

Figure 5.5. The log file for the development environment

The contents of the log file vary greatly between environments, and for good reason: the development log file contains *every* SQL statement that's sent to the database server, including the details of how long it took to process each statement. This information can be very useful if you're debugging an error or looking for some additional insight into what is going on. However, it's not appropriate in a production environment—a large number of queries might be executing at any one time, which would result in an enormous log file.

We'll revisit these log files in Chapter 6, when we examine the entries written to them by the `ActionController` and `ActionView` modules.

Generating a Controller

Now that we have our model in place, let's build a controller. In the same way that we generated a model, we generate a controller by running the **script/generate** script from our application's root folder.

Running the generate Script

Run the `generate` script from the command line again, but this time, pass `controller` as the first parameter:

```
$ ruby script/generate controller
```

The output of this command is depicted in Figure 5.7.

As you may have deduced from the output, calling the **generate** script to create a controller requires us to pass the desired name of the controller as a parameter. Other parameters that we could pass include any actions that we'd like to generate.

Let's try it out. Type in the following:

```
$ ruby script/generate controller Stories index
```

The output of the `generate` script, shown in Figure 5.6, tells us exactly what it's doing. Let's analyze each of these lines of output.

```
Core:shovell scoop$ script/generate controller Stories index
       exists  app/controllers/
       exists  app/helpers/
       create  app/views/stories
       exists  test/functional/
       create  app/controllers/stories_controller.rb
       create  test/functional/stories_controller_test.rb
       create  app/helpers/stories_helper.rb
       create  app/views/stories/index.html.erb
Core:shovell scoop$
```

Figure 5.6. Generating a Story controller

Figure 5.7. Sample output from the controller generator

Understanding the Output

The meaning of the messages output by the controller generator should be growing quite familiar by now.

- First, the `generate` script skipped over the creation of a couple of folders, because they already exist in our project.

▓ Next, the **app/views/stories** folder was created. As I mentioned when we first looked at `ActionView` in the section called "`ActionView` (the View)" in Chapter 4, the templates for our newly created `StoriesController` will be stored in this folder.

▓ After skipping over one more folder, `generate` created four new files:

app/controllers/stories_controller.rb

This file houses the actual class definition for our `StoriesController`. It's mostly empty, though; all it comes with is a method definition for the `index` action, which, admittedly, is empty as well. Don't worry—we'll expand it soon!

```
                                                          06-stories_controller.rb

class StoriesController < ApplicationController
  def index
  end
end
```

Astute readers will notice that our `StoriesController` doesn't inherit from the `ActionController::Base` class in the way we'd expect. The `ApplicationController` class that we see here is actually an empty class that inherits directly from `ActionController::Base`. The class is defined in the **application.rb** file, which lives in the **app/controllers** folder, if you're curious. The resulting `StoriesController` has exactly the same attributes and methods as if it had inherited directly from `ActionController::Base`. Using an intermediary class like this provides a location for storing variables and pieces of functionality that are common to all controllers.

test/functional/stories_controller_test.rb

This file contains the functional test for our controller. We'll skip over it for now, but we'll expand the test cases that this file contains in the section called "Testing the StoriesController" in Chapter 9.

app/helpers/stories_helper.rb

This is the empty **helper** class for the controller (helpers are chunks of code that can be reused throughout your application). We'll look at helpers in more detail in Chapter 6.

app/views/stories/index.html.erb

This file is the template that corresponds to the `index` action that we passed as a parameter to the `generate` script. For the moment, it's the only one in the **app/views/stories** directory, but as we create others, they'll be stored alongside **index.html.erb** and given names that match their actions (for example, the `show` action will end up with a template named **show.html.erb**).

With this knowledge, we're finally in a position to breathe life into our little Rails monster, in the true spirit of Frankenstein.

Watch Your Controller Class Names!

You'll notice the controller class that was created by the `generate` script is called `StoriesController`, though the first parameter that we specified on the command line was simply `Stories`. If our parameter had been `StoriesController`, we'd have ended up with a class name of `StoriesControllerController`!

Starting Our Application ... Again

It's time to fire up our application again. While our previous experience with Mongrel was somewhat uneventful, our application should do a little more this time.

Start up the web server with the following command:

```
$ ruby script/server
```

Once the server has completed its startup sequence, type the following address into your web browser: http://localhost:3000/stories. If everything goes to plan, you should be looking at a page similar to the one in Figure 5.8.

Figure 5.8. Accessing our `StoriesController` from a browser

What does this display tell us? Well, this simple (and not especially pretty) page confirms that:

1. The routing between controllers and views is working correctly—Rails has found and instantiated our `StoriesController` class, based on the URL that we asked it to retrieve.

2. The `index` action is the default action that's called when no explicit action is specified in the URL (all that we specified was a controller name, using the path **/stories**). When you consider that most web servers usually load a file called **index** by default (**index.html**, **index.php**, **index.jsp**, **index.aspx** etc.), this seems like a sensible default.

3. Our controller is able to locate its views—the HTML for the page we see rendered in the browser is contained in the file that's mentioned on screen (**app/views/stories/index.html.erb**).

If you think about it, this is actually quite an accomplishment, given that we've really only executed two commands for generating code from the command line.

So that we can complete the picture, let's pull some data from our model into our `index` action.

Creating a View

We can use two approaches to build views for our Rails application. One is to make use of scaffolding; the other is to "go it alone."

We'll look at scaffolding very briefly, but we won't be using it much in the development of our Shovell application. I'll introduce just enough of this topic to give you a taste, then leave it up to you to decide whether or not you find it worthwhile in your own projects.

After that, we'll roll up our sleeves and build some views from scratch.

Generating Views with Scaffolding

In the early days of Rails, scaffolding was one of the features that the Rails community used as a selling point when promoting the framework. Ironically, this feature also received a considerable amount of criticism, though this was largely due to critics failing to fully understand the intended uses of scaffolding.

So what is scaffolding, anyway?

Scaffolding is a tool that quickly creates a web interface for interacting with your model data. The interface lists the existing data in a table, providing an easy way to add new records and manipulate or delete existing ones.

While there used to be a way to use scaffolding in a temporary fashion (as a one-line addition to one of your controllers, which would then perform all sorts of behind-the-scenes magic), these days scaffolding is Yet Another Generator invoked through the **script/generate** command.

When a scaffold is generated, you end up with a model, a controller with several actions, and numerous view templates for these actions. The generated code can then be built on and extended over time as you progress with your application. Features provided by the template code can then be tweaked or implemented in a different manner, and code that doesn't suit your project can be removed.

We won't be generating any permanent scaffolding in this project, but I do encourage you to experiment with this approach in your own projects, as there may be cases in which you'll find it useful. The syntax to generate a model with scaffolding code is as follows (the inline help is available in Figure 5.9):

```
$ ruby script/generate scaffold Story name:string link:string
```

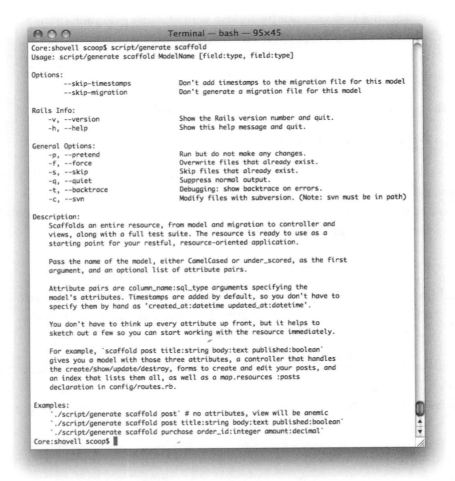

Figure 5.9. The inline help for script/generate scaffold

Destroy What You Create!

If you ever mess up a call to **script/generate**, you may find its alter ego **script/destroy** very helpful. This takes exactly the same arguments as **script/generate** but attempts to reverse what it did, removing newly generated files and modifications to existing files. You can think of the two scripts as the up and down methods of a migration.

An example screen from a generated scaffold for our Story model is shown in Figure 5.10.

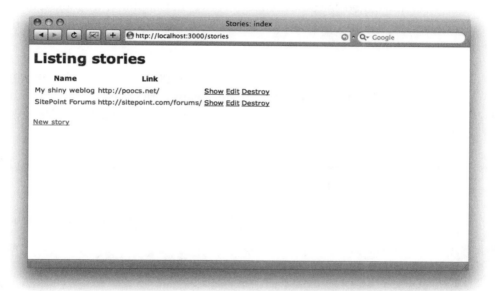

Figure 5.10. Example screen from a generated scaffold

 Scaffolding Limitations

Please keep in mind that scaffolding is a tool designed for quick interaction with models, and should only be used as such. It is by no means intended to be a fully automated tool for generating web applications (or even administration interfaces).

Scaffolding is also not without its limits in providing automated access. For example, it can't cope with ActiveRecord associations such as "a Story belongs to a User," which we saw in the section called "ActiveRecord (the Model)" in Chapter 4. Additionally, since most applications end up requiring a fully fledged administrative interface, you're often better off just creating the real thing rather than fiddling around with a dummy interface.

Scaffolding is certainly a powerful feature of Rails, and it's rewarding to get the instant visual feedback that comes with having some views created for us. However, it's now time for us to create some views of our own, which will give us a much better insight into what each part of the MVC stack does.

Creating Static Pages

Back in the section called "`ActionView` (the View)" in Chapter 4, we looked briefly at the `ActionView` module, but only in theory. Let's create some custom views that we can actually view using a web browser.

As a quick refresher, `ActionView` represents the view part of the model-view-controller architecture. Files that are used to render views are called templates, and they usually consist of HTML code interspersed with Ruby code. These files are referred to as **ERb templates**.

One of these templates (albeit a not so interesting one) has already been created for us—it's the **index.html.erb** file that's located in **app/views/stories**:

07-index.html.erb

```
<h1>Stories#index</h1>
<p>Find me in app/views/stories/index.html.erb</p>
```

Looks familiar, doesn't it? This is the HTML code that we viewed in our web browser earlier in this chapter. As you can see, it's a **static** page (meaning that it doesn't contain any Ruby code). **Dynamic** pages (pages that pull in data from a database, or from some other source) are much more interesting! We'll have a closer look at dynamic pages now.

Creating Dynamic Pages

Let's begin our adventure in building dynamic pages. We'll add a value—the current date and time—to the HTML output of our view. Although simple, this value is considered to be dynamic.

Open the template file in your text editor and delete everything that's there. In its place add the following line:

```
08-index.html.erb
<%= Time.now %>
```

Here, we call the `now` class method that lives on the `Time` class, which is part of the Ruby standard library. This method call is wrapped in ERb tags (beginning with `<%=` and ending with `%>`).

You may remember from the section called "`ActionView` (the View)" in Chapter 4 that the equal sign attached to the opening ERb tag will cause the return value of `Time.now` to be output to the web page, rather than executing silently.

If you refresh your browser now, the page should display the current time, as shown in Figure 5.11. Just to confirm that this value is indeed dynamic, reload your page a few times—you'll notice that the value does indeed change.

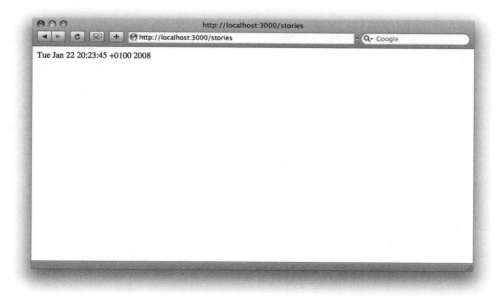

Figure 5.11. Our first dynamic page: displaying the current time

Passing Data Back and Forth

There's one fundamental problem with what we've done here. Can you spot it?

In order to adhere to the model-view-controller architecture, we want to avoid performing any hefty calculations from within any of our views—that's the job of the controller. Strictly speaking, our call to Time.now is one such calculation, so it should really occur within the controller. But what good is the result of a calculation if we can't display it?

We introduced the concept of passing variables between controllers and views briefly in the section called "ActionView (the View)" in Chapter 4, but at that point, we didn't have any views that we could use to demonstrate it in action. Now's our chance!

We learned that any instance variable that's declared in the controller automatically becomes available to the view as an instance variable. Let's take advantage of that fact now. Edit **/app/controllers/stories_controller.rb** so that it contains the following code:

```
09-stories_controller.rb

class StoriesController < ApplicationController
  def index
    @current_time = Time.now
  end
end
```

Next, replace the contents of **app/views/stories/index.html.erb** with the following:

```
10-index.html.erb

<%= @current_time %>
```

I'm sure you can guess what's happened here:

1. We've moved the "calculation" of the current time from the view to the controller.

2. The result of the calculation is stored in the instance variable @current_time.

3. The contents of this instance variable are then automatically made available to the view.

The result is that the job of the view has been reduced to simply displaying the contents of this instance variable, rather than executing the calculation itself.

Voilà! Our application logic and our presentation logic are kept neatly separate.

Pulling in a Model

All we need to do now is pull some data into our view, and we'll have the entire MVC stack covered!

In case you deleted all of your model records when we experimented with scaffolding earlier, make sure you create at least one story. Type the following into a Rails console:

```
>> Story.create(
➥     :name => 'SitePoint Forums',
➥     :link => 'http://www.sitepoint.com/forums/')
```

To display this model data within a view, we need to retrieve it from within the controller, like so:

11-stories_controller.rb

```
class StoriesController < ApplicationController
  def index
    @story = Story.find_by_name('SitePoint Forums')
  end
end
```

We'll also change our view accordingly:

12-index.html.erb

```
A random link:
<a href="<%= @story.link %>"><%= @story.name %></a>
```

Reload the page to see the result—it should look like Figure 5.12.

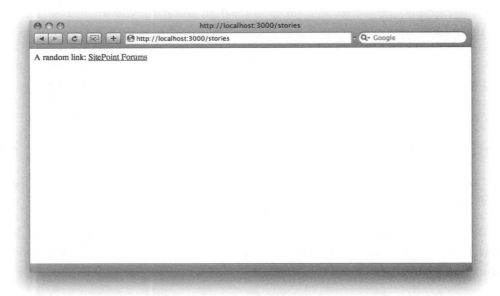

Figure 5.12. MVC in action: a view displaying model data via the controller

Of course, Rails wouldn't be doing its job of saving you effort if it required you to manually create links the way we just did. Instead of typing out the HTML for a link, you can use the link_to function, which is much easier to remember and achieves the same result. Try it for yourself:

13-index.html.erb *(excerpt)*

```
A random link:
<%= link_to @story.name, @story.link %>
```

One other point: I'll be the first to admit that the text on the page is a little misleading. Our link is not exactly random—it simply retrieves the same link from the database over and over again.

It's actually quite easy to make our application retrieve random stories, though. Simply modify the part of the controller that fetches the story so that it looks like this:

16-stories_controller.rb *(excerpt)*

```
@story = Story.find(:first, :order => 'RANDOM()')
```

This modification selects a single story, just like before (using the `:first` parameter). However, this time the database is being instructed to shuffle its records before picking one. When you reload your page, random stories should now appear—assuming you have more than one story in your database, that is! You might like to save a few more stories (using `Story.create` in a Rails console) and see the random link feature of our Shovell application in action.

There we have it: the beginnings of our story-sharing application. Admittedly, displaying a random story from our database is only a small achievement, but hey—it's a start!

Summary

This chapter saw us create some real code for each of the components of an MVC application. We generated a model with a corresponding migration to handle the storage of our stories; we generated a controller to handle communication between the models and the views; and we created a view that dynamically renders content supplied by our controller.

With the functionality provided by `ActiveRecord`, we've been creating, updating, and deleting data from our SQL database without resorting to any SQL.

I also introduced you to the `rake` tool, which can be used to run migrations and other tasks. And we learned about the YAML data representation language that's used to store test fixture data for our application.

In Chapter 6, we'll add a layout to our application using HTML and CSS; we'll talk about associations between models; and we'll extend the functionality of our application.

Let's get into it!

Helpers, Forms, and Layouts

In Chapter 5, we put in place some basic architecture for our application—a model, a view, and a controller—and were able to display a link to a random story that was stored in the database. Though the foundation of our application is sound, users can't really interact with it yet.

In this chapter, we'll use some helpers to implement the basic functionality for our application: the capability that allows users to submit stories to the site.

We'll also make a start on building our test suite. In this chapter, we'll create some functional tests to confirm that the submission form is working as intended. We'll expand on this suite of tests in the coming chapters.

Calling upon Our Trusty Helpers

No, I'm not talking about Santa's little helpers. Let me explain.

In Chapter 5, we discussed the importance of keeping application logic in a controller, so that our views contain only presentational code. While it hasn't been apparent in the simple examples that we've looked at so far, extracting code from a view and moving it into a controller often causes clumsy code to be added to an application's controllers.

To address this problem, another structural component exists: the **helper**. A helper is a chunk of code that can be reused throughout an application, and is stored in a **helper file**. A helper usually contains relatively complicated or reusable presentation logic; since any views that utilize the helper are spared this complexity, the code in the view is kept simple and easy to read, reflecting our adherence to DRY principles. Dozens of helpers are built into Rails, but you can, of course, create your own to use throughout your application.

An example of a good candidate for a helper is code that renders a screen element on a page. Repeating this type of code from one view to another violates the DRY principle, but sticking it all into a controller doesn't make sense either.

As we saw in the section called "Generating a Controller" in Chapter 5, when we generate a controller (using the `generate` script that we've come to know and love), one of the files that's created is a new helper file called *controllername*_**helper.rb**. In the case of our `StoriesController`, the helper file associated with this controller is **stories_helper.rb**, and lives in **app/helpers**.

In previous versions of Rails, helpers associated with a particular controller were available *only* to the views of that particular controller, except for those defined in the file **app/helpers/application_helper.rb**, which were available to any view. In Rails 2 every helper is available to every view, no matter which controller it's associated with. This is due to the `helper :all` statement in the `ApplicationController`, generated with every new application.

We'll be relying on a few of Rails' built-in helpers for much of the story submission interface that we'll build in this chapter.

Enabling Story Submission

In our brief foray into the world of scaffolding in the section called "Generating Views with Scaffolding" in Chapter 5, we saw that it's possible in Rails to create a quick (and dirty) front end for our data, though this approach doesn't necessarily constitute best practice.

In this section, we'll build a web interface for submitting stories to our Shovell web site without relying on any scaffolding. First, we'll create a view template that contains the actual submission form, then we'll add a new method to our `StoriesController` to handle the task of saving submitted stories to the database. We'll also implement a global layout for our application, and we'll create some feedback to present to our users, both when they're filling out the form and after they've submitted a story.

Creating a Form

The topic of HTML forms is one that even seasoned front-end developers have traditionally found intimidating. While it would be possible to create our form elements manually, it's not necessary—Rails offers a number of helpers and shortcuts that make the creation of forms a breeze. One of those is the `form_for` helper, which we'll look at now.

Introducing the `form_for` Helper

Rails offers a few different helper functions for writing forms. `form_for` is the most common among these and is recommended for use when generating a form that's bound to one type of object. By "bound," I mean that each field in the form maps to the corresponding attribute of a single object, rather than to corresponding attributes of multiple objects. At its most basic, using the `form_for` helper to bind a simple form to a `Story` object would look something like this:

```
<% form_for @story do |f| %>
  <%= f.text_field :name %>
  <%= f.text_field :link %>
<% end %>
```

This syntax boasts a few points that are worth highlighting:

- The first and last lines use the ERb tags for silent output (`<% … %>`), while each line within the form uses the ERb tags that display output to the browser (`<%= … %>`).

- The parameter that immediately follows `form_for` is the object to which the form will be bound (`@story`).

- The fields that make up the form live inside a block. As you'll no doubt remember from the section called "Blocks" in Chapter 3, a Ruby block is a statement of Ruby code that appears between the keywords do and end, or between curly braces. This is the first time we've encountered a block within an ERb file, but the principle is the same.

- A new object, which I've named f in this case, as shorthand for "form," must be passed as a parameter to the block. This object is of type FormBuilder, which is a class that contains instance methods designed to work with forms. Using these methods, we can easily create the HTML form input elements such as text_field, password_field, check_box, and text_area.

We receive a number of benefits in exchange for following this syntax:

- The form tags that signify the start and end of our HTML form will be generated for us.

- We gain access to a number of instance methods, via the FormBuilder object, that we can use to create fields in our form. In the example, we've used the text_field method to create two text fields; these fields will be mapped to our @story object automatically.

- Appropriate name and id attributes will be applied to each of these fields; these attributes can then be used as hooks for CSS and JavaScript, as we'll see later in this chapter.

- Rails automatically figures out to which URI this form should be posted to when submitted by the web browser if our model has been defined as a resource (a term that you will recall from the section called "The REST" in Chapter 4). More on this in a moment.

As you can see, using form_for and the FormBuilder object that comes with it is a powerful way to create comprehensive forms with minimal effort.

Creating the Template

Now that we have a handle on form_for, let's use it to create the form that site visitors will use to submit stories to Shovell.

A form is a presentational concept, which means that it should be stored as a view. Our form will allow users to submit *new* stories to Shovell, so we'll give this view the name new. Let's make a template for it: create a new file called **new.html.erb** in the **app/views/stories** folder. It should contain the following:

01-new.html.erb

```erb
<% form_for @story do |f| %>
<p>
  name:<br />
  <%= f.text_field :name %>
</p>
<p>
  link:<br />
  <%= f.text_field :link %>
</p>
<p>
  <%= submit_tag %>
</p>
<% end %>
```

Let's break down the ERb code here:

```erb
<% form_for @story do |f| %>
```

As we just discussed, the form_for helper creates a form that's bound to a specific object—in this case, it's bound to the @story instance variable.

```erb
<%= f.text_field :name %>
```

This line creates a text field called name, which is mapped to our @story object. It will display a text field in which the user can enter the name of the story he or she is submitting.

```erb
<%= f.text_field :link %>
```

This line creates another text field, this time named link, which is also mapped to our @story object. It will display a text field in which the user can enter the URL of the story he or she is submitting.

```
<%= submit_tag %>
```

This helper generates the HTML code for a **Submit** button to be displayed in our form. This is a **stand-alone helper**—it's not part of the `form_for` helper.

Next, make sure that your web server is running (refer to Chapter 2 if you need a refresher on starting the server). Open your web browser and type the following URL into the address bar: http://localhost:3000/stories/new. You should see—yikes!—an error similar to Figure 6.1.

If you see a different error message when you try to open this URL, I recommend that you monitor the console window from which you launched your web server. This process is the heart of our application; if it's not beating, you won't be able to access any of the functionality that we're going to add in this chapter. Any errors that appear in the console should give you an idea of what went wrong.

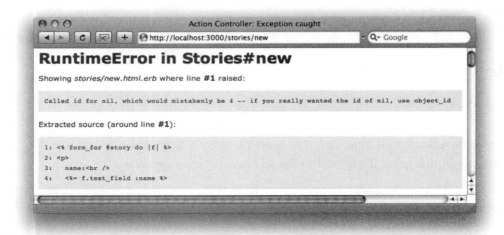

Figure 6.1. An error message is shown when trying to access our new form

Now, what happened here? Well, we handed the `form_for` helper the instance variable called `@story`, but we never actually assigned an object to that variable, so it ended up being `nil`. Adhering to the MVC principles, we need to turn to the controller as being responsible for putting a value into `@story`, which we'll do in the next section.

Modifying the Controller

To create an action that will populate the @story instance variable, edit the file
app/controllers/stories_controller.rb so that it looks as follows (I've indicated the
method to be added in bold):

```
                                                      02-stories_controller.rb
class StoriesController < ApplicationController
  def index
    @story = Story.find(:first, :order => 'RANDOM()')
  end
  def new
    @story = Story.new
  end
end
```

It doesn't matter whether you place this new method above or below the existing
index method. Some people prefer to sort their methods alphabetically, while others
group their methods by purpose; the decision is entirely up to you and has no impact
on the functionality of your application.

The code that we've added to our new method simply instantiates a new Story object
and stores it in the @story instance variable. As it's an instance variable, @story
will now be available to our view and thus to the form_for helper.

Reloading the page in your browser should now yield Figure 6.2 ... yet another error!

Figure 6.2. Even after implementing the "new" action, we still get an error on our submission form

As I said in the section above, one benefit of using the `form_for` helper to set up our form is that it automatically figures out where to submit the form. Now it's showing that there's clearly something missing from our equation here. To be precise, we haven't declared `Story` as a resource anywhere. So let's do that now.

Resources in Rails

Although the creators of Rails would certainly love to make it so that every model you generate automatically ends up being declared a resource, we're not quite there yet—and, admittedly, it doesn't make sense to make it so in every case.

Resources in Rails are declared in the file responsible for the **Routing Configuration**, **config/routes.rb**. In Rails, the routing module is responsible for mapping URLs to controllers and actions. Take the following URL for example:

```
/stories/new
```

The routing module maps this URL to the `new` action of `StoriesController`. It does this due to the default routing configuration we generated way back when we first used the `rails` command. Here are the contents of the **routes.rb** file with its comments removed:

```
ActionController::Routing::Routes.draw do |map|
  map.connect ':controller/:action/:id'
  map.connect ':controller/:action/:id.:format'
end
```

As outlined above, the first part of the URL is mapped to the controller and the second part is mapped to the action.

This being the default configuration, mapping resources is a little different. Resources always consume the second spot in the URL—we're talking about resource-centric development, after all. So for any given resource (the first of which we'll declare in just a moment), the paths along with their respective HTTP verbs outlined in Table 6.1 are recognized.

Table 6.1. The Mapping of URLs to Controller Actions

URL	Action
GET /stories	index
GET /stories/new	new
POST /stories	create
GET /stories/1	show
GET /stories/1/edit	edit
PUT /stories/1	update
DELETE /stories/1	destroy

When you're looking at the table, the actions can be divided into two groups: actions that operate on a single story (show, edit, update, and destroy) and those that don't (index, new, and create). The actions that do operate on a single, specific story use the second part of the URL to identify the resource they are operating on with its numeric *id*.

That leaves us with seven different ways to interact with stories. But are we supposed to define all those by hand for every resource our application is going to have? Rails wouldn't be Rails if we had to jump through all those hoops. So let's take a look at the magic that's behind map.resources.

Mapping a New Resource

We can discuss the theory of resources in Rails until we're blue in the face, but nothing gets the brain working like actually doing it for yourself. In the **config/routes.rb** file, simply add the following line:

03-routes.rb *(excerpt)*

```
ActionController::Routing::Routes.draw do |map|
  map.resources :stories
  map.connect ':controller/:action/:id'
  map.connect ':controller/:action/:id.:format'
end
```

This one line of code will give us all sorts of exciting features. Among them is a working—albeit unstyled—story submission form we can see upon reloading the page in the browser. The result is shown in Figure 6.3. We'll explore the remainder of those features in the upcoming chapters.

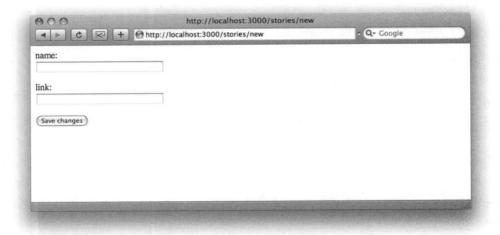

Figure 6.3. Our unstyled story submission form

Analyzing the HTML

The time has come to find out what kind of HTML the Rails helpers have generated. If you check the HTML for this page (using your browser's **View Source** option) you should see something that looks like this:

```
<form action="/stories" class="new_story" id="new_story"
    method="post"><div style="margin:0;padding:0"><input
    name="authenticity_token" type="hidden"
    value="ecf4a9e81b187d3a6d70fc065a7e17f93e5b2dec" /></div>
<p>
  name:<br />
  <input id="story_name" name="story[name]" size="30"
      type="text" />
</p>
<p>
  link:<br />
  <input id="story_link" name="story[link]" size="30"
      type="text" />
</p>
<p>
  <input name="commit" type="submit"
      value="Save changes" />
</p>
</form>
```

This markup is basically what we would expect: two text fields and a **Submit** button have been created for us, and everything has been wrapped up in a `form` element. Rails has also figured out the correct target URL (the `action` attribute of the `form` element) to create a new `Story` object according to the RESTful URL mapping outlined in the last section. Submission of the form will lead us to the `create` action of `StoriesController`, which we have yet to implement.

What's also of note is that strange `<div>` element in the markup, which has an equally strange hidden `<input>` element named `authenticity_token` inside it. This is one aspect of Rails' attempt to counteract so-called Cross-Site-Request-Forgery (CSRF) attacks, ensuring that submitted forms originate at the current web application, as opposed to a third party. The content `authenticity_token` is based on the user's session and is verified against a token set for the application (in **config/environment.rb**, if you're curious). If there is a mismatch, an error is raised and the form submission is discarded.

Okay, so our markup looks fine. But if you were to submit the form in its current state, you wouldn't be exactly thrilled with the results: we'd just receive another error, because the `create` method in `StoriesController` does not yet exist. Let's add some code to save the story data to the database.

Saving Data to the Database

We know from when we made `Story` a resource, implementing the URL mapping, that the submission of the form will `POST` the entered form data to the `create` action of `StoriesController`, which we'll create now. Add a method to the **app/controllers/stories_controller.rb** file like this:

```
                                            04-stories_controller.rb (excerpt)

def create
  @story = Story.new(params[:story])
  @story.save
end
```

The `params` object in the first line of our method is a hash that contains all of the content that the user submitted; you can revisit hashes in Chapter 3 if you'd like a refresher.

All of the form data passed to Rails will be added to the `params` hash. If you look once more at the HTML source of the submission form, you'll notice that the `input` element `name` attributes all have a `story[]` prefix. This prefix groups all of the submitted form fields for the story we're creating in `params[:story]`.

We can then reference individual elements within the hash by passing the name of the attribute (as a symbol) to the hash. For example, the value of the `name` attribute could be accessed as `params[:story][:name]`. You get the idea.

The point of all this is that user data submitted via the form can be assigned to an object very easily. All we need to do is pass the `params[:story]` hash to the `Story.new` method, and we have ourselves a populated `@story` object.

Not coincidentally, this is exactly what we've done in the first line of our method:

```
@story = Story.new(params[:story])
```

The newly created `@story` object is then sent the `save` method to store it permanently into our database.

Now, before you go ahead and enter some data into your form and click **Save changes**, let's pause for a second and think about what Rails would do if you did submit the form. Can you hazard a guess?

If we were to try and submit the form in its current stage, we'd end up with *yet another* error screen stating that Rails was unable to locate the `create.html.erb` template.

After Rails has finished processing the code in the controller action, it will (unless instructed otherwise) go ahead and try to render a template named after the controller and action, which, in this case, would be **app/views/stories/create.html.erb**.

But we don't actually want to render anything. We have saved the object to the database and can return to the random story selector that we created in Chapter 5, located within the `index` action.

Redirecting with URL helpers

If we don't want to render a template after an action has finished, preferring to go somewhere else instead, we need to use the `redirect_to` method. This method takes a single argument, namely the destination of the redirection. What *is* the destination of the redirection? Well, we know we've accessed the story randomizer at `http://localhost:3000/stories`, so could we simply redirect there with the following command?

```
redirect_to 'http://localhost:3000/stories'
```

We certainly could. But since it's likely that we need to use these kinds of URLs all over the place, it seems a little tedious to go down that path. And, after all, `form_for` was able to figure out paths on its own, why wouldn't `redirect_to`, too?

Albeit a lot of magic and mind-reading on the part of Rails, it turns out that we *do* need to tell Rails what we want it to do in this case. But to ease our pain, there are quite a few methods—known as **URL helpers**—provided free from the `map.resources` call in the **config/routes.rb** file that we used to define our stories as resources.

Table 6.2 shows a list of URL helpers that are being defined for every `Story` resource.

Table 6.2. URL Helpers for the `Story` Resource

`stories_path`	`/stories`
`new_story_path`	`/stories/new`
`story_path(@story)`	`/stories/1`
`edit_story_path(@story)`	`/stories/1/edit`

The helpers use singular or plural naming conventions depending on whether they're dealing with a specific story (singular) or no specific story (plural).

You may wonder why there's no such thing as a `destroy_story_path(@story)` or `create_stories_path`. Well, these don't exist because the actual URL generated from those would not be any different from `story_path(@story)` and `stories_path`, respectively. Remember that they just differ by the actual HTTP verb used to access the resource. We'll learn in the forthcoming chapters how to specify a different HTTP verb.

Now that we know about the URL helpers available to us, it's easy to spot the helper we need to use for our `redirect_to` call to redirect the browser back to the story index: `stories_path`. The new `create` method should now look as follows:

05-stories_controller.rb *(excerpt)*

```ruby
def create
  @story = Story.new(params[:story])
  @story.save
  redirect_to stories_path
end
```

Submitting the form now—after filling in a proper name and story link, of course!—should store your story submission and redirect you back to the random story selector. That's good! However, our application does look a little sparse. Let's make it pretty.

Creating a Layout

In Rails, a **layout** is a specialized form of a view template. Layouts allow page elements that are repeated globally across a site to be applied to every view. Examples of such elements include HTML headers and footers, CSS files, and JavaScript includes.

Layouts can also be applied at the controller level. This ability can be useful if, for example, you want to apply different layouts to a page depending on whether it's being viewed by an administrator or a regular user.

We'll begin our foray into layouts by creating a global layout for the entire application.

Establishing Structure

Layouts should be stored in the **app/views/layouts** folder. A layout template can basically be given any name, as long as the file ends in **.html.erb**. If the filename is **application.html.erb**, Rails will adopt this as the default layout.

Let's take advantage of that convention, and create a file named **application.html.erb** in the **app/views/layouts** folder, populating it with this code:

06-application.html.erb

```
<!DOCTYPE html PUBLIC "-//W3C//DTD XHTML 1.0 Strict//EN"
    "http://www.w3.org/TR/xhtml1/DTD/xhtml1-strict.dtd">
<html xmlns="http://www.w3.org/1999/xhtml"
    xml:lang="en" lang="en">
  <head>
    <meta http-equiv="Content-type"
        content="text/html; charset=utf-8" />
    <title>Shovell</title>
    <%= stylesheet_link_tag 'style' %>
  </head>
  <body>
    <div id="content">
      <h1>Shovell</h1>
      <%= yield %>
    </div>
  </body>
</html>
```

There's nothing too radical going on here—we've created a regular XHTML document, and it includes a proper DOCTYPE declaration. However, a couple of ERb calls here warrant some explanation.

```
<%= stylesheet_link_tag 'style' %>
```

This code generates the HTML that includes an external style sheet in the page. By passing the string `style`, we ensure that the `<link>` tag that's generated will point to the URL **/stylesheets/style.css**. We'll create this style sheet in a minute.

Help at Hand

Rails ships with a number of helpers that are similar to `stylesheet_link_tag`, in that they make generating HTML pages easy. They mostly save tedious typing—and thus potential errors. Similar helpers include `image_tag` and `javascript_include_tag`.

```
<%= yield %>
```

This line is the point at which the content for our specific view is displayed. Now, telling our layout to "yield" might not seem the most intuitive thing to do here, but it does actually make sense. Let me explain.

Remember that our layout will be used by many different view templates, each of which is responsible for displaying the output of a specific action. When the layout receives the command `yield`, control is handed to the *actual* view template being rendered—that is, the layout *yields* to the view template. Once that template has been rendered, control returns to the layout, and rendering is resumed for the rest of the page.

Since we've linked a style sheet, we'd better make use of it.

Adding Some Style

We'll use CSS to make our page look good.

Easy CSS

Don't worry if CSS is not your forte. All you need to do for this project is type out the CSS rules exactly as you see them—or, even better, simply copy and paste them from the code archive. If you're interested in improving your CSS skills, a good place to start is with Rachel Andrew and Dan Shafer's book, *HTML Utopia: Designing Without Tables Using CSS*.[1]

---

[1] http://www.sitepoint.com/books/css2/

To apply a style sheet to your application, create a file called **style.css** in the **public/stylesheets** folder, and drop in the following code:

06-style.css

```css
body {
  background-color: #666;
  margin: 15px 25px;
  font-family: Helvetica, Arial, sans-serif;
}
#content {
  background-color: #fff;
  border: 10px solid #ccc;
  padding: 10px 10px 20px 10px;
}
```

Reload the page in your browser. You should see a slightly prettier version of the form, as shown in Figure 6.4.

Figure 6.4. The new story form with a layout

Excellent! We now have a form that functions correctly, is well structured under the hood, *and* looks good on the outside.

However, our app doesn't deliver any feedback to the user to let them know whether or not a story submission was successful. Enter: the flash!

Enabling User Feedback with the Flash

Yes, you read that correctly: **flash**.

And no, we're not going to be switching to Adobe's Flash technology to provide submission feedback. "Flash" also happens to be the name for the internal storage container (actually a kind of hash) that Rails uses for temporary data. In this section, we'll use the flash to pass temporary objects between actions. We'll then apply some validation to the data that's entered.

Adding to the Flash

When I say that the flash is used to store *temporary* items, I'm not talking about items that exist in memory and aren't saved to the database. Items stored in the flash exist for the duration of exactly one action, and then they're gone.

What good is that? Well, using the flash allows us the convenience of communicating information between successive actions without having to save information in the user's browser or the database. The flash is well positioned to store short status messages, such as notifications that inform the user whether or not a form submission or login attempt was successful.

Flash content is usually populated from within a controller action. Using the flash is very easy: to place a message in the flash, simply pass it an identifying symbol (the **flash area**) and a corresponding message. Here's an example:

```
flash[:error] = 'Login unsuccessful.'
```

In our story-sharing application, we want to put a message into the flash immediately after the story is saved, to let the user know that the submission was successful. Add the following line to the create action of your StoriesController:

08-stories_controller.rb (excerpt)

```
def create
  @story = Story.new(params[:story])
  @story.save
```

```
    flash[:notice] = 'Story submission succeeded'
    redirect_to stories_path
end
```

 Conventions for Flash Areas

In general, Rails applications use flash areas named after common UNIX logging levels to indicate the level of severity of a message. The common area names are `:notice`, `:warning`, and `:error`.

In this case, the message is not critical, so we've chosen to use `:notice`. However, the name of the flash area is entirely up to you.

Retrieving Data from the Flash

To retrieve contents from the flash (usually done in the successive action), just access the flash from a view in the same way that you would access any other hash in Rails. You don't need to explicitly populate it in the controller, nor do you have to purge the Flash once the view has been rendered—Rails takes care of this for you.

Since flash content is universally applicable, we'll change our layout file (which is located at **app/views/layouts/application.html.erb**) so that it renders a notification box as long as there is content available to render. Modify your layout file as follows:

09-application.html.erb *(excerpt)*

```
<div id="content">
  <h1>Shovell</h1>
  <% unless flash[:notice].blank? %>
    <div id="notification"><%= flash[:notice] %></div>
  <% end %>
  <%= yield %>
</div>
```

The condition that we've added here checks whether the `flash[:notice]` variable is blank; if not, the code renders a simple HTML `div` element to which an `id` is attached. Rails considers an object to be blank if it's either `nil` or an empty string.

Before we switch to the browser to test this addition, let's add a few rules to our style sheet to display our notification:

```
                                                    09-style.css (excerpt)
#notification {
  border: 5px solid #9c9;
  background-color: #cfc;
  padding: 5px;
  margin: 10px 0;
}
```

If you submit another story now, you should see a nice green box on the subsequent page informing you that the submission succeeded, as shown in Figure 6.5. If you're curious, reload the landing page to make sure the contents of the flash disappear.

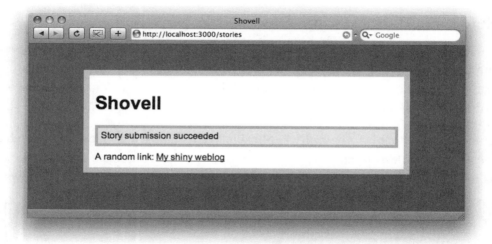

Figure 6.5. Providing feedback after story submission

However, our form submission process is still flawed: it's possible for a user to submit stories without entering a name. Or a link. Or both!

Applying Validations

To ensure that all the stories submitted to Shovell contain both a name and a link before they're saved, we'll make use of the `ActiveRecord` functionality called **validations**.

Validations come in a variety of flavors: the simplest flavor says, "Check that this attribute (or form input) is not empty." A more complex validation, for example, might be, "Make sure this attribute (or form input) matches the following regular expression."[2] There are varying degrees of complexity in between. A more complex validation might be used, for example, to validate an email address.

Validations are defined in the model. This ensures that the validation is always applied, and, therefore, that an object is always valid, before its data is saved to the database.

Let's look at a simple validation. To add validations to our Story model, edit the model class in **app/models/story.rb** so that it looks like this:

11-story.rb (excerpt)

```ruby
class Story < ActiveRecord::Base
  validates_presence_of :name, :link
end
```

You'll notice that the line we've added here is fairly verbose, so it's quite readable by humans. This line makes sure that the name and link attributes have a value before the model is saved.

Tweaking the Redirection Logic

We want to ensure that the user will only be redirected to the story list if the model passes its validation checks. To do so, we need to modify the create action in our controller as follows:

12-stories_controller.rb (excerpt)

```ruby
def create
  @story = Story.new(params[:story])
  if @story.save
    flash[:notice] = "Story submission succeeded"
    redirect_to stories_path
  else
```

---

[2] A regular expression is a string of characters that can be used to match another string of characters. The syntax of regular expressions can be confusing, with particularly long expressions looking much like random characters to a newcomer to the syntax. One of the most common uses of regular expressions is validating whether or not an email address is in the correct format.

```
      render :action => 'new'
    end
end
```

As you can see, we've added an `if` clause so that it checks to see whether **@story.save** returns true.

The validations we defined will be called before the `save` method writes the object to the database. If the validations fail, this method will return false—the object will not be saved, and the user will not be redirected.

It's quite common to use Ruby statements directly within conditions, as we've done with the `save` method here. In general, many of the methods provided by Rails core classes return true or false, which makes them an excellent choice for use in conditions.

In the `else` part we instruct the controller to rerender the template associated with the `new` action, which is our story submission form. This enables the user to correct his or her submission and resubmit without having to reenter the form values. Please note that the `render` call does *not* execute any of the controller code associated with the `new` action.

Fantastic! Our logic for processing the form is sound. If you were to try to submit a blank name or link now, our app would not allow the object to be saved, the redirect would not occur and the form would be rerendered. However, we still need to give the user some guidance for correcting any errors that result from a failed validation.

Improving the User Experience

Looking at the generated HTML of the rerendered form gives us a hint as to how we might implement some additional feedback for the user when a validation error occurs:

```html
<div class="fieldWithErrors">
  <input id="story_name" name="story[name]" size="30" type="text"
     value="" />
</div>
```

As you can see, using the Rails `form_for` helper has paid off. It has wrapped our text field in a `div` element, and assigned it a `class` called `fieldWithErrors`. We could style this `div` with a red border, for example, to indicate that this field threw an error. In fact, let's do just that. Add the following rule to the **style.css** file:

13-style.css *(excerpt)*

```
.fieldWithErrors {
  border: 5px solid #f66;
}
```

The helper's other neat trick is that it populates each field with values that the user entered, as Figure 6.6 shows.

It's also good practice to tell our users what *exactly* is wrong with a particular field—further down the road, we may want to add a validation to our model to ensure that each URL is submitted only once.

Add the following line to the top of the **new.html.erb** template:

14-new.html.erb *(excerpt)*

```
<%= error_messages_for 'story' %>
```

Now, if a user submits the form without entering content into every field, the browser will display:

- a useful error message that indicates how many fields are blank
- some textual hints as to the nature of the error for each field
- a red border that clearly highlights which fields need attention

See Figure 6.6 for an example.

Figure 6.6. Story submission form with validation output

A pretty functional form submission process, no? And it doesn't look too shabby, either.

However, before we begin loading our application with additional features, we should add some unit and functional test coverage, to make sure that future modifications don't break any of our existing functionality.

Testing the Form

Getting into the habit of writing tests for newly added code is more than just a good idea—it may save your hide in the future!

As I've mentioned before, by writing tests for *all* of your code, you can evolve a suite of automated testing facilities as your application evolves. This suite can then be run periodically or on demand to reveal errors in your application.

You can take a couple of approaches to creating a test suite for your application. One of them—the more radical, in fact—is referred to as **test-driven development** (TDD). When adhering to TDD principles, you *first* write a test, make sure it fails, then fill in the code that causes the test to pass. This approach works best when you've had some experience with the programming language you're writing your application in.

The opposite approach is to write the code first, and make sure it passes *you* (the human testing engine). Once this preliminary test has been passed, you write some automated testing code, then run your application against the automated test. We'll be using this second approach for the rest of the development of our story-sharing application.

A Rails test suite can be split into three fundamental parts:

unit tests

Unit tests cover model-level functionality, which generally encompasses an application's core business logic. Unit tests can test validations, associations (which we'll be covering in Chapter 7), and generic methods that are attached to models.

functional tests

Functional tests in Rails cover controller-level functionality and the accompanying views. A functional test can be quite specific: ensuring, for example, that a certain HTML element is present in a view, that a variable is populated properly, or that the proper redirection takes place after a form has been submitted.

integration tests

Integration testing goes beyond the relatively isolated approaches of functional and unit testing. An integration test allows you to test complete stages of user interaction with your application. The registration of a new user, and the story submission process as a whole, are good candidates for integration testing.

In this chapter, we'll look at functional and unit testing; we'll cover integration testing in Chapter 11.

Generally speaking, test cases in Rails exist as classes that descend from `ActiveSupport::TestCase`. However, when we generated our models and controllers in Chapter 5, the generate script created some skeleton files for us. These are located in the **test** folder, which is where all of the files that make up our testing suite reside.

Testing the Model

While our Story model doesn't have a great deal of functionality yet, it does have some validations, and we should definitely make sure that they operate as expected. We'll add them to the skeleton test file, then run the test to confirm that our validations are behaving themselves!

Analyzing the Skeleton File

The skeleton test file for our Story model is located at **test/unit/story_test.rb**. When you open it, you should see the following code:

15-story_test.rb (excerpt)

```
require File.dirname(__FILE__) + '/../test_helper'

class StoryTest < ActiveSupport::TestCase
  # Replace this with your real tests.
  def test_truth
    assert true
  end
end
```

That first line aside, what we have here is a basic class definition by the name of StoryTest. The name of this class, which was created when the file was generated, suggests that its purpose is for testing our Story model—and so it is.

The require command at the top of the file is a simple example of one file gaining access to the functionality of another file; the external file in such arrangements is known as an **include file**. By including this file, we gain access to a large amount of testing-related functionality.

Of course, Rails includes other files all the time, but we don't see dozens of require commands littered throughout our code. Why not? The Rails conventions allow it to deduce what is needed, when it is needed, and where it can be found. And this is another reason why following Rails conventions is so important.

Using Assertions

Code is tested in Rails using **assertions**. Assertions are tiny functions that confirm that something is in a certain state. A simple assertion may just compare two values to make sure that they're identical. A more complex assertion may match a value against a regular expression, or scan an HTML template for the presence of a certain HTML element. We'll look at various types of assertions in this section.

Once they have been written, assertions are grouped into **tests**. A test is an instance method that is prefixed with `test_`. An example of a test is the `test_truth` method in the previous code listing. These tests are executed one by one via the `rake` command that we looked at in Chapter 5. If one of the assertions in a test fails, the test is immediately aborted and the test suite moves on to the next one.

Now that we know what assertions are, and how they work, let's write one!

Writing a Unit Test

The `test_truth` method in our unit test is just a stub that was created by the `generate` script. Let's replace it with a real test:

```
16-story_test.rb (excerpt)

def test_should_not_be_valid_without_name
  s = Story.create(:name => nil, :link =>
➥       'http://www.testsubmission.com/')
  assert s.errors.on(:name)
end
```

We've named our method `test_should_not_be_valid_without_name`. As you may have guessed, this method will test the validation of the name. Let's examine each line within the method:

```
  s = Story.create(:name => nil, :link =>
➥       'http://www.testsubmission.com/')
```

This line creates a new `Story` object—a task that we might perform in a regular controller action. Note, however, that this time we've purposely left the required `name` attribute blank (`nil`). As the `create` method will attempt to save the new object

immediately, the validations that we defined in the model will be checked at the
same time.

At this point, we can check the result of the validation by reading the `errors` attribute of our newly created object.

```
assert s.errors.on(:name)
```

Every model object in Rails has an `errors` attribute. This attribute contains the
results of any validations that have been applied to it—if the validation failed, errors
will exist "on" that attribute. In this case, we deliberately left the `name` attribute
empty; passing the symbol `:name` to `errors.on`—to test for errors on the `name` attribute—should therefore return true, and our `assert` statement confirms exactly that.

The `name` attribute is not the only required attribute for our `Story` model, though—the
`link` attribute must be assigned a value before a story can be saved. We've already
added one test, so adding a second should be fairly straightforward. Let's add a test
that covers the validation of the `link` attribute:

17-story_test.rb (excerpt)

```
def test_should_be_valid_without_link
  s = Story.create(:name => 'My test submission', :link => nil)
  assert s.errors.on(:link)
end
```

Easy, huh?

Lastly, to complete our first batch of tests, we'll add a test that checks whether or
not a new `Story` object can be successfully created and saved when being instantiated
with all the required attributes, thereby passing all of our validations:

```
                                                    18-story_test.rb (excerpt)
def test_should_create_story
  s = Story.create(
    :name => 'My test submission',
    :link => 'http://www.testsubmission.com/')
  assert s.valid?
end
```

In this test, a new `Story` object is created, and all mandatory attributes are assigned a value. The assertion then confirms that the created object has indeed passed all validations by calling its `valid?` method—this method returns true if no validation errors are present.

Running a Unit Test

With this testing code in place, let's run our small unit test suite. From the applications root folder, execute the following command:

```
$ rake test:units
```

This command will execute all the test cases located in the **test/unit** folder one by one, and alert us to any assertions that fail. The output of a successful test execution should look something like Figure 6.7.

As you can see, `rake` gives us a nice summary of our test execution. The results suggest that a total of three test cases and three assertions were executed, which is exactly what our test suite contains at the moment.

You'll notice some dots between the **Started** and the **Finished** lines of the test suite output: one dot for each test passed. Whenever an assertion fails, an uppercase `F` will be displayed, and if one of your tests contains an error, an uppercase `E` will be displayed, followed by details of the error that occurred.

Figure 6.7. Running a successful suite of unit tests

Instead of just boldly assuming that our tests work correctly, let's change a test so that we *know* it's going to fail. In our `test_should_create_story` method, modify the last line so that its output is reversed:

```
assert ! s.valid?
```

Save the file and run the unit testing suite again:

```
$ rake test:units
```

Your output should display an F, indicating test failure, as shown in Figure 6.8. A description of the assertions that may have caused the test to fail is also displayed.

Armed with this information, locating and fixing an error is easy. We're provided with the name of the test that failed (`test_should_create_story`), the test case to which it belongs (`StoryTest`), and the line on which it failed (line 7). Thus, the (admittedly forged) culprit is easily located and fixed.

```
Core:shovell scoop$ rake test:units
(in /Users/scoop/shovell)
/System/Library/Frameworks/Ruby.framework/Versions/1.8/usr/bin/ruby -Ilib:test "
/Library/Ruby/Gems/1.8/gems/rake-0.8.1/lib/rake/rake_test_loader.rb" "test/unit/
story_test.rb"
Loaded suite /Library/Ruby/Gems/1.8/gems/rake-0.8.1/lib/rake/rake_test_loader
Started
F..
Finished in 0.131339 seconds.

  1) Failure:
test_should_create_story(StoryTest)
    [./test/unit/story_test.rb:18:in `test_should_create_story'
     /Library/Ruby/Gems/1.8/gems/activesupport-2.0.2/lib/active_support/testing/
default.rb:7:in `run']:
<false> is not true.

3 tests, 3 assertions, 1 failures, 0 errors
rake aborted!
Command failed with status (1): [/System/Library/Frameworks/Ruby.framework/...]

(See full trace by running task with --trace)
Core:shovell scoop$
```

Figure 6.8. Unit testing with a failed test

For now, undo the change you made to the last line of `test_should_create_story`, so that the test will again pass:

```
assert s.valid?
```

That's it—we've tested the model. We'll add more tests in later chapters as we add more functionality to the model.

Testing the Controller

The functional testing of controllers is, at first glance, not very different from testing models—it's just a different part of the MVC stack. However, there *is* some extra housekeeping involved in setting up the environment properly.

Analyzing the Skeleton File

Once again, a skeleton functional test was created as a result of our generating the `StoriesController`. This skeleton file resides in **test/functional/stories_controller_test.rb**:

```
                                    19-stories_controller_test.rb (excerpt)

require File.dirname(__FILE__) + '/../test_helper'

class StoriesControllerTest < ActionController::TestCase
  # Replace this with your real tests.
  def test_truth
    assert true
  end
end
```

On first inspection, this *looks* similar to the StoryTest class that we saw in the previous section. We also have a test_truth dummy test, which we'll overwrite once again.

Writing a Functional Test

To add the first test for our StoriesController, replace the test_truth method in the skeleton functional test file with the following code:

```
                                    20-stories_controller_test.rb (excerpt)

def test_should_show_index
  get :index
  assert_response :success
  assert_template 'index'
  assert_not_nil assigns(:story)
end
```

Let's look at each line in this method.

```
def test_should_show_index
```

As you may have deduced from the name of the method, what we're checking here is that the index action is correctly displayed in the user's browser when the /index path is requested.

```
get :index
```

This line simulates a user requesting the `index` action of the `StoriesController` class. It uses the HTTP request method `GET`; similarly, the methods `post`, `put`, and `delete` exist for testing actions requiring that respective HTTP verb.

```
assert_response :success
```

The `assert_response` assertion checks that the HTTP response code we receive is the code that we expect.[3]

```
assert_template 'index'
```

By invoking `assert_template`, we ensure that the request we made is actually rendered with the template that we expect, not a template with a different name.

Shortcuts for Cryptic HTTP Codes

HTTP codes are numeric, so sometimes they're hard to remember. As a result, Rails has implemented a few aliases for the more common codes. In this example we've used the `:success` symbol, which maps internally to the `200 OK` response code that is returned when a page request is successful. Other mappings that can be used with the `assert_response` function include `:redirect` for HTTP redirect headers and `:missing` for the all-too-common "404 Not Found" error that occurs when a request is made for a file that doesn't exist.

```
assert_not_nil assigns(:story)
```

This final assertion is not as intuitive as the others, but it's actually quite straightforward. `assert_not_nil` tests whether or not the instance variable `@story` is set to `nil` (that's the easy bit). The `assigns(variable_name)` construct makes available to the functional test all of the instance variables that have been declared within the controller's actions. The `@story` object is one such variable, so passing the `:story` symbol to the test allows the `@story` variable to be used as part of the test.

We also need some fixtures for this test. As we learned in Chapter 5, fixtures are dummy model objects that provide a consistent data set against which our tests can

---

[3] A complete list of HTTP response codes can be found at http://en.wikipedia.org/wiki/List_of_HTTP_status_codes.

run. Fixtures are model based, so there's a fixture file for every model class in our application. By default, Rails makes all YAML files stored in **test/fixtures/** available to our tests. This means that we don't need to specify explicitly which fixtures we want to load for each test.

Running a Functional Test

Now that we've created our test case, we can invoke the functional test suite. Once again, we turn to the trusty `rake` tool:

```
$ rake test:functionals
```

The output that results from the successful execution of our test suite is shown in Figure 6.9.

Figure 6.9. Running a successful functional test suite

Writing More Functional Tests

There are two actions for which we haven't yet written a test: the `new` and `create` actions. We'll want to create a few different tests for these actions. Let's do that now.

For the purpose of testing the inner workings of our new action in GET mode, we'll use a test case that we'll name `test_should_show_new`. Add the following method below the `test_should_show_index` test that we created previously:

21-stories_controller_test.rb *(excerpt)*

```ruby
def test_should_show_new
  get :new
  assert_response :success
  assert_template 'new'
  assert_not_nil assigns(:story)
end
```

This is quite straightforward. Apart from a few textual differences, this test is almost identical to that for `test_should_show_index`. However, our work isn't done yet!

There's a `form` element in the new template, and we should certainly test that it appears correctly. Here's another test to do just that:

22-stories_controller_test.rb *(excerpt)*

```ruby
def test_should_show_new_form
  get :new
  assert_select 'form p', :count => 3
end
```

The `assert_select` helper function that we've used here is a very flexible and powerful tool for verifying that a certain HTML element is present in the document that's returned from a request. `assert_select` can even verify the hierarchy of the HTML element, regardless of how deeply it is nested. It can also test the element's attributes: for example, the value of its `class` or `id`. In fact, it's so flexible that we could potentially devote an entire chapter to its features alone.[4]

But now we're getting sidetracked. Back to this line! `assert_select` checks for the existence of one `form` element in which three `p` elements are nested; the count is supplied using the `:count` argument. These three paragraphs contain the fields that comprise our story submission form.

---

[4] An `assert_select` cheat sheet is available at the web site of Assaf Arkin, the tool's author: http://labnotes.org/svn/public/ruby/rails_plugins/assert_select/cheat/assert_select.html

How do we specify an element in this hierarchy? Easy: by following the simple rules of CSS selectors.

In this example, we want to reference a paragraph element that resides within a form element. Now, if we were writing a CSS rule to style these paragraph elements to be bold, it would look like this:

```
form p {
  font-weight: bold;
}
```

In the same way that we reference paragraphs in CSS, the parameter that we use with assert_select is simply 'form p'. We'll look at a few more of the CSS selector features of assert_select in the tests we write in later chapters.

Lastly, to test the posting of a new story, we'll write a few more short tests for the create action:

23-stories_controller_test.rb (excerpt)

```
def test_should_add_story
  post :create, :story => {
      :name => 'test story',
      :link => 'http://www.test.com/'
    }
  assert ! assigns(:story).new_record?
  assert_redirected_to stories_path
  assert_not_nil flash[:notice]
end
```

Let's break this test down line by line.

```
post :create, :story => {
    :name => 'test story',
    :link => 'http://www.test.com/'
  }
```

As I mentioned earlier in this chapter, post is another way to invoke an HTTP request programmatically from a test. post takes a few parameters—in this case, we're simulating the submission of a story. To do this, we need to pass a hash that contains values for the required attributes of a story: symbols representing the `name` and `link` attributes.

Immediately after our `post` call has been issued, the following line checks the results:

```
assert ! assigns(:story).new_record?
```

Here, we're using the `new_record?` method of the `@story` instance variable to confirm that the record has actually been saved to the database. Since we want the assertion to tell us if it *hasn't* been saved at this point, we use the exclamation mark (`!`) to reverse the return value of the `new_record?` call.

When a story submission has been successful, our application issues a redirection. We can test that this redirection occurs using `assert_redirected_to`:

```
assert_redirected_to stories_path
```

Lastly, we assert that the contents of the `notice` flash area is not `nil`:

```
assert_not_nil flash[:notice]
```

Whew! Our rapidly expanding test suite is evolving to the point where we can be very confident that the story submission process is functioning correctly.

The final test case we'll add covers the situation in which posting a new story fails. We'll cause the submission to fail by omitting one of the required fields:

24-stories_controller_test.rb *(excerpt)*

```
def test_should_reject_missing_story_attribute
  post :create, :story => { :name => 'story without a link' }
  assert assigns(:story).errors.on(:link)
end
```

In the first line of this code, we attempt to post a story without a `link`:

```
post :new, :story => { :name => 'story without a link' }
```

After this submission attempt, we use the `errors` attribute to verify that there's an error condition on the `link` attribute, just as we did in the unit test earlier in the chapter:

```
assert assigns(:story).errors.on(:link)
```

That's it! We've written all the tests we need for the time being. Now, let's run the suite.

Running the Complete Test Suite

Now that we have these additional tests in place, we'll need to run all of our tests again. However, this time, we'll use a slightly different approach: instead of invoking our unit and functional tests separately, we'll use a `rake` task to run these test suites successively:

```
$ rake test
```

The output of a successful test run should look like Figure 6.10.

Congratulations! Not only have you created a full test suite, but, on running it, you've found that your application is error-free—a discovery that should earn even the most seasoned developer a self-pat on the back. To finish up, let's turn our thoughts to the application's performance as we inspect the log files generated by `ActionPack`.

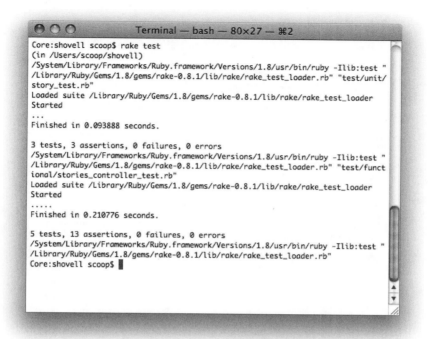

Figure 6.10. Running the complete test suite

Revisiting the Logs

We took a brief look at the extensive logging functionality that `ActiveRecord` provides in the section called "Where's the SQL?" in Chapter 5—this gave us a glimpse into the kind of automation, in terms of SQL generation, that happens behind the scenes in Rails.

If you liked what you saw back then, you'll be glad to learn that `ActionPack` is also a prolific logger. An example of some of the entries that `ActionPack` wrote to the development log file are shown in Figure 6.11.

Figure 6.11. Contents of the development log file showing `ActionPack` entries

As you look at these entries, you'll notice a full record of your activities within the application has been logged, complete with SQL statements, page redirections, page requests, templates rendered, and more.

The level of detail in Rails's log files is of real benefit when you're hunting down a problem with your code—the logs provide real insight into what's actually happening as a page is requested. The same level of detail is captured for unit and functional tests in the test log file, which is located in **log/test.log**.

The timing values that are written to the log file are particularly interesting. Consider the following snippet:

```
Completed in 0.00970 (103 reqs/sec) | Rendering: 0.00321 (33%) |
DB: 0.00115 (11%) | 200 OK [http://localhost/stories]
```

From this log entry, we can conclude that:

- 11% of the time it took Rails to pump out this page was spent talking to the database

- only 33% of the total time was spent in actually assembling the page

While 33% might sound like a large portion of the total time—which it is—by looking at the actual number of seconds involved in the process, we see that rendering the page took less than 0.01 seconds.

Rails also provides us with a rough estimate of how many instances of this particular page could potentially be served per second (in this case, it estimates 103 page requests per second). Note, though, that this is a very rough estimate; we're running our app in the development environment, which is certainly not optimized for speed. The application is also unlikely to be located on the same server as the one that will be running the application in production. As such, the real numbers for this statistic may vary greatly.

We won't dig any deeper into the logs, but be aware that it's worth keeping an eye on your log files. Incidentally, this is the same information that has been flying past in the terminal window you launched your web server from, too. This is another way that you can check your application's log entries in real time, although you'll probably find using a text editor more practical.

We'll revisit the log files once more when we reach Chapter 11.

Summary

We certainly increased the functionality of our application in this chapter; we even made it look a little prettier. We used the Rails form helpers to create a fully functional web interface for submitting stories in a RESTful way, and we added a global layout to our application, complete with style sheets.

Along the way, we looked briefly at the flash, Rails's short-term memory container that can be used to pass messages between successive actions. We also added some validations to our Story model, to make sure that our story submissions adhere to our own high standards—or that, at the very least, that each story has a title and a URL!

Finally, we wrote our first unit and functional test cases, which we used to automate the testing of our models, controllers, and views. We also took a scroll through the Rails log files to see what kind of logging the `ActionPack` module performs, and how those log entries are useful when we debug our application.

In the next chapter, we'll add the much-anticipated voting feature to our story-sharing application—and we'll do it using cutting-edge Ajax technology, spiced up with some Web 2.0 visual effects. Yes, it's going to be one good-looking chapter! On with the show!

Ajax and Web 2.0

The success of a social bookmarking or content-sharing application doesn't rest solely on the submission of stories by users; there must also be some way for site visitors to gain an idea of the *value* of each content item.

Now, in the world of social bookmarking, popular opinion rules. That's why, on our Shovell site, the value of each story will be gauged by its popularity as indicated by the number of votes the story receives from Shovell users.

In this chapter, we're going to expand the feature set of our story-sharing application to include this crucial voting functionality. And there's no better way to do so than with the technology behind one of Web 2.0's biggest buzzwords: Ajax! We'll cover Ajax and the JavaScript libraries that come with Rails, Prototype and script.aculo.us, in the coming pages.

Generating a Vote Model

At the core of our app's voting functionality lies a data model—a Vote—which we'll need to create. Once that's in place, we'll create and apply the necessary changes to our database schema. We learned how to do this using migrations in Chapter 6, so there's no reason to return to the old ways now!

Creating the Model

Using the `generate` script (by now, you should be feeling reasonably at home with this!), let's add a new model to our application:

```
$ ruby script/generate model Vote story_id:integer
```

Just like the last time we generated a new model, we gave the `generate` script some insight into the attributes the new model is going to have, which we'll explore in a moment. The result of running the command is shown in Figure 7.1.

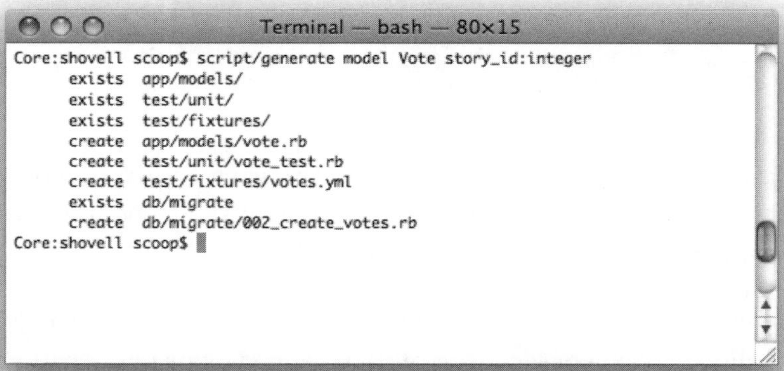

```
● ○ ○              Terminal — bash — 80×15
Core:shovell scoop$ script/generate model Vote story_id:integer
      exists  app/models/
      exists  test/unit/
      exists  test/fixtures/
      create  app/models/vote.rb
      create  test/unit/vote_test.rb
      create  test/fixtures/votes.yml
      exists  db/migrate
      create  db/migrate/002_create_votes.rb
Core:shovell scoop$ 
```

Figure 7.1. Generating a `Vote` model

As you might expect, this command generates a new migration file (among others), **db/migrate/002_create_votes.rb**; let's look at it right now.

Examining the Vote Migration

The migration file that was generated for us contains the basic code to create a `votes` table in our database. This is the second migration for our project, so it has been assigned the number `002`. Currently, the `self.up` method should look like this:

```
                                          01-002_create_votes.rb
def self.up
  create_table :votes do |t|
    t.integer :story_id

    t.timestamps
  end
end
```

As you can see, to create the schema, we're following the format we used in Chapter 5, but this time, the column types are different. Let's look at them briefly:

```
    t.integer :story_id
```

This line creates a `story_id` column of type `integer`. It's going to be used to store the numerical ID of a story that has received a vote from a user. This column will be populated using associations, which we'll talk about in the next section.

Rails has a handful of "magical" column names; two of the most handy are `created_at` and `updated_at`, each of type `datetime`. Since they're so useful, Rails has a shortcut for creating those two columns in a migration. It even includes that shortcut by default every time we create a new migration:

```
    t.timestamps
```

Whenever a new model is saved to the database using the `save` method, Rails will automatically populate the column called `created_at` with the current date and time.

Its companion, `updated_at`, operates in a similar manner. It automatically populates the column with the current date and time of any successive call to the `save` method, although we won't be making use of this column for the `Vote` model. (A vote, once cast, is a vote, right?)

As with the last migration we created, the `self.down` method is fine as is—reversing this migration simply gets rid of the whole table.

Applying the Migration

Our migration is in place, so let's apply it using the `rake` tool once more:

```
$ rake db:migrate
```

The result of applying the migration is shown in Figure 7.2.

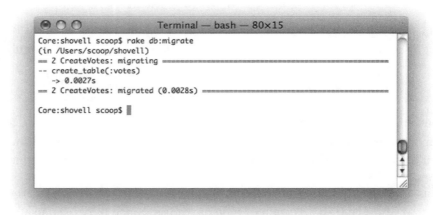

Figure 7.2. Applying the second migration

Excellent! Now, I suggest you sit down before we begin the next topic, because things could get a little heavy. It's time for you and me to have an in-depth talk about relationships.

Introducing Relationships

Contrary to received wisdom, relationships don't have to be hard work.

No, I'm not talking about human relationships—I'm talking about the **relationships** (also commonly referred to as **associations**) between objects in our model. We touched on some of this stuff back in Chapter 4 when we talked about the features of `ActiveRecord`. Now we finally have a practical use for all that theory.

The `Vote` model that we just created needs to be associated with our `Story` model. After all, what good is a vote if you don't know which story it's for?

As we saw back in Chapter 4, Rails can cater for a variety of associations between models. One of the more popular associations is the **one-to-many relationship**, which we'll add to our model now.

Introducing the `has_many` Clause

A one-to-many relationship exists when a single record of type A is associated with many records of type B.

In our application, a single story is likely to be associated with many votes. This relationship is shown in Figure 7.3.

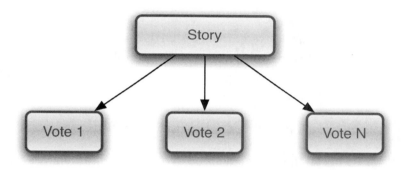

Figure 7.3. The one-to-many relationship between stories and votes

Relationships are usually declared bidirectionally, so that the relationship can be utilized from both sides. Let's begin by examining the `Story` model's relationship to a `Vote`; we'll look at the reverse relationship later in the chapter.

To define the first aspect of the relationship, edit the `Story` class, located in **app/models/story.rb**, adding the line in bold below:

02-story.rb *(excerpt)*

```
class Story < ActiveRecord::Base
  validates_presence_of :name, :link
  has_many :votes
end
```

The addition of this one line has ignited a flurry of activity behind the scenes—fire up a Rails console, and I'll show you what I mean. First, retrieve an existing Story record from the database:

```
$ ruby script/console
>> s = Story.find(:first)
=> #<Story id: 2, name: "SitePoint Forums", …>
```

Next, invoke this object's newly acquired votes method:

```
>> s.votes
=> []
```

The name of this method is derived directly from the has_many :votes relationship that we defined in our class definition (we'll talk more about declaring associations in Chapter 9). Invoking the method grabs all votes for the Story and returns them in an Array (which, obviously, is empty right now).

So, how would we go about adding some votes to this story?

The easiest way is to call the create method of the object returned by story.votes, like so:

```
>> s.votes.create
=> #<Vote id: 1, story_id: 2, …>
```

This approach instantiates a new Vote object, and saves the object to the database immediately. It works because we haven't specified any validations for the Vote model yet, so there's nothing to prevent empty fields from being saved. However, if you assume that the record we just saved to the database is completely empty, you couldn't be more off the mark.

Let's take a look at the number of votes that have been created. Call the size method for our Story's associated votes, like so:

```
>> s.votes.size
=> 1
```

This is another method to which we gained access by defining the `has_many` relationship. It instructs Rails to calculate the number of records associated with the current model object. A result of 1 indicates that the `Vote` object that we just created does indeed contain some information, since one `Vote` is associated with the `Story` we retrieved.

To find out more, let's retrieve the same `Vote` object independently from the `Story` it's been associated with, and inspect its attributes:

```
>> v = Vote.find(:first)
=> #<Vote id: 1, story_id: 2, …>
>> v.attributes
=> {"story_id"=>2, "id"=>1, "created_at"=>
   Tue Feb 05 11:04:55 0100 2008, "updated_at"=>
   Tue Feb 05 11:04:55 0100 2008}
```

As you can see, not only has our `Vote` object automatically been populated with a creation and update date (the two start out being the same value), but a value has been assigned in its `story_id` field. This value was obtained from the `id` attribute of the `Story` object that was used to create the vote. (In this case, the value is equal to 2, as that's the `id` of the first `Story` in my database.) Figure 7.4 shows this relationship.

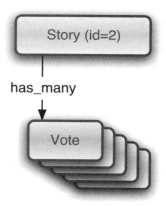

Figure 7.4. A `Story` has many `Votes`

To complete our relationship definition, let's add its counterpart—the `belongs_to` clause—to the `Vote` model.

Introducing the `belongs_to` Clause

As we learned in the previous section, as in life, there are usually two sides to the story when it comes to relationships.

Now we'll add the second part of our one-to-many relationship. First, edit the Vote model class (in **app/models/vote.rb**) as follows:

03-vote.rb

```ruby
class Vote < ActiveRecord::Base
  belongs_to :story
end
```

Now that we've defined the relationship within both models that are affected by it, not only can we access the votes of a Story, we can also access the story of a Vote. And I'm sure you can guess how we'd do the latter—back to the Rails console!

```
>> v = Vote.find(:first)
=> #<Vote id: 1, story_id: 2, …>
>> v.story
=> #<Story id: 2, name: "SitePoint Forums", …>
```

Reloading the Rails Console

If you make a change to your models or controllers while you have a running Rails console, you'll find you cannot call any of your new code—your console needs to reload your models and controllers. Doing this is as simple as issuing the `reload!` console command. You'll then see the following:

```
>> reload!
Reloading...
=> true
```

You'll also have to recreate any existing instances of your models, because they will still be using the old class.

With the addition of just one line to our Vote class definition, we've gained access to the associated Story object. As the code listing above shows, access to this object is possible via a new instance method (`story`) on the model—this method is available as a direct result of the relationship clause that we put in place, and obtains its name from the first parameter of the association call (`belongs_to :story`).

Figure 7.5 shows how this relationship works.

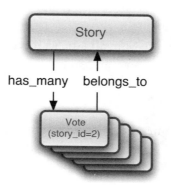

Figure 7.5. A `Vote` belongs to a `Story`

How's Our Schema Looking?

Now that we've established both sides of our one-to-many relationship, let's look at how the information representing this relationship is stored in the database.

If you recall each of the migrations that we've created and applied so far, you'll notice that, although the `Vote` model contains a `story_id` column, the `Story` model doesn't contain a corresponding `vote_id` column.

In fact, this column isn't necessary. There's no need to store association information in both models when defining a one-to-many relationship; the information is always stored on the "many" side of the relationship. With this information in place, Rails is intelligent enough to query the correct table when we instruct it to find objects that have an association.

Also note how the terminology used to define the relationship is an accurate reflection of what's going on—the `Votes` *belong to* the `Story` (hence the `belongs_to` call). And the `Vote` model represents the "many" side of the relationship, so each `Vote` stores its own reference to its associated `Story`.

Now that we understand the data structures that underlie our voting functionality, let's jump into building some user interactivity.

Making a Home for Each Story

In terms of viewing stories that have been submitted to Shovell, our users currently only have access to a page that displays a random story. To address this issue, we'll add a new action that displays a single story, along with all of its details, before we implement the voting actions themselves. The story page will serve as a reference point for any given story on the Shovell site, as it will contain a range of information—voting actions, voting history, and so on—about the story.

Determining Where a Story Lives

The first step in displaying our stories is to find out what the URLs to access a single Story need to look like and which action we need to teach StoriesController to handle these requests.

If you flip back to the section about resources in Rails which we've talked about in Chapter 6 and take another look at the table with the mappings of URLs to controller actions, you'll find the promising mention of a show action to handle URLs like /stories/2. This action is exactly what we're going to implement over the next few pages.

Before we implement said show method in StoriesController, let's think for a moment about what it's going to do. Our controller action needs to go ahead and retrieve a story with a specific ID from the database. This ID is contained in the URL; Rails Routing extracts it from there and makes it available to us as params[:id]. The controller then needs to hand the object it finds to the view, which is in turn responsible for displaying it.

We'll start by adding the following method to our StoriesController class. Once again, the order of the method definitions within the class definition is not important.

04-stories_controller.rb *(excerpt)*

```
def show
  @story = Story.find(params[:id])
end
```

The single line of code in our show method executes a find by passing the value of params[:id] to it. By doing so, we're instructing ActiveRecord to retrieve from the database all rows with an `id` that's equal to the value in the URL requested by the user; there should only ever be a single row returned.

The result of that find operation is then assigned to the instance variable `@story`, which is automatically made available to the corresponding view internally by Rails. Speaking of which, let's create that view now.

Displaying Our Stories

Lastly, we need a template with which to display a story. Create a new template file at **app/views/stories/show.html.erb**, and fill it with the following simple HTML and ERb code:

```
                                                                   05-show.html.erb
<h2><%= @story.name %></h2>
<p><%= link_to @story.link, @story.link %></p>
```

All this does is display the name of the `Story`, wrapped in `<h2>` tags. It also adds a link to the URL that's stored as part of the story.

Let's check that this functionality works as expected. Open the following URL in your browser (if you've deleted some of your stories, substitute a higher number at the end): http://localhost:3000/stories/2.

As you can see in Figure 7.6, our story has its own page that displays its name and a link to the story content.

 Is Your Server Running?

As with our other examples, connecting to your application requires the Rails web server to be running. If you need a refresher on how to launch it, flip back to the section called "Starting Our Application" in Chapter 2.

Figure 7.6. The first version of the show action

Improving the Story Randomizer

While we're at it, let's change our front page so that the random link it displays no longer uses the story's external URL. Instead, we'll direct users to the story's internal page, to which we'll add some voting functionality very soon.

Open up the template responsible for the index action of StoriesController (located at **app/views/stories/index.html.erb**) and change the link_to call so that it reads as follows:

```
                                                        06-index.html.erb (excerpt)

<%= link_to @story.name, story_path(@story) %>
```

The fact that a story_path function exists for our use is a direct result of the **map.resources :stories** call in the route configuration—this is another benefit of using Rails Resources and following their conventions, which include using the action show to display a single resource. The story_path function accepts a Story object that's used dynamically to generate the URL we're looking for.

Reload the index page at http://localhost:3000/stories. It should now link to the internal story page, as demonstrated in Figure 7.7.

Figure 7.7. The index page linking to the story page

If you thought that was fairly simple and straightforward a way to generate a link to a story, it gets even better! The above `link_to` call can be shortened to just the following:

```
<%= link_to @story.name, @story %>
```

Rails's `link_to` helper will automatically invoke the `story_path` helper behind the scenes, all because of that simple one-line declaration that made `Story` into a resource in the first place.

Well, this is already fairly functional. But I think we can do better in terms of readability within the URLs we're exposing to our users. So let's take a look at the concept of a **clean URL.**

Implementing Clean URLs

The URLs we put to use in the last section are fairly simple. And they're definitely simpler than those we're plagued by on our daily travels through some niches of the Internet. But we can do better!

To recap, we've employed a URL like the following to refer to a single story:

```
/stories/1
```

This is all well and good, but an `id` of 1 isn't exactly meaningful to our users—they're more likely to remember the title of a story. Even if the title was slightly modified (with special characters removed, escaped, or replaced), it would still make for a more usable URL—and be much friendlier to our search engine friends as well!

So, in referring to a story titled "My Shiny Weblog," the following URL would be perfect:

```
/stories/my-shiny-weblog
```

The implementation we're about to commence comes close to the ideal outlined above. Upon finishing this section, we'll have our stories shown at URLs such as this one:

```
/stories/1-my-shiny-weblog
```

As you can see, the URL *still* contains the `id` of the `Story`, but in addition to that it contains a simplified version of the story name. To implement this URL, we'll pull a little Ruby trick that's worth exploring in the console first.

Converting from Strings to Numbers

We've already talked about different object classes that are available in Ruby, and more or less any other programming language on the planet. And there are ways to convert between them. Of course, there are some conversions that make sense and others that don't. In this section we'll look at the conversion of a `String` object into an `Integer` object, and a neat side effect of that.

First off, why would you want to convert an object to a different class? Well, everything our web application receives from a user's browser is treated as a string, because the HTTP protocol doesn't specify values with a class. So better to be safe than sorry, given that `String` is the most universal choice and able to represent almost *everything*.

With that out of the way, it's fairly clear that the value 1 we receive in `params[:id]` from a URL like `/stories/1` is actually not a number, but a string. The difference is illustrated by the following Rails console output:

```
>> 1.class
=> Fixnum
>> "1".class
=> String
```

But how do we make a number out of a string representation of a number? To convert a string into an integer (whole numbers, without a decimal component, which is what the number 1 can be seen as), every `String` object ships with a `to_i` method:

```
>> "1".to_i
=> 1
```

The flipside of this is the `to_s` method provided by the `Fixnum` class:

```
>> 1.to_s
=> "1"
```

Armed with that knowledge, here's the little trick that will make our permalinks work with minimal effort:

```
>> "1-my-shiny-weblog".to_i
=> 1
```

So how does that work? `String`'s `to_i` method simply discards anything after the first numeric content it encounters, leaving us just with the ID of the story nicely extracted. Now we just need to get that simplified title into our story URLs, which is the topic of the next section.

Investigating Link Generation

When Rails's URL generation helpers need to generate URLs that point to specific objects such as the `Story` we've seen above, they actually ask the model being passed in how it wants to be represented.

The view template we created for the `show` action originally included a call to the `story_path` helper. This is basically a shortcut that Rails gives us for declaring `Story` a resource. Okay, I know you've come across this point a number of times now, but it's really important and well worth repeating.

If we weren't to use resources and needed to do without `story_path`, we'd have to use the following code to achieve the same result:

```
url_for :controller => 'stories', :action => 'show', :id => @story
```

But even that snippet of code carries a bit of Rails magic. If you pass an `ActiveRecord` model to `url_for`, it will automatically call the `to_param` method of the model (`@story` in the example above). This method, by default, returns the value of the `id` attribute.

So the above `url_for` call is actually equivalent to:

```
url_for :controller => 'stories', :action => 'show',
    :id => @story.to_param
```

And it's this `to_param` method that we can use to our advantage in sneaking our simplified title into the URL.

I know you're champing at the bit to reach the next section and make a start with the nifty Ajax stuff, so quickly throw this method into the `Story` class definition (stored in `app/models/story.rb`):

07-story.rb (excerpt)

```
class Story < ActiveRecord::Base
  def to_param
    "#{id}-#{name.gsub(/\W/, '-').downcase}"
  end
end
```

This rather cryptic snippet of code **overrides** the `to_param` method defined by the `ActiveRecord::Base` class. Now it no longer returns just the `id` but also includes a simplified version of the story's name. It's this new return value that we'll use in URLs pointing to stories.

In the new `to_param` method, I'm using *regular expressions* to turn non-alphanumeric characters in the story name (basically everything that's not a number or alphabetical character) into a dash and convert everything else to lowercase. This string is then appended to the original `id` of the story to generate the new, more representative URL. Of course, like a lot of methods in Rails, you're free to play with it in the console as well:

```
>> s = Story.find :first
=> #<Story id: 2, name: "SitePoint Forums", …>
>> s.name
=> "SitePoint Forums"
>> s.to_param
=> "2-sitepoint-forums"
```

At this point we can let Rails go and do its magic. We don't need to do anything else to make our clean URLs work. Give it a try—reload the story index in your browser (http://localhost:3000/stories) and marvel at your nice new clean URLs!

So right now, we're ready to start implementing the app's voting functionality. However, as we're going to do this using Ajax techniques, we'll take another slight detour to learn a bit about Ajax and see how it's implemented in Rails.

Ajax and Rails

We mentioned back in Chapter 1 that Rails is a full-stack framework, encompassing code on the client, the server, and everything in between. **Ajax** is a technique for communicating between client and server, so the Rails implementation of Ajax is therefore one of the key parts that makes up this "full-stack."

Introducing Ajax

Ajax stands for Asynchronous JavaScript and XML, but represents a technique that encompasses more than just these specific technologies. You've no doubt heard of the term, which has become one of the prime buzzwords behind the so-called Web 2.0 movement. Strictly speaking, though, Ajax isn't a new invention—it's actually existed for quite some time.

Basically, Ajax enables a web browser to continue to communicate with a web server without having to completely reload the page it's showing—a technique that's also known as **remote scripting**. This communication may include the exchange of form data, or the requesting of additional data to be incorporated into a page that has already been displayed. The end result is that a web application that uses Ajax has the potential to compete with more traditional desktop applications by providing the user with a more dynamic and responsive experience.

At the heart of Ajax is the `XmlHttpRequest` object. `XmlHttpRequest` was originally invented by Microsoft in the late 1990s for Internet Explorer 5, to improve and enhance the user experience of Microsoft's web-based email interface. It has since been implemented in all modern browsers. In 2005, a user-experience designer named Jesse James Garrett invented the term Ajax to describe the approach of using the `XmlHttpRequest` object, along with XHTML, CSS, and the Document Object Model (DOM), to create interactive web sites that *feel* like desktop applications.[1]

While compatibility with certain web browsers was lacking when the first applications that used Ajax hit the Web, this is no longer as much of an issue—all popular web browsers support the `XmlHttpRequest` object, including Internet Explorer, Firefox, Safari, and Opera.

Ajax has been used in many popular web applications, such as Digg, Flickr,[2] del.icio.us,[3] GMail,[4] and the 37signals applications that we talked about in Chapter 1.

As we'll soon see, implementing Ajax in Rails is as easy as implementing a regular link.

Remote Scripting with Prototype

Being an early adopter of new technologies usually necessitates diving into other people's code—code that usually does not represent best practice—as well as persisting with debugging tools, if such a tool even exists. Not so with Ajax and Rails.

Rails was one of the first—if not *the* first—frameworks to ship with (and even encourage) the use of Ajax in web applications. Rails comes bundled with the **Prototype** JavaScript library,[5] which is responsible for all of the dynamic interaction between

---

[1] The term Ajax was first mentioned in this essay:
https://www.adaptivepath.com/ideas/essays/archives/000385.php

[2] http://flickr.com/

[3] http://del.icio.us/

[4] http://mail.google.com/

[5] Although Prototype is bundled with Rails, it can be downloaded as a stand-alone JavaScript library from the Prototype web site [http://prototypejs.org/], and used independently.

browser and application. As it's so easy to use, many Rails-powered web applications were Ajax-enabled from day one.

Adding Visual Effects with script.aculo.us

When web developers first embraced Ajax, it introduced a number of new user in-terface problems. Interaction designers are still searching to find the best solution for several of these! These challenges arose from the fact that the way in which users interact with a web application that utilizes Ajax is fundamentally different from the way they use an app that does not. Back in the Web 1.0 days before Ajax, most users were able to anticipate when communication was occurring between client and server, and when it wasn't. The interaction was very start-stop in nature, because each back-and-forth transmission resulted in the delivery of a new page to the client.

With Ajax, the web browser might never really stop communicating with the server. We're therefore faced with a problem: how do we let the user know that communic-ation has taken place?

Let me illustrate this point with an example. When users click on an element, such as a link or a button, on a web page that uses Ajax, they expect a new page to load. After all, this is what's happened with every other link that they've clicked on the Web in the past. Instead, a small amount of content on the page is updated, while everything else stays in place, unchanged. The change that takes place is so minor, though, that the users don't notice it. They begin to wonder whether they might have missed the link when they clicked it, so they try clicking it again. Figure 7.8 shows a hypothetical example of this kind of confusion in action; blink and the frames appear much the same.

Figure 7.8. An Ajax-powered to-do list without visual feedback

In fact, the only thing that's missing is feedback from the application about what's going on. What would be great in this situation is some kind of visual feedback to let the users know that their click has been processed, so that the results of that action become more obvious. For this very purpose, Rails core team member Thomas Fuchs invented the **script.aculo.us** JavaScript library, which works with the Prototype library to provide various visual effects. Rails ships with this library by default, and we'll use it to provide feedback to the user.[6]

While they might look like gratuitous eye candy at first, when used sparingly, the visual effects provided by script.aculo.us can provide great user feedback for the Ajax actions handled by Prototype. For example, you can use effects to drop elements off the bottom of the page when a user deletes them, to highlight specific elements that have just been updated, or to "shake" the entire login form if a user supplies an incorrect password.

In addition to these visual effects, script.aculo.us was later expanded to include some other nifty functionality, such as:

drag-and-drop

These helper functions allow for the easy reordering of lists, but could also be applied to a drag-and-drop shopping cart, for example.

edit-in-place

This functionality allows a user to edit text that is displayed on the page (a heading, or a regular paragraph, for example) simply by clicking on it. The text turns into a text field into which the user can type to change the text; the edits are saved without the page having to be reloaded. You might already have used similar functionality on Flickr, for example.

auto-completion of strings

This functionality allows your web application to perform a database lookup as users type text into a form field. This capability could be used to complete path names on a remote server or to suggest search terms, an implementation pioneered by Google Suggest.[7]

---

[6] While script.aculo.us is bundled with Rails, it can, like Prototype, be downloaded from its own web site [http://script.aculo.us/].

[7] http://labs.google.com/suggest/

An additional benefit of using Rails's built-in helpers to enable Ajax functionality in your application (compared with writing all of the Ajax code from scratch) is that they make it easy to provide a fallback option for browsers that don't support Ajax—a concept known as **graceful degradation**. The browsers that fall into this category include older versions of web browsers, some browsers on newer platforms such as mobile phones or PDAs, and browsers for which the user has deliberately disabled JavaScript. Visitors using these browsers will still be able to use your web application. It won't be as dynamic as it is for other users, but at least they won't be faced with an application that doesn't work at all—a scenario that's almost guaranteed to drive them away from your site.

Armed with this knowledge of Prototype and script.aculo.us, we'll make use of the Rails Ajax helpers to implement functionality that allows users to vote on stories in our Shovell application without waiting for page reloads. We'll also provide those users with a nice visual effect to highlight the altered element after their vote actions are successful.

Making Stories Shove-able

Okay, we've walked through the ins and outs of Ajax. We've discussed the capabilities of the two JavaScript libraries that are bundled with Rails—Prototype and script.aculo.us—and explored the role played by each of them. We're now in a good position to add voting functionality to our application, and to indicate to users that their votes have been recorded. We'll also provide a fallback option for users whose browsers don't support Ajax.

Just to be extra-cheeky, we'll refer to each story's vote as a **shove**, rather than a digg—users can then "shove" stories that they think are worthy of publication on the site's homepage.

Controlling Where the Votes Go

Before we can tackle the design details of that funky "shove" button, we need to lay down the foundation of where the votes go as soon as they're cast. We need another controller!

Here's the `script/generate` call for generating a new controller (`VotesController`) with a single action (`create`):

```
$ ruby script/generate controller Votes create
```

The output of that command is shown in Figure 7.9.

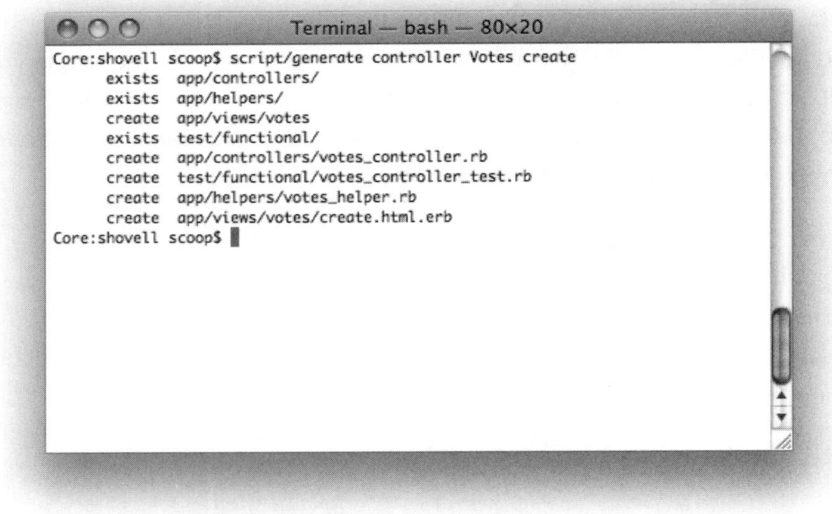

```
●○○              Terminal — bash — 80×20
Core:shovell scoop$ script/generate controller Votes create
      exists  app/controllers/
      exists  app/helpers/
      create  app/views/votes
      exists  test/functional/
      create  app/controllers/votes_controller.rb
      create  test/functional/votes_controller_test.rb
      create  app/helpers/votes_helper.rb
      create  app/views/votes/create.html.erb
Core:shovell scoop$ █
```

Figure 7.9. Generating a VotesController

Additionally, being RESTful citizens, we're going to declare a new set of resources in **config/routes.rb**. You might be tempted to declare Vote as a stand-alone resource. But what good is a vote without a story? It turns out, Rails has something in store to adapt our use of a one-to-many relationship between a story and its votes to the resource declarations. Change the routing configuration as follows:

08-routes.rb (excerpt)

```
ActionController::Routing::Routes.draw do |map|
  map.resources :stories, :has_many => :votes
  : routes…
end
```

Now, what did this get us? At this point, it makes sense to introduce a helpful rake task that simply gives you a list of all the RESTful Routes and their helper names that Rails generates for you based on the configuration in **config/routes.rb**:

```
$ rake routes
```

Go ahead and run the command for yourself and see if you can spot what the declaration of `:has_many => :votes` in the routing configuration got us in terms of URL helpers. The result of the command run locally on my machine can be found in Figure 7.10.

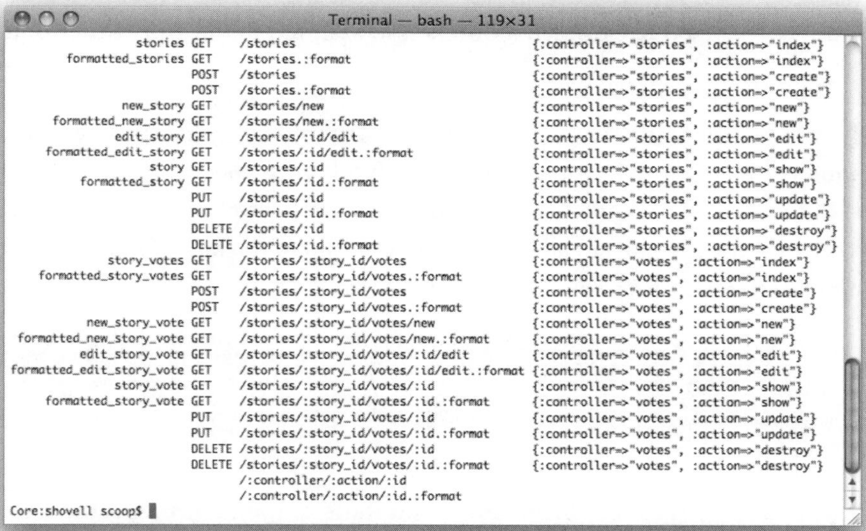

Figure 7.10. The output of the rake routes command

You've guessed right if you've pointed at all the routes with a declaration of `:controller => "votes"` in them. What's interesting to see here is that the URLs look like this:

```
/stories/:story_id/votes
```

What we've created here is a so-called **nested route**. That is, a vote object is nested below the story object and cannot be accessed by simply going to a URL like `/votes` or `/votes/1`, but must be accessed with a prefix naming the associated story first, such as `/stories/1/votes`.

Also of note is the naming of the URL helpers. Instead of employing the standard `votes_path` method to refer to the votes index, our nested route has provided us with the `story_votes_path` method. Similarly, the helper to access a single vote would not be `vote_path` but `story_vote_path`. We'd receive an error if we tried to use incorrectly named helpers. Also, we need to specify the parent story of the vote when generating vote URLs. Confused yet? Let's see it in practice!

Including the JavaScript Libraries

First, though, we need to perform a quick side-step to enable Ajax functionality in Shovell.

As both of the helpers that we're going to use—Prototype, for dealing with the `Xml-HttpRequest` object, and script.aculo.us, for displaying visual effects—are implemented in JavaScript, we need to include the appropriate JavaScript files into our application's layout. To do so, add the following line to the **app/views/layouts/application.html.erb** file, somewhere in the `head` section:

09-application.html.erb (excerpt)

```
<%= javascript_include_tag :defaults %>
```

This line calls the `javascript_include_tag` Rails helper, passing it the `:default` parameter. It causes a total of five JavaScript files to be added to our application:

prototype.js

This file contains the entire Prototype library, which provides our Ajax functionality.

effects.js

This is the visual effects part of the script.aculo.us library.

dragdrop.js

This file contains the JavaScript methods required for adding drag-and-drop functionality, also from the script.aculo.us library.

controls.js

The auto-completion methods are contained within this part of the script.aculo.us library.

application.js

This is an empty file that we can use to store our own custom JavaScript functions. It's located in the **public/javascripts** folder of our application.

To confirm that the helper is indeed doing its job, take a look at the source of any of the pages that exist in our application right now. Remember, since we added these files to the application's layout template, this change will be visible on *every* page. In the header of the page source, you should find `<script>` tags that closely resemble the following:

```
<script src="/javascripts/prototype.js?1202241846"
    type="text/javascript"></script>
<script src="/javascripts/effects.js?1202241846"
    type="text/javascript"></script>
<script src="/javascripts/dragdrop.js?1202241846"
    type="text/javascript"></script>
<script src="/javascripts/controls.js?1202241846"
    type="text/javascript"></script>
<script src="/javascripts/application.js?1202241846"
    type="text/javascript"></script>
```

If you're curious about that weird numerical suffix that follows each of the JavaScript files, don't be: this number simply represents the amount of time in seconds between January 1, 1970 (the "Unix epoch"), and the time at which the file was last modified. This information is included in order to force browsers to reload the file in question whenever the file is modified. Normally browsers cache supplementary files such as style sheets and JavaScript files, so this is a good way to force the browser to discard the cached version and apply the new file.

It's Not All or Nothing!

If you like, you can be more selective about what you include in your own application, depending on whether you plan to use all of the functionality provided in the JavaScript files that ship with Rails. This might save some download time for your users, since their browsers won't have to load JavaScript files that your app doesn't use anyway. Rails also ships with functionality to combine multiple JavaScript files into a single download when your application moves into its production environment.

Giving Stories a Shove

The next step is to change our existing show view (located at **app/views/stories/show.html.erb**) to display the current number of votes that the story has received; we also need to add a link that allows users to vote on stories. Modify your view so that it looks like this:

```
                                                          10-show.html.erb
<h2>
  <span id="vote_score">
    Score: <%= @story.votes.size %>
  </span>
  <%= @story.name %>
</h2>
<p>
  <%= link_to @story.link, @story.link %>
</p>
<div id="vote_form">
  <% form_remote_tag :url => story_votes_path(@story) do %>
    <%= submit_tag 'shove it' %>
  <% end %>
</div>
```

Let's take a look at what's new here:

```
<h2>
  <span id="vote_score">
    Score: <%= @story.votes.size %>
  </span>
  <%= @story.name %>
</h2>
```

The heading that previously displayed just the name of the story now also contains a <span> tag that holds its vote score. To calculate this number, we simply use the size method on the votes association that we saw earlier to add up the number of votes submitted for that story. We've also given the span element a unique id, which we'll use later as a hook to update the score when a user casts a vote. We'll add some CSS to float this span to the right of the page, too.

We've also added the following:

```
<div id="vote_form">
  <% form_remote_tag :url => story_votes_path(@story) do %>
    <%= submit_tag 'shove it' %>
  <% end %>
</div>
```

This is where the magic happens! The extra `div` houses a form created by the `form_remote_tag` helper. This function generates the bits of HTML and Javascript that are necessary to invoke the form submission using Ajax, rather than submitting it as a regular page-loading form.

What we handed to `form_remote_tag` is a call to one of the nested resource helpers we've talked about earlier (the ones that might have made you feel a little dizzy, remember?), specifically to the `story_votes_path` helper. This helper takes `@story` as its argument, to specify that we're dealing with votes associated with that given story.

Specifically, we'd like to create a new vote for this story, which means we need to send a `POST` request to `/stories/1/votes`, which Rails then routes to the `create` action of `VotesController` (see the output on `rake routes` for a refresher).

Styling the Scoreboard

Next, let's expand our CSS (it lives in the file located at **public/stylesheets/style.css**), to style and position our new elements:

11-style.css (excerpt)

```css
#vote_score {
  float: right;
  color: #9c9;
}

#vote_form {
  margin: 10px 0;
}

#vote_form input {
  padding: 3px 5px;
  border: 3px solid #393;
  background-color: #cfc;
  text-decoration: none;
```

```
  color: #393;
}

#vote_form input:hover {
  background-color: #aea;
}
```

There's nothing too mysterious happening here—it's all cosmetic stuff. But who said cosmetics weren't important?

If you access one of your stories through your browser (using the link to a random story on **http://localhost:3000/stories**, for example) you should see a page similar to the one in Figure 7.11. However, clicking the **shove it** link won't do much right now (except that your application may spit out some weird warnings and error messages).

Figure 7.11. Showing a story with voting score and vote link

Storing the Votes

To store the votes that have been submitted, we'll implement the `create` method of our `VotesController` we generated earlier in this chapter. Here it is:

```
                                          12-votes_controller.rb (excerpt)

class VotesController < ApplicationController

  def create
    @story = Story.find(params[:story_id])
    @story.votes.create
  end

end
```

This new method doesn't contain anything we haven't seen before. In the first line of the method, we find the appropriate story record using the unique ID of `Story` for which a vote has been cast. This ID is given to us by Rails in the form of `params[:story_id]`, since `params[:id]` is in this case reserved for a potential ID of a `Vote` object. You can also see this pattern displayed in the routes list we looked at earlier (the route syntax looked like this: `/stories/:story_id/votes`).

The second line creates and saves a new `Vote`. It only contains auto-generated values, such as the creation date, and the IDs that receive a value because of the `Vote`'s association with a `Story`.

If you were to try clicking the **shove it** link on your story page now, it would store your vote. But nothing on the page would change yet—we can only perform so much magic at once, even in Rails-land.

To update the voting score that's displayed on the page and highlight it with a visual effect, we'll use a new kind of Rails template: an RJS template.

Introducing RJS Templates

While the regular **.html.erb** templates with which we're so familiar deal with a whole page (or partial pages, as we'll see later), templates with an **.rjs** extension (short for *Rails JavaScript*) are used to modify parts of an existing page. When we use **RJS templates**, the information that's transferred to the user's browser is a series of JavaScript instructions that modify, extend, and apply visual effects to HTML elements. In contrast, **.html.erb** templates transfer HTML elements themselves.

You don't need to add anything special to your controllers or actions in order to have them use .rjs templates; simply place a template that has the extension .rjs right alongside all your other regular views, and it will be ready for use.

Let's create an RJS template for our create action of VotesController now. In fact, the generator we used to generate the controller template has already created a file called **create.html.erb** in **app/views/votes** for us which we won't use, so you might just as well rename its extention from .html.erb to .rjs.

This template will handle the updating of a story's voting score (the number of "shoves"), and it'll highlight the score after the update, using a visual effect. Modify the template like so:

```
13-create.rjs
page.replace_html 'vote_score', "Score: #{@story.votes.size}"
page[:vote_score].visual_effect :highlight
```

That's all: just two lines of code! Let's look at what each line does.

First of all, you'll notice that the window to the world of RJS is the page object. This object provides us with two different approaches for using RJS templates:

- The first approach focuses on *what* you do to an element on the page: "replace the content of an HTML element," for example, or "show this visual effect." This approach involves calling a specific instance method on the page object; the method usually takes as a parameter the HTML element to be modified (referenced by its id attribute).

- The second approach revolves around the question of *which element* you want to work with first. We can access the HTML element in question—once again identified by its id attribute (well, a Ruby symbol of the same name as its id, anyway)—by treating the page object like a hash that contains all the elements on the page. The actual functionality is then invoked as an instance method on the element.

The two lines of code I showed above purposely use the two different approaches, because I wanted to demonstrate each in an example. You could just as easily (and probably should) choose one approach and use that consistently. We'll leave our

RJS template as is, but as an exercise, you might like to try modifying the code so that your approach to using RJS templates is consistent.

The first line is responsible for updating the story's score after a new vote has been cast:

```
page.replace_html 'vote_score', "Score: #{@story.votes.size}"
```

The `replace_html` method of the `page` object takes two arguments: the `id` of the element whose contents you'd like to replace (`vote_score`, this time as a string, not a symbol), and the actual text that you want to assign to the element.

One new thing here is the `#{}` syntax that we've used between the quotes of the last argument. Using this syntax gives us the ability to add dynamic values to our strings—in this case, we're adding the value of `@story.votes.size`, which, if you recall, returns the number of votes that the story has received. To use this functionality, you must use double quotes instead of single quotes; the `#{}` syntax does *not* work with single quotes.[8]

In this example, the code between the parentheses is a simple method call. However, it is possible to put any Ruby code in there. Be mindful, though, not to violate the MVC terms and conditions by placing any complex calculations within your views—that stuff really belongs in your controller code.

The second line of our RJS template provides some visual feedback:

```
page[:vote_score].visual_effect :highlight
```

This second line of our RJS template uses the second syntax that we discussed for the `page` object. It asks for the element with the `id` of `vote_score`, and applies the visual effect `highlight` to it. By default, this effect will highlight the background of the element in question with a light yellow, then fade it back to white. The color of the fade can be customized easily, like most of Rails' defaults.

After the user clicks the **shove it** voting link, the score will update, and the element will be highlighted with the yellow fading background. It's difficult to show the

---

[8] For performance reasons, it's generally a good idea to use single quotes whenever you *don't* need to replace values in a string dynamically.

dynamic update and highlighting effect in black-and-white print (I've done my best in Figure 7.12), so you'll just have to go ahead and try it yourself.

Figure 7.12. The "yellow fade" visual effect

Isn't it amazing how much you can do with as little code as this?

Ensuring Graceful Degradation

To implement a fallback action for browsers that don't support Ajax, we actually just need to take care of the different treatment for browsers with and without Javascript support on the behalf of the `create` action of `VotesController`, since the HTML generated by the `form_remote_tag` helper we've used to generate our voting form is already fully compatible with both worlds.

Our plan is to redirect users back to the story page after we've processed their votes with their non-Javascript browsers while users with Ajax-enabled browsers can watch as the total number of votes is updated and highlighted without a page reload. To instruct our votes controller to take appropriate action, whether it's dealing with an Ajax request or a regular HTTP POST request, we need to modify the create action in our VotesController class like so:

```
                                                14-votes_controller.rb (excerpt)
class VotesController < ActionController::Base Application Controller
  def create
    @story = Story.find(params[:story_id])
    @story.votes.create

    respond_to do |format|
      format.html { redirect_to @story }
      format.js
    end
  end
end
```

The newly added respond_to block acts as the switchboard for the different requests we need to account for.[9] By indicating the action that must be taken for each of the different requests, our application will do what's appropriate without duplicating any of the code that stores the vote.

In the code block that's passed to the respond_to clause, we list the alternatives that we intend to support in our modified show action. Note that the alternatives listed here (format.html and format.js) are not filenames—format is an object that's provided to the code block in order to find out "which format the client wants." For each supported request type, a corresponding instance method is defined; each line can be read as "if the client wants this format, do that." Let's look at each of them:

```
    format.html  { redirect_to @story }
```

If we're dealing with a regular HTTP POST request, we want to redirect the user back to the story page. The redirect_to function should be familiar to you from Chapter 6. It also uses the same shorthand syntax we've used for link_to earlier in this chapter.

---

[9] Rails uses the HTTP Accept header to determine the request type. This header, among others, is supplied by the user's web browser when it connects to the server.

Our former Ajax-only `create` action implicitly rendered the only available template it found (the RJS template) after the vote had been processed. However, since we've introduced a decision into the mix, we need to tell Rails explicitly to support the rendering of an RJS template, in case we're dealing with an Ajax request. That instruction is delivered by this line:

```
format.js
```

Type Less in Rails

Speaking of shorthand syntax, I've got an even shorter version of our gracefully degraded form for you, in case you were wondering why you suddenly needed to type in all these characters to get such a, well, simple thing as a form that simultaneously caters to both traditional and Ajax-enabled browsers, submits to a nested route, and looks pretty. Turns out you *don't*!

```
<div id="vote_form">
  <% form_remote_for [ @story, Vote.new ] do |f| %>
    <%= f.submit 'shove it' %>
  <% end %>
</div>
```

Now we're using `form_remote_for`, which is `form_remote_tag`'s slightly more specialized cousin. If we hand that helper an array containing the parent story and a new `Vote` object, we get exactly the same result as before, only with a little less typing. You've got to love that!

Since inconsistently named files is a pet peeve of mine, we'll now perform a quick, mostly cosmetic housekeeping task and rename the RJS template again, this time from **create.rjs** to **create.js.rjs** to match the syntax used in the `respond_to` block above. Also, the *official* naming scheme for a template with two extensions is for the first to declare the content type (we've seen HTML and Javascript so far) and the second declare the language that the template is written in (we've seen ERb and RJS so far). If you're as fussy as I am about keeping things nice and tidy, you may now do the same.

Introducing Partials

I've mentioned before that templates ending in **.html.erb** can be used to display certain pieces of the page independently of the rest of the page. When used in this way, these files are called **partials**. Partials can be helpful for dealing with parts of a page that are constantly being reused (such as a navigation menu), or for retrieving and formatting the items in a collection (such as a list).

In this section, we'll use partials to implement a voting history box for our story page. The history box will show the dates and times at which each vote for a story was submitted.

Adding Voting History

We'll implement the voting history as a list, using the HTML elements for an unordered list (ul). Each vote will be represented as a list item (li) that shows the voting timestamp. The list items themselves will be rendered as partials, so a single template that contains a single list item will be rendered as often as there are votes for a given story.

To begin with, we'll modify the show template located at **app/views/stories/show.html.erb** to render an unordered list of the votes a story has received. To accomplish this, we'll add to the template code right above the paragraph container that houses the story link, like so:

15-show.html.erb (excerpt)

```
<ul id="vote_history">
  <% if @story.votes.empty? %>
    <em>No shoves yet!</em>
  <% else %>
    <%= render :partial => 'votes/vote',
               :collection => @story.votes %>
  <% end %>
</ul>
<p>
  <%= link_to @story.link, @story.link %>
</p>
```

In this code, we've started out with a very straightforward `ul` element that has a unique `id`, and we've added a condition using an `if … else … end` construct. This causes the message **No shoves yet!** to be displayed whenever a story that has not received any votes is rendered:

```
<% if @story.votes.empty? %>
  ⋮ template code…
<% else %>
  ⋮ template code…
<% end %>
```

While the `if` construct is familiar to us from Chapter 3, the `votes.empty?` part is new. The `empty?` method brought to us by declaring the association between votes and stories will return false if a story has associated votes, and true if not.

It's in this call to `render` that we add the partial to our page:

```
<%= render :partial => 'votes/vote',
           :collection => @story.votes %>
```

We instruct Rails to render a template for every `Vote` that has been added to a story. The `render :partial` syntax can be used to render a partial once or many times (as in this case)—it's the addition of the `:collection` argument that indicates we'll be rendering the partial multiple times.

The value `votes/vote` of the `:partial` option actually asks Rails to look for a `vote` partial in the `votes/` sub-directory of `app/views/`, since this is the place where we're going to store the new partial.

Creating the Partial

Partials, like regular full-page templates, have a **.html.erb** extension and are stored right alongside their full-page cousins in an application's directory structure. A partial is identified by an underscore (_) prefix in its filename. Let's create the new partial at **app/views/votes/_vote.html.erb**, and populate it with the following line of code:

```
                                                    16-_vote.html.erb
<li><%= vote.created_at.to_formatted_s(:short) %></li>
```

That's all there is to it! This line simply wraps the date on which a vote was made (the value of which is stored in the `created_at` attribute) in a pair of `<li>` tags.

Note that we have access to an object named `vote`. Rails has created this object for us—it does so for every partial—and the object takes the name of the partial (`vote`, in this case). This object is automatically set to the current element of the collection that's being rendered.

The upshot of all this is that a partial needn't concern itself with determining which `Vote` it's currently processing, or where that `Vote` sits within the larger collection of votes. The partial simply operates on a single `vote` object and lets Rails take care of the rest.

Styling the Voting History

If we printed the date and time exactly as they appear in the database, we'd produce something rather awkward in appearance:

```
2008-02-01 11:47:55
```

To address this issue, we've made use of Rails' date-formatting helper. This helper, appropriately named `to_formatted_s`, is available as an instance method for objects of the classes `Date` and `Time`. The helper takes a single argument: one of several pre-defined symbols representing the format that should be applied to the output. Some of the formats include `:short` and `:long`; for a `Time` object, these render as `01 Feb 11:47` and `February 01, 2008 11:47` respectively.

Again, to make things a little more pleasing to the eye, we'll add a few CSS rules to our style sheet to define what our voting history box should look like. These rules arrange our voting history nicely, but they also introduce some minor CSS quirks that relate to floated elements. Thankfully, we can rectify these problems easily by adding a few more lines to our style sheet. The additions are marked in bold below:[10]

---

[10] The explanation of what's happening here—and why these cryptic CSS rules are necessary—is well beyond the scope of this book. However, if you're interested in learning more, this topic (amongst myriad others) is explained in Rachel Andrew's *The CSS Anthology: 101 Essential Tips, Tricks & Hacks* [http://www.sitepoint.com/books/cssant1/].

17-style.css *(excerpt)*

```css
#content {
  background-color: #fff;
  border: 10px solid #ccc;
  padding: 10px;
  overflow: hidden;
}
* html #content {
  height: 1%;
}
⋮ CSS code…
#vote_history {
  padding: 5px;
  margin: 0;
  list-style: none;
  border: 3px solid #ccc;
  background-color: #eee;
  float: right;
  color: #999;
  font-size: smaller;
}
```

With all of this code in place, go ahead and reload a story page in your browser—the result should look similar to Figure 7.13 (depending on how much fun you had clicking the **shove it** link earlier).

While the page is looking good, there are a few more details we should add: the history should be updated whenever the **shove it** link is clicked, we should really sort the votes by descending ID (so that the newest is displayed at the top), and we should limit the number of votes that are displayed.

Figure 7.13. Showing a story with voting history

We can achieve the first task easily by adding some code to our RJS template, located at **app/views/votes/create.js.rjs**. These additions will deal with the voting actions:

```
                                          18-create.js.rjs (excerpt)
                                          .Votes. Size
page.replace_html 'vote_score', "Score: #{@story.votes_count}"
page[:vote_score].visual_effect :highlight        ⟋
page[:vote_history].replace_html :partial => 'vote',
          :collection => @story.votes
```

Can you see where we're heading with this? Once again, we've used the `page` object to gain access to the `vote_history` HTML element. This element is then replaced with a new value. The syntax for replacing the element is the same syntax that we used for the original `render` call in our **show.html.erb** template. The name of the partial is passed using `:partial`, and the collection of votes (available via `@story.votes`) is passed using a symbol called `:collection`.

When we pass `:partial` and `:collection` to the `replace_html` method of an RJS template like this, the method will behave just like the regular call to `render` that we used in **show.html.erb**. In this case, it will render exactly the same collection of partials that our view displays. Using the partial in more than one location is a nice way to avoid writing duplicate code.

Tweaking the Voting History

Lastly, we'll add an instance method to the association between the Vote and the Story model to return a limited number of votes sorted by descending ID. Why would we write this as a separate method, and not just retrieve the data from within the view? Well, for a couple of reasons. For one, MVC principles state that we shouldn't be retrieving any data from our view. But the fact that we'll be calling this method from a couple of separate places means that moving it to the model makes even more sense.

Let's create the method first, then we'll add the references to it. Edit the Story class so that it looks like this:

19-story.rb (excerpt)

```
class Story < ActiveRecord::Base
  : story class…
  has_many :votes do
    def latest
      find :all, :order => 'id DESC', :limit => 3
    end
  end
end
```

This latest method will take advantage of the story's association with the Vote model, and will use a regular find call to retrieve the records we want, up to a total of three records (as specified by the :limit => 3 parameter). The :order => 'id DESC' argument will ensure that they're ordered so that the newest vote is located at the top.

When :all Doesn't Really Mean All

Even though :all is passed as the first argument, this find call will *not* retrieve all the votes from the database. It will only fetch votes associated with the current Story object and the :order and :limit arguments will be used in the database query, so a maximum of three votes will be returned to our application.

Ordering Records in Rails

In case you're curious, the `:order` argument is actually a tiny piece of SQL. DESC, quite obviously, stands for descending; there's also **ASC** for ascending, which is often left off as it's the default.

The rest of the `:order` argument constitutes a column name by which the records will be ordered (or multiple column names separated by commas—if you want to order by multiple columns—like so: `:order => 'id, created_at'`). Rails itself currently offers no way to specify the ordering of records in pure Ruby.

Having added this new method to the `Story` class, you can go ahead and replace the two occurrences of `@story.votes` that are present in our views with `@story.votes.latest`. The first occurrence is the `render` call in **show.html.erb**:

20-show.html.erb *(excerpt)*

```
<%= render :partial => 'vote',      ← 'votes/votes'
           :collection => @story.votes.latest %>
```

The second occurrence is the last line of the RJS template **create.js.rjs**:

21-create.js.rjs *(excerpt)*

```
page[:vote_history].replace_html :partial => 'vote',
                     :collection => @story.votes.latest
```

Excellent. Reloading the story page should produce the expected results, with the number of votes being limited to three, and the votes ordered by descending ID. Hitting the **shove it** link will update the voting history and place the new vote at the top of the list. Have a look at Figure 7.14 to see how the updated page looks.

Figure 7.14. The final story page with voting history

Testing the Voting Functionality

In Chapter 6, we mentioned that our plan is to provide test coverage for all of the functionality in our application. Let's expand our growing test suite by adding some unit and functional tests.

Testing the Model

While most of the work in this chapter has been on the controller side, we still made some changes to the model: we modified our `Story` model, we added a `Vote` model, and we defined an association between the two. We also added an instance method called `latest_votes` to retrieve the most recent votes of a given `Story`. All of these features can be tested programmatically, so let's write some unit tests to cover them.

Preparing the Fixtures

Before we write any tests, we'll add some test data to the fixtures for our `Vote` model, which resides in **test/fixtures/votes.yml**:

```
                                                              22-votes.yml
one:
  story: one

two:
  story: one
```

We generated the original contents of this file using the `generate` script earlier in this chapter, but I've made some enhancements here. Both `story` attributes point to the first `Story` named `one` in the **stories.yml** fixture file, illustrating the point that one `Story` can have multiple `Votes`.

Testing a `Story`'s Relationship to a `Vote`

At this stage, we're ready to add a test that covers the `Story`'s relationship to the `Vote` model. To do this, open the file **test/unit/vote_test.rb** and change the `VoteTest` class to read as follows:

```
                                                    23-vote_test.rb (excerpt)
class VoteTest < ActiveSupport::TestCase
  def test_story_association
    assert_equal stories(:one), votes(:one).story
  end
end
```

The new `test_story_association` test undertakes the testing of the `Story`'s relationship to the `Vote` model. While the underlying Rails association has very good internal test coverage, it's good practice to test all associations that you create as you test your application's behavior.

```
    assert_equal stories(:one), votes(:one).story
```

The `assert_equal` assertion, as the name implies, confirms that two expressions are absolutely equal. In this case, we're simply comparing the return values of two methods.

What's new on this line is the `stories(:one)` and `votes(:one)` syntax, which references our fixture data by name. Making use of a fixture file in a test doesn't just load the contents of the file into the database—it also gives us a convenient way to access each record in the fixture file, without having to resort to manual retrieval methods (for example, using `Vote.find(1)` to retrieve the first vote). The records we defined in the **votes.yml** fixture file above are named `one` and `two`. Simply passing these identifiers as symbols to the `votes` method returns the corresponding record.

To give an example, take a look at these two calls—they'd be equal, given the **votes.yml** fixture we created earlier:

```
Vote.find(1)
votes(:one)
```

Incidentally, a method with a name identical to the name of the fixture file (minus the `.yml` extension) is made available for every fixture we include in a test case. As we've created two fixtures so far, we have access to both the `votes` and `stories` methods.

In our assertion line, we compare the `Story` named `one` with the `Story` object that's associated with the `Vote` named `one`. We know that this assertion should be `true`, because we associated both votes in the fixture file with the first story.

Testing a `Vote`'s Relationship to a `Story`

To test the complementary part of the relationship between our models, edit the **test/unit/story_test.rb** file. To cover the association with a test, we'll add the following method just below the existing tests:

24-story_test.rb (excerpt)

```
class StoryTest < ActiveSupport::TestCase
  ⋮ unit tests…
  def test_should_have_a_votes_association
    assert_equal [ votes(:one), votes(:two) ],
      stories(:one).votes
  end
end
```

This assertion confirms that the votes associated with the `Story` are indeed the votes that we named `one` and `two`. Here, we're manually assembling an array of votes in the order in which we expect them to appear, and comparing that array with the votes that are returned by the `votes` method. If the two arrays match, we know our code works!

Testing the Voting History Order

To test the functionality provided by the `latest_votes` method we added, we'll add two more tests to the **story_test.rb** file, below the others:

25-story_test.rb (excerpt)

```ruby
def test_should_return_highest_vote_id_first
  assert_equal votes(:two), stories(:one).votes.latest.first
end

def test_should_return_3_latest_votes
  10.times { stories(:one).votes.create }
  assert_equal 3, stories(:one).votes.latest.size
end
```

Let's look at these tests line by line.

The `test_should_return_highest_vote_id_first` test confirms that the `:order` part of the `latest_votes` method is indeed operating correctly.

```ruby
assert_equal votes(:two), stories(:one).votes.latest.first
```

The assertion compares the first element of the array returned by the `latest` method with the `Vote` object to which we expect it to be equal (the fixture with the highest id attribute).

To test whether the `:limit` part of our `latest` method does indeed do its job, we need to add a few more votes to the database, as our fixture file currently contains only two votes. However, because it's unlikely that we'll be using a large number of votes in any other test, we'll create the additional votes right there in the test, using a simple block of Ruby code:

```ruby
10.times { stories(:one).votes.create }
```

This line programmatically creates ten votes on the fly by calling the `create` method on the `votes` association of the first `Story`.

These dynamically created votes will automatically be wiped from the database before the next test starts, so they won't affect any other tests.

The assertion then goes ahead and compares the size of the array returned by `latest` with the expected number of three, which is the maximum number of votes that `latest` should return.

Running the Unit Tests

At this point, we're ready to run our unit tests with all of the newly added coverage. You remember how to do that, right? Use the `rake` tool:

```
$ rake test:units
```

The output should look similar to Figure 7.15.

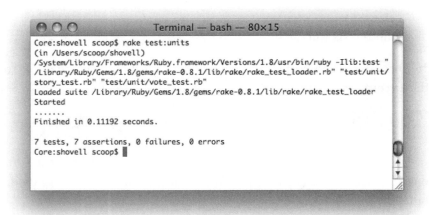

Figure 7.15. Running unit tests

Testing the Controller

Now that we've created tests that cover all the extra functionality we added to our model in this chapter, we'll do the same for the new controller actions—`show` in `StoriesController` and `create` in `VotesController`—and their accompanying views.

Testing Page Rendering

We'll add two tests for the show action to **test/functional/stories_controller_test.rb**; the first will be a test that deals with the basics of displaying a story. The code for the first test looks like this:

```
                                      26-stories_controller_test.rb (excerpt)

def test_should_show_story
  get :show, :id => stories(:one)
  assert_response :success
  assert_template 'show'
  assert_equal stories(:one), assigns(:story)
end
```

This code doesn't do anything we haven't seen before—we request a page (the "show story" page) using HTTP GET, and make sure that the page returns a code indicating that it displayed successfully. We then check that the template name is correct, and make sure that the story we've requested via its id is indeed the story we expected.

The next test we'll create will cover the new HTML elements that we added to the story page—specifically those relating to the voting functionality. The test is as follows:

```
                                      27-stories_controller_test.rb (excerpt)

def test_should_show_story_vote_elements
  get :show, :id => stories(:one)
  assert_select 'h2 span#vote_score'
  assert_select 'ul#vote_history li', :count => 2
  assert_select 'div#vote_form form'
end
```

This is quite a a comprehensive test. It checks for the presence of correctly nested HTML tags on the rendered page, as well as proper element attributes. Let's examine it one line at a time:

```
assert_select 'h2 span#vote_score'
```

This assertion introduces more of the CSS selector syntax that can be used with `assert_select`, which we first encountered in Chapter 6. Just as you would regularly style an element on a page by referring to its ID, `assert_select` allows us to test for the presence of an element with a given ID using the exact same syntax we'd apply to style an element on the page.

Here, we're checking for a `span` tag with an `id` of `vote_score` nested within an `h2` element. This test actually confirms that we have a proper story header in place, and that the current voting score appears beneath it.

The next assertion also uses `assert_select`:

```
assert_select 'ul#vote_history li', :count => 2
```

Here, we check for the presence of a `ul` element that has a unique `id` of `vote_history` and a specific number of `li` elements nested within it (these reflect the entries of the voting history for this particular story).

Our final check confirms the presence of a `div` element with a unique `id` of `vote_form` with a nested `form` inside of it:

```
assert_select 'div#vote_form form'
```

We now have a high level of confidence that our pages are displaying everything we expect them to! Now, let's add some tests for our voting functionality.

Testing Vote Storage

To test the basics of the vote-casting functionality, add the following test to **test/functional/votes_controller_test.rb**. It simply confirms that new votes are stored correctly:

28-votes_controller_test.rb (excerpt)

```
class VotesControllerTest < ActionController::TestCase
  def test_should_accept_vote
    assert stories(:two).votes.empty?
    post :create, :story_id => stories(:two)
    assert ! assigns(:story).votes.empty?
  end
end
```

The test uses a before-and-after check to confirm that this action, which is supposed to modify data, is indeed doing its job. Let's look at each line in turn.

The first line confirms that the story initially has no votes:

```
assert stories(:two).votes.empty?
```

We then submit the vote using HTTP POST:

```
post :create, :story_id => stories(:two)
```

Finally, we confirm that the vote we submitted was stored successfully, and is indeed associated with our story:

```
assert ! assigns(:story).votes.empty?
```

Okay, we now have a basic test in place for the application's basic voting functionality. But our voting pages aren't exactly basic—they use that fancy Ajax stuff, remember? Can we test that, too? You bet we can!

Testing Ajax Voting

Let's test an Ajax voting action. Add the following test to your rapidly expanding collection of functional tests:

```
                                            29-votes_controller_test.rb (excerpt)
def test_should_render_rjs_after_vote_with_ajax
  xml_http_request :post, :create, :story_id => stories(:two)
  assert_response :success
  assert_template 'create'
end
```

Let's walk through each line of this test.

The first line is our test's way of pretending to perform an actual Ajax request:

```
xml_http_request :post, :create, :story_id => stories(:two)
```

Obviously, this isn't really an Ajax request—it doesn't make use of a browser, and there's no XmlHttpRequest object in sight. But, by prefixing the regular post call with the xml_http_request method, our request receives a header that fools the application into thinking that this is a real Ajax request.

The next block of statements checks for a proper response, and confirms that the correct template was rendered:

```
assert_response :success
assert_template 'create'
```

There's nothing here that we haven't seen before, so let's move on to our last test.

Testing Regular HTTP Voting

We still need to test the process of vote submission using regular HTTP POST (that is, without Ajax). To do so, we'll add one more test to the **votes_controller_test.rb** file:

30-votes_controller_test.rb (excerpt)

```
def test_should_redirect_after_vote_with_http_post
  post :create, :story_id => stories(:two)
  assert_redirected_to story_path(stories(:two))
end
```

Let's examine each line in this test. The first line casts the vote with a simple HTTP GET:

Post

```
post :create, :story_id => stories(:two)
```

After the vote has been submitted, we just need to check whether the user is properly redirected to the story page. This is accomplished with an assert_redirected_to assertion:

```
assert_redirected_to story_path(stories(:two))
```

Excellent! All of our new functionality is covered. Time to run the tests!

Running the Full Test Suite

Invoking the full test suite (using the `rake test` command) will run through a total of 26 assertions contained in ten tests. The results of a successful test suite execution should look something like Figure 7.16.

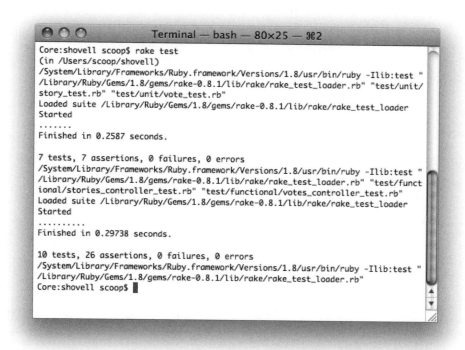

```
Core:shovell scoop$ rake test
(in /Users/scoop/shovell)
/System/Library/Frameworks/Ruby.framework/Versions/1.8/usr/bin/ruby -Ilib:test "
/Library/Ruby/Gems/1.8/gems/rake-0.8.1/lib/rake/rake_test_loader.rb" "test/unit/
story_test.rb" "test/unit/vote_test.rb"
Loaded suite /Library/Ruby/Gems/1.8/gems/rake-0.8.1/lib/rake/rake_test_loader
Started
.......
Finished in 0.2587 seconds.

7 tests, 7 assertions, 0 failures, 0 errors
/System/Library/Frameworks/Ruby.framework/Versions/1.8/usr/bin/ruby -Ilib:test "
/Library/Ruby/Gems/1.8/gems/rake-0.8.1/lib/rake/rake_test_loader.rb" "test/funct
ional/stories_controller_test.rb" "test/functional/votes_controller_test.rb"
Loaded suite /Library/Ruby/Gems/1.8/gems/rake-0.8.1/lib/rake/rake_test_loader
Started
..........
Finished in 0.29738 seconds.

10 tests, 26 assertions, 0 failures, 0 errors
/System/Library/Frameworks/Ruby.framework/Versions/1.8/usr/bin/ruby -Ilib:test "
/Library/Ruby/Gems/1.8/gems/rake-0.8.1/lib/rake/rake_test_loader.rb"
Core:shovell scoop$
```

Figure 7.16. Running the full test suite

Summary

In this chapter we've equipped Shovell with some fully fledged voting functionality, and we've done it using cutting-edge technologies like Ajax combined with some good-looking Web 2.0 effects.

Along the way, we covered the principles of the Rails routing helpers, and we added to our application a page that shows the details of a story that has already been submitted.

We also looked at using RJS templates to modify the contents of pages that have already been rendered, and discussed how we can use visual effects to enhance the usability of our application. We even covered partials—mini page templates that help reduce the amount of template code required to get the job done.

Finally, we established test coverage for all the functionality that we added to our Shovell application in this chapter, so that we'll know immediately if any future change to the application code breaks our existing functionality.

In the next chapter, we'll implement some protective measures in Shovell with user authentication—with some additional benefits!

Protective Measures

Over the last few chapters, we've spent a good deal of time implementing new features for our story-sharing application. However, we've yet to put any effort into preventing those features from being misused.

In this chapter, we'll implement some user authentication techniques that will allow us to protect certain actions from use by individuals who have not registered with, or logged into, the site.

Introducing Sessions and Cookies

Before we write any code, let's learn a bit more about the technology behind user logins, including sessions and cookies.

If you already have some experience with sessions and cookies, you may prefer to skim through this section, or jump forward a few pages to the section called "Modeling the User"—that's where we'll get back into writing the code that will bring these concepts to life.

Identifying Individual Users

Generally speaking, HTTP—the protocol that a web browser uses to talk to an application—is a **stateless protocol**. This means that it doesn't make any assumptions about, or rely upon, previous requests between the client and the server.

This is the crucial difference between stateless protocols and other protocols, including instant messaging systems such as AIM or ICQ: when you start up an instant messenger client, it logs in to the instant messaging server, and remains connected for the time that you use the service. Stateless protocols, such as HTTP, request only a single item—a web page, an image, a style sheet, or a Flash movie, for example—during each connection. Once the item has been requested, the connection is closed. If the requested item is a web page, it is impossible for the application to tell what the users are doing—they may still be reading the page, they may have followed a link to another site, or they may have shut down the machine altogether.

In the world of HTTP, it's also impossible to tell whether two pages requested in succession were actually requested by the same user. We can't rely on the IP address of the user's computer,[1] as that computer might sit behind a proxy server or firewall, in which case it's entirely possible that thousands of other users share the IP address displayed by that machine.

Obviously, we need to use another technique to identify individual visitors. Without it, we'd have to force every user to log in to each and every page of our Shovell application, and that's just not cool. This is where sessions and cookies come into play.

What's a Cookie?

A **cookie** is a tiny snippet of information that a web site places on a user's computer. The cookie is bound to the web site that placed it there—no other site is able to access the cookie. You've probably encountered cookies when using the Web in the past, possibly without even knowing it.

A cookie consists of a name/value pair. For example, a cookie with the name `color` might have the value `green`. Additionally, the cookie's name must be unique—if a

---

[1] An IP address is a number that uniquely identifies a computer connected to the Internet. You've no doubt encountered them before; here's an example: 123.45.67.123.

cookie is set with the same name as one that already exists, the older cookie will be overwritten.

All web browsers give users control over the cookies that web sites set on their machines (although some make cookie management easier than others). Firefox, for example, provides a handy tool for inspecting—and removing—the cookies that have been set on a machine. To display the Firefox cookie manager shown in Figure 8.1, select **Tools > Options** (**Firefox > Preferences** on a Mac), click **Privacy**, select the **Cookies** tab, and click **View Cookies**. Go take a look—chances are that many of the sites you have visited have left a cookie, without even telling you about it!

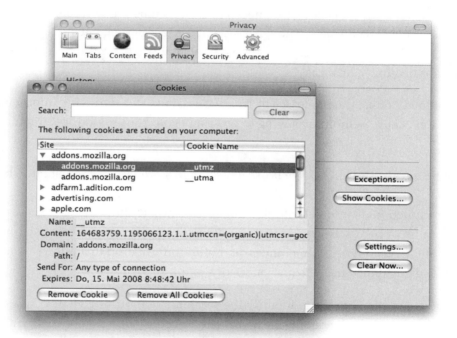

Figure 8.1. The Firefox cookie manager

Cookies usually have an expiration date; a browser will delete a cookie automatically once its expiration date has passed. It makes sense for sites to set expiration dates on cookies, because they occupy space on the user's computer. Also, once a cookie is set, it can't be modified by the application that set it, so a cookie that had no expiration date could wind up sitting on the user's hard disk forever.

A site can set the expiration date of a cookie in two ways:

- by setting an explicit date (for example, December 31, 2008)
- by setting the cookie to expire when the user closes the browser

The latter is the default behavior for Rails' session cookies ... which brings us to the next topic: **sessions**.

What's a Session?

Sessions are just what we need to identify returning visitors. A session is like a small container that's stored on the server for each user; it can be used as a temporary storage location for everything that needs to be remembered between successive page views made by the user. Though a session is a less permanent storage solution, the data stored in the session shouldn't be treated any differently from data stored in the application's database.

As an added bonus, the processes of creating sessions and retrieving information from them occurs without us having to write any code, or provide specific instructions.

For our Shovell application, we'll use a session to store information about where a user has come from; we'll use that information when the user attempts to access pages or functionality, to determine whether we should allow the user access, or redirect him or her to the login form. Sessions can also be used to store shopping cart content, custom user preferences, and other information that allows us to enhance and customize users' experiences of a site.

Rails uses a **session cookie** to identify the session of a returning visitor. A session cookie, by default, will contain the actual session content in a safely encrypted fashion, although it's possible to store the session content on the server or in the database if you so desire later on.

In fact, if you've been following the code in this book, you may notice that a session cookie has been set by our application already—check your browser's cookie manager for a cookie set by `localhost` or `localhost.local`, with the name `_shovell_session`. This is a cookie that Rails sets for us automatically, to provide us with a session that we can use within our application.

Sessions in Rails

In Rails, a session is automatically created for each of your application's users, and can be used to store and retrieve data without requiring any special code.

The session container for a user is accessed just like any other hash. To add a new value to the session, simply assign the value that you wish to store to a hash key that doesn't yet exist in the session, like so:

```
session[:page] = 'Index page'
```

The result of this assignment is that a cookie will be written to the user's machine as shown in Figure 8.2 (in this case, the cookie name is _shovell_session). This cookie contains an encrypyted representation of what you stored in the session previously. With the cookie in place, any data stored in the session becomes available for all successive pages that this user visits.

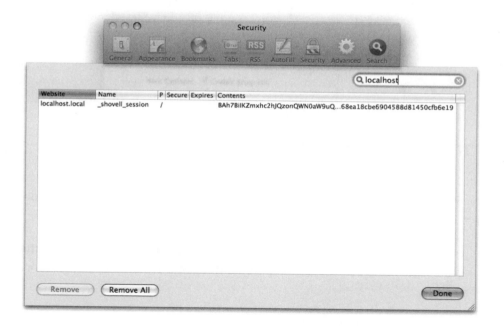

Figure 8.2. A cookie set by our Rails application

The retrieval of session values is equally simple. To access the value we stored in the previous code snippet, and display it in a view, we'd use the following syntax:

```
<%= session[:page] %>
```

It's actually possible to store data other than strings in a session container—you can use a session to store any type of data you like. The only prerequisite for the storage of such objects is that your application has access to the class definition of the object that's stored. However, in practice, sessions should only be used to store simple objects, such as `String` and `Fixnum` objects. And since anything you store in the session will be stored in the user's browser, the objects you store had better be small!

The Physical Location of a Session

As I mentioned, we can store the contents of a session on the server or in different types of databases, as well as the default location of the session cookie itself.

While this solution is fine for local development, it may not work quite so well in a production environment. This procedure lacks some control, not least by its inability to purge data from the user's session and thus prevent data from becoming stale (out of sync with data in our database).

Although an in-depth discussion on the different session storage options is beyond the scope of this book, we'll briefly explore some of the alternatives in Chapter 12.

Modeling the User

Right! Now that we've stepped through the theory, let's get back to the topic at hand: protective measures. In this section, we're going to lay an architectural foundation for providing user authentication in Shovell.

The first step is to generate a new model named `User`. Since we've covered the generation of models before, I'm not going to dwell on this step for long. Let's do it!

Generating a User Model

From the **shovell** folder, run the `generate` script shown below to generate the base class of the `User` model, along with its migration files, unit tests, and fixtures:

```
$ ruby script/generate model User login:string
      password:string name:string email:string
```

The output of this script is shown in Figure 8.3.

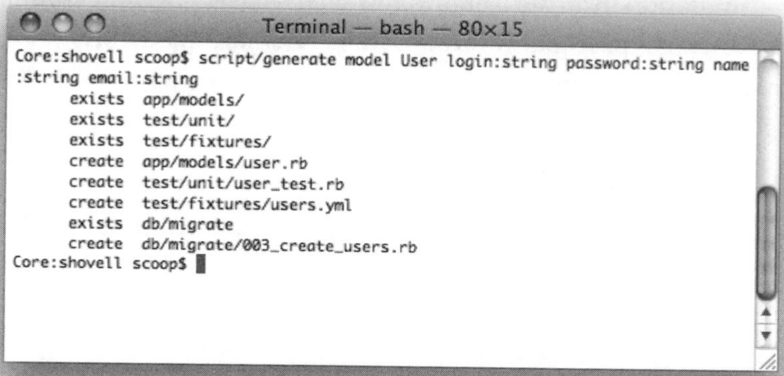

Figure 8.3. Generating the User model

To create the database table for this model, modify the generated migration file located at **db/migrate/003_create_users.rb** to look like this:

01-003_create_users.rb

```
class CreateUsers < ActiveRecord::Migration
  def self.up
    create_table :users do |t|
      t.string :login
      t.string :password
      t.string :name
      t.string :email

      t.timestamps
    end

    add_column :stories, :user_id, :integer
    add_column :votes, :user_id, :integer
  end
  def self.down
    drop_table :users
```

```
    remove_column :stories, :user_id
    remove_column :votes, :user_id
  end
end
```

We'll use this migration to create a brand-new `users` table. The four columns defined above will hold users' personal information: usernames, passwords, names, and email addresses. Actually, the table has seven columns if you include the automatically created `id` column as well as the `created_at` and `updated_at` columns that are a result from the `t.timestamps` call above.

In addition to creating this new table, we'll insert a new column into each of the existing `stories` and `votes` tables, which will store the `id` of the user who created a particular story or vote, respectively.

While we would normally split migrations into the components that handle small, isolated changes, in this case it makes sense to group the creation of the `users` table with the modification of the two other tables. We'll keep our schema changes together as one migration, as they're so closely related. We use the good old `rake` tool to apply the migration we've just written:

```
$ rake db:migrate
```

Figure 8.4 shows the result of a successful migration. We now have in place the database structure necessary to begin writing some code for our `User` model.

Adding Relationships for the `User` Class

As you've probably gathered from our past endeavors with `ActiveRecord`, a model doesn't require a whole lot of code in order to be functional.

The `User` class is no exception; the only changes we'll make to it now are to specify the relationship between it and our two other models. This will help us keep track of which user submitted a particular story or vote.

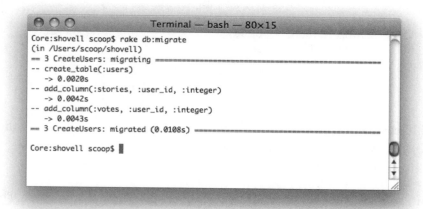

Figure 8.4. Applying the migration

Open the `User` class definition, located at **app/models/user.rb**, and modify it as follows:

```
                                                                    02-user.rb
class User < ActiveRecord::Base
  has_many :stories
  has_many :votes
end
```

This code sets up a one-to-many relationship between the `User` class and each of the `Story` and `Vote` classes.

As you already know, relationships can (and should) be defined for both of the participating models. So our next step is to add complementary relationship definitions to the `Story` and `Vote` classes (located at **app/models/story.rb** and **app/models/vote.rb** respectively):

```
                                                            03-story.rb (excerpt)
class Story < ActiveRecord::Base
  belongs_to :user
  : class definition…
end
```

```
                                          04-vote.rb (excerpt)

class Vote < ActiveRecord::Base
  belongs_to :user
  ⋮ class definition…
end
```

These bidirectional relationship definitions allow us to retrieve not only the Vote and Story objects associated with a particular User, but also the User object associated with a particular Story or Vote.

All right, enough of the architectural building blocks—let's create a user. Then we can start to protect some of our actions from users who haven't logged in.

Creating a User

Creating a User object is no different from creating any other ActiveRecord object. It's easily accomplished from the Rails console (feel free to create an account for yourself, rather than using my name!):

```
>> u = User.new
=> #<User id:nil, …>
>> u.name = 'Patrick Lenz'
=> "Patrick Lenz"
>> u.login = 'patrick'
=> "patrick"
>> u.password = 'sekrit'
=> "sekrit"
>> u.email = 'patrick@limited-overload.de'
=> "patrick@limited-overload.de"
>> u.save
=> true
```

 Implementing Hashed Password Storage

Yes, we *are* using plaintext passwords here. Storing passwords as plaintext is a big security risk—all your users' accounts are accessible if someone with evil intentions manages to get access to your database. To improve the security of your application, only store cryptographic hashes of the passwords (with a unique random string called a salt prepended to it). That way, if your database is accessed the passwords will not be readable and your users protected.

> Be sure to implement hashed password storage for yourself before you launch your application to the world; the `Digest` module[2] that comes bundled with Ruby has the tools for the job.

Developing Login Functionality

In order to handle login and logout actions (and cater for new user registrations down the track), we'll need another controller to complement our existing controllers `StoriesController` and `VotesController`. Once that's in place, we can create some functionality to let users log in and out. It's exciting stuff!

Creating the Controller

We'll name this new controller `SessionsController` (since it's not dealing with the creation and deletion of users, but rather with the creation and deletion of their sessions), and generate it using the `generate` script, as usual:

```
$ ruby script/generate controller Sessions new create destroy
```

Passing the additional *new*, *create*, and *destroy* parameters as arguments to the `generate` script will automatically create blank `new`, `create` and `destroy` actions in our new `SessionsController`, which saves us a few lines of typing. It will also create empty `ActionView` templates in the **app/views/sessions/** folder, with the names **new.html.erb**, **create.html.erb**, and **destroy.html.erb**. Since we don't need a template for the `create` action (this action is destined to just redirect elsewhere after it performs its job), you're free to remove **create.html.erb**. Figure 8.5 shows the output of the above generate call.

---

[2] http://www.ruby-doc.org/stdlib/libdoc/digest/rdoc/

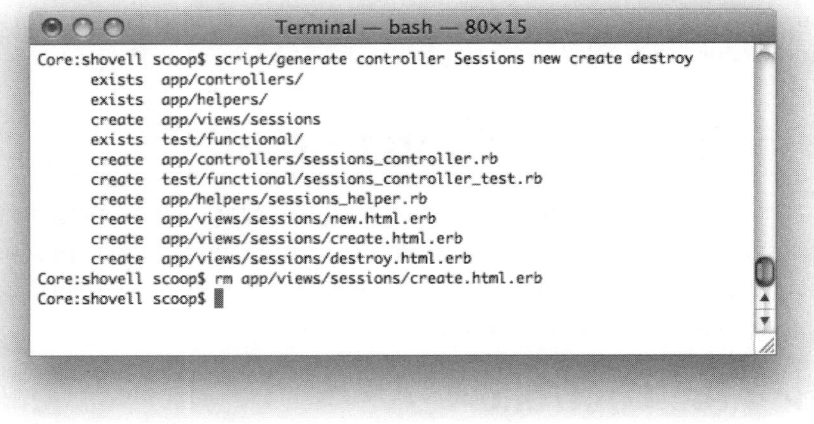

Figure 8.5. Generating a `SessionsController` class

Before closing off this section, we need to revisit our routing configuration (stored in **config/routes.rb**), since we want to build our `SessionsController` in a RESTful way. Add the following line to make sure Rails knows our intentions and provides the appropriate helpers to generate RESTful URLs for the session that's about to begin:

05-routes.rb (excerpt)

```
ActionController::Routing::Routes.draw do |map|
  : more routes…
  map.resource :session
end
```

Please note that we've used the *singular* form of `map.resource` instead of the plural form (`map.resources`) that we've been using for stories. When using the singular form, Rails knows we're talking about a **singleton** resource, which means that only one of it ever exists at a time. This is true here in the context of a `User` object, which is only ever going to have a single session at a time. As such, all the RESTful URLs for sessions will take the singular form, rather than the plural form, of the model name we've seen so far. For example, the URL that creates a new session will be: /session/new.

All right, let's go ahead and create some forms.

Creating the View

To better understand what happens when we use extra parameters to generate `ActionView` templates, type http://localhost:3000/session/new into your web browser.

The result you see should be similar to Figure 8.6—it's basically a friendly message to let us know where we can find the template that's being displayed in the browser.

Figure 8.6. The generated login template

Remember to Start Your Server!

As always, to use our Shovell application, you must have the web server running. Flip back to Chapter 2 if you need a refresher on this.

Let's modify this template and turn it into an actual login form. As Rails indicates in the browser, the template's located at **app/views/sessions/new.html.erb**:

06-new.html.erb

```
<% form_tag session_path do %>
  <p>Please log in.</p>
  <p>
    <label>Username:</label>
    <%= text_field_tag 'login' %>
```

```
  </p>
  <p>
    <label>Password:</label>
    <%= password_field_tag 'password' %>
  </p>
  <p><%= submit_tag 'login' %></p>
<% end %>
```

Once again, we've created a form using simple HTML markup and a few of the Rails form helpers. This time, our form doesn't deal with a specific model object, so we can't use the `form_for` helper that we used back in Chapter 6. Instead, we use the standard `form_tag` helper that defines the surrounding form with a `do` and `end` block:

```
<% form_tag session_path do %>
  ⋮ login form…
<% end %>
```

This generates the all-important `<form>` and `</form>` HTML tags. It uses the `sessions_path` URL helper that we got by telling the Rails Routing configuration that we want RESTful handling of the session's URLs in the last section. To check that they're being created correctly, reload the modified page in your browser and view the source of the page.

The `text_field_tag` and `password_field_tag` helpers generate HTML `input` elements with the `type` attribute set to `text` and `password`, respectively:

```
<p>
  <label>Username:</label>
  <%= text_field_tag 'login' %>
</p>
<p>
  <label>Password:</label>
  <%= password_field_tag 'password' %>
</p>
```

These elements will render the text fields into which our visitors will enter their usernames and passwords. The *login* and *password* parameters that we're passing to each of these helpers assigns a name to the HTML tag that's generated; it also causes this value to show up in the `params` hash, which, as we'll see later on, will prove to be very useful.

Now that we've put our form in place, we can establish some functionality behind it.

Adding Functionality to the Controller

We're ready to implement the actual login functionality within the `create` controller action. You'll find the controller class in the file **app/controllers/sessions_controller.rb**. Add the following code to the `create` method of this class:

```
07-sessions_controller.rb
class SessionsController < ApplicationController
  ⋮ controller code…

  def create
    @current_user = User.find_by_login_and_password(
      params[:login], params[:password])

    if @current_user
      session[:user_id] = @current_user.id
      redirect_to stories_path
    else
      render :action => 'new'
    end
  end

  ⋮ controller code…
end
```

As Figure 8.7 shows, we've expanded the previously empty `create` action to handle the submission of the login form. We attempt to fetch a user using the `login` and `password` values that the visitor provided. Notice that we use one of the `ActiveRecord` dynamic finder methods to do this:

```
@current_user = User.find_by_login_and_password(
    params[:login], params[:password])
```

Figure 8.7. The completed login form

If we're able to locate a user whose record matches the visitor-entered username and password combination (which means @current_user is not nil, which is a true condition for the if clause), we store within the current visitor's session the id of the User object that was retrieved. The user is then redirected to the story index, which Rails gave us the shorthand stories_path for:

```
if @current_user
  session[:user_id] = @current_user.id
  redirect_to stories_path
else
  ⋮
end
```

If we *don't* find a corresponding user in the database, we'd like to rerender the login form. Maybe the user mistyped the password or forgot the username, in which case we'd like to enable him or her to try again:

```
if @current_user
    ⋮
else
    render :action => 'new'
end
```

ActiveRecord Objects and the Session Container

Be careful when you're storing `ActiveRecord` objects in the session container. `ActiveRecord` objects may change at any time, but the session container won't necessarily be updated to reflect the changes. For example, in our Shovell application, a story object might be viewed by one user, and modified by a second user immediately afterwards. If the entire story was stored in the session container, the first user's session would contain a version of the story that was out of date (and out of sync with the database).

To ensure that this scenario doesn't eventuate, it's best to store only the primary key of the record in question—the value of the `id` column—in the session container. Here's an example:

```
session[:user_id] = myCurrentUser.id
```

On successive page loads, we retrieve the `ActiveRecord` object using the regular `Model.find` method, and pass in the key that was stored in the session container:

```
current_user = User.find session[:user_id]
```

This is all well and good, and if you were to try logging in at http://localhost:3000/session/new using the initial user that we created a few pages back, you would indeed be redirected to the story page. Go on, try it out—it works! However, there's still something missing.

Since we've stored only the user's `id` in the session container, we need to make sure that we fetch the `User` object for that user before we hand execution control to another controller action. If we failed to fetch the rest of the user's details, we wouldn't be able to display the username of the currently logged-in user—which we aim to do on every page in our application.

So, before we proceed too much further, let's look at some of the theory behind one of the features of Rails that allows us to execute code globally: filters.

Introducing Filters

A **filter** is a function that defines code to be run either before or after a controller's action is executed. Using a filter, we can ensure that a specific chunk of code is run no matter which page the user's looking at.

Once we've discussed how filters work, I'll show you how to use one to fetch a `User` object from the database when a user logs in. We'll use another filter to redirect to the login page any anonymous visitors who attempt to access a protected page.

Before Filters

The first type of filter we'll look at is the **before filter**. As you might expect, a before filter executes *before* the code in the controller action is executed.

Like all filters, a before filter is defined in the head of the controller class that calls it. Calling a before filter is as simple as invoking the `before_filter` method and passing it a symbol that represents the method to be executed. The filter can also accept as a parameter a snippet of Ruby code; this code is used as the filter code. However, this practice is discouraged, as it makes for code that's difficult to maintain.

Here's a hypothetical example in which a controller method is called using a symbol:

```
class FoosController < ApplicationController
  before_filter :fetch_password
  def fetch_password
    : method body…
  end
end
```

After Filters

Like a before filter, an **after filter** is defined in the controller class from which it is called. The method to use is appropriately named `after_filter` and, not surprisingly, these filters are executed *after* the controller's action code has been executed. Here's an example:

```
class FoosController < ApplicationController
  after_filter :gzip_compression
  def gzip_compression
    : method body...
  end
end
```

Around Filters

A combination of before and after filters, the **around filter** executes both before *and* after the controller's action code.

In a nutshell, around filters are separate objects that have `before` and `after` methods. These methods are automatically called by the filter framework. Despite being a combination of its simpler siblings, the around filter is significantly more advanced; therefore, we won't cover it in this book.

A Word on Filter Methods

As we've learned, filters take as a parameter a symbol that represents the controller method to be executed. Consider the hypothetical example of our `FoosController` once more:

```
class FoosController < ApplicationController
  before_filter :fetch_password
  def fetch_password
    : method body...
  end
end
```

This all seems fine, until you realize that every method that you implement in a controller can actually be executed directly by a user, using a web browser. For example, in the code listing above, a user would be able to execute the `fetch_password` method of `FoosController` simply by visiting http://localhost:3000/foos/fetch_password.

Wait a minute—that's not what we want! The security implications of such an implementation are potentially disastrous, so we definitely want to hide these kinds of methods from the general public.

When we discussed object oriented programming back in the section called "Ruby Is an Object Oriented Language" in Chapter 3, we talked about the interface that an object provides to the outside world—the interface with which other objects can interact. All of the class and instance methods that an object shares this way are called **public methods**, and this is, in fact, the only type of method we've used up to this point.

However, Ruby has two types of methods that are not public: private methods and protected methods.

private methods

Private methods are available only from within the classes in which they're stored, period. These methods cannot be accessed in any way from another object. In the following example, the keyword `private` signals that all methods that follow it are implemented as private methods:

```
class Formula1Car
  private
    def secret_tuning_option
    ⋮ method body…
    end
end
```

protected methods

Like private methods, protected methods are unavailable to the outside world. However, a protected method remains available to classes that inherit from the class in which the protected method is defined. For example, in the following code listing, objects of class `FerrariF1` would have access to the protected method `launch_control`, which is defined in the parent class `Formula1Car`:

```
class Formula1Car
  protected
    def launch_control
    ⋮ method body…
    end
end

class FerrariF1 < Formula1Car
end
```

The point of all this is that you should *always* implement filter methods as non-public methods, in order to protect them from being executed independently from the filtering role for which they were intended. This is exactly what we'll do now.

Managing User Logins

Okay, we've covered filter theory, so let's modify our application to fetch the currently logged-in User from our database. Once we've done that, we'll display the user's name on the page, and provide the ability for the user to log out again.

Retrieving the Current User

We're going to use filters to fetch the current user for each and every page of the Shovell site. That phrase—"each and every page"—should give you a hint as to where we'll apply the filter. Filters can be inherited from parent classes and, as we don't want to write numerous filter declarations, we'll stick our filter in the parent class for all of our controllers: ApplicationController.

Methods and filters that are defined in this class are available to all classes that inherit from ApplicationController (located at app/controllers/application.rb), which is just what we want: *in Rails 2.3 application-controller.rb*

```
                                                     08-application.rb
class ApplicationController < ActionController::Base
  : controller code…
  before_filter :fetch_logged_in_user

  protected

    def fetch_logged_in_user
      return unless session[:user_id]
      @current_user = User.find_by_id(session[:user_id])
    end
end
```

Let's take a look at each of the lines that make up the fetch_logged_in_user method:

```
    return unless session[:user_id]
```

This line is fairly straightforward. There's no point retrieving a User object if the user hasn't logged in yet (in which case there's no user_id stored in the session)—we can simply exit the filter method without executing the rest of the code.

The next line tries to fetch from the database a User object with an id that's equal to the id stored in the visitor's session container:

```
@current_user = User.find_by_id session[:user_id]
```

The fetched object will be assigned to the instance variable @current_user, which will then become available to actions in our controller as well as our views.

We've purposely used the find_by_id method here, rather than find, even though on the surface it appears that the two would produce the same results. In fact, find displays an error if it can't retrieve a record that matches the *id* that's passed to it, while find_by_id exits more gracefully. It's conceivable that a user may revisit our site after his or her account has been deleted (perhaps because the user submitted the same boring stories over and over again), so we need to make sure the application will handle these cases in a user-friendly manner. Spitting out a bunch of technical-looking errors is not the solution we're looking for, hence our use of find_by_id.

Session Security Revisited

As we saw earlier, the value of session[:user_id] is, albeit stored in the user's web browser, stored in an encrypted fashion. This means that a user can't, for example, impersonate another user by simply changing the contents of his or her session.

The only way that a user could circumvent the security measures that we've put in place so far would be either to guess the session ID, or to identify it using a brute force attack[3] ... that is, apart from grabbing another user's laptop while he's in the bathroom!

As Rails uses a randomized string of 128 hexadecimal characters for the session ID as well as a secret key set in the Rails application itself (that is never exposed to the site's users) to verify the data integrity of the session container contents,

---

[3] A brute force attack involves looping through a list of every possible combination of alphanumeric characters (or sometimes a list of dictionary-based passwords) until a matching phrase is found.

> it's highly unlikely that a malicious user could gain another user's id using either of these approaches.

Our next task will be to display the name of the current user in the global application layout.

Displaying the Name of the Current User

Since we require that our users log in just once to access the entire application, let's add to our global application layout (the file located at **app/views/layouts/application.html.erb**) some code that will display the name of the currently logged-in user. Make the following changes to this file:

09-application.html.erb (excerpt)

```erb
<div id="content">
  <div id="login_logout">
    <% if @current_user %>
      Logged in as:
      <%= @current_user.login %>
      <em><%= link_to "(Logout)", session_path,
                :method => :delete %></em>
    <% else %>
      <em>Not logged in.</em>
      <%= link_to 'Login', new_session_path %>
    <% end %>
  </div>
  <h1>Shovell</h1>
  : page body...
<div>
```

Let's step through these changes. Using a simple `if` condition, we display a link to the action that's most appropriate, based on the user's login status:

```erb
<% if @current_user %>
```

The condition checks whether the instance variable `@current_user` evaluates to `nil`.

Once we've made sure that the user is actually logged in, we display the user's name along with a link to log out again, which we'll implement in the `SessionsController` in a moment. We indicate that we want the link to use the HTTP DELETE request type by passing the :method => :delete argument to the link_to method. We wrap the link in an <em> tag to make it stand out a little:

```
Logged in as:
<%= @current_user.login %>
<em><%= link_to "(Logout)", session_path,
            :method => :delete %></em>
```

If a visitor is *not* logged in, we display a link that the user can follow to the login form:

```
<%= link_to 'Login', new_session_path %>
```

As you can see, our sessions are REST all over. We've been using the bare session_path to handle both the login action (at POST /session) and the logout action (the code of which is still missing, but it'll live at DELETE /session) and new_session_path for the actual login form (living at GET /session/new).

To make the page look a little nicer, let's add a snippet of CSS to the global style sheet that's located at **public/stylesheets/style.css**:

10-style.css (excerpt)

```
#login_logout {
  float: right;
  color: #999;
  font-size: smaller;
}
```

This code dims the text colors a little, floats the container to the right, and makes the font size a little smaller. If you reload the page after logging in, you should see the results shown in Figure 8.8. That's much better!

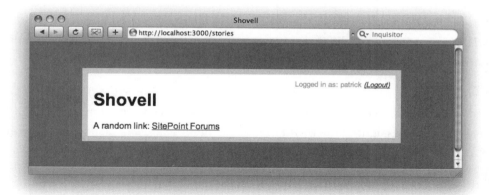

Figure 8.8. Displaying the current user

Next, we'll implement the logout functionality.

Allowing Users to Log Out

Providing our users with a manual logout function is much more user-friendly than forcing them to close their browsers to log out. We'll implement this method in our SessionsController class, located in **app/controllers/sessions_controller.rb**:

```
11-sessions_controller.rb (excerpt)

class SessionsController < ApplicationController
  : controller code...
  def destroy
    session[:user_id] = @current_user = nil
  end
end
```

Logging a user out of the application is a matter of setting two variables to nil:

- the user_id that's stored in the user's session
- the instance variable that holds the current user

Both of those tasks are completed with one line of code:

```
session[:user_id] = @current_user = nil
```

This line of code prevents our before filter (the `fetch_logged_in_user` method) from retrieving anything from the database. As we're setting both the current user *and* the user id stored in the session to `nil`, no more `User` objects for this user remain in memory. The user has therefore been logged out of the system.

I've taken this opportunity to introduce another piece of shorthand syntax that's used often in Ruby code: we've assigned `nil` to two variables at once. Strictly speaking, we're assigning the result of the statement `@current_user = nil` (which happens to be `nil`) to `session[:user_id]`.

With that code in place, adding a simple message to **app/views/sessions/destroy.html.erb** will confirm for the user that the logout was successful:

12-destroy.html.erb

```
<h2>Logout successful</h2>
<%= link_to 'Back to the story index', stories_path %>
```

Let's check that this all works as we expect. Click that **(Logout)** link in the top right-hand corner of the page. If everything goes to plan, you should be logged out of the application and presented with a page like the one shown in Figure 8.9. Additionally, the username that was previously displayed in the upper right-hand corner should not be present on any successive page that you visit—you should see a **Login** link instead.

Figure 8.9. Successfully logging out of the application

Now that users are able to log in and out of the application, we're in a position to make certain actions available only to logged in users. However, before we begin to make these additions, let's add to our site an element that has been sorely lacking so far: navigation.

Adding a Navigation Menu

You're probably growing a little tired of typing http://localhost:3000/stories/new over and over again. Let's create a diminutive navigation menu at the bottom of every page, so that we can move easily between the different pages we've created.

To do so, modify the file **app/views/layouts/application.html.erb**. Right above the closing </body> tag at the bottom of the file, place the following unordered list, which contains our navigation menu:

```
                                           13-application.html.erb (excerpt)
<body>
  ⋮ page body…
  <ul id="navigation">
    <li><%= link_to 'Front page stories', stories_path %></li>
    <li><%= link_to 'Submit a new story!', new_story_path %></li>
  </ul>
</body>
```

We've got two links in our menu at this point:

- a link to the story index (which currently displays a random story from the pool)
- a link to the story submission form

As usual, we'll also expand our style sheet to make the menu look pretty; the result is shown in Figure 8.10:

```
                                                    14-style.css (excerpt)
#navigation {
  list-style: none;
  padding: 5px 0;
  margin: 0;
  text-align: center;
}
```

```
#navigation li {
  display: inline;
  padding: 0 5px;
}
#navigation li a {
  color: #fff;
}
```

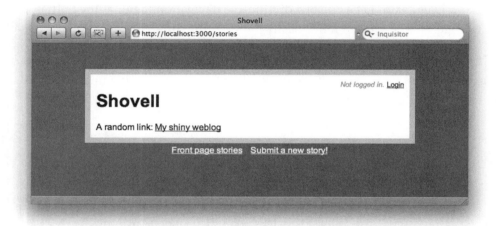

Figure 8.10. Story index with navigation

That's much better. With the navigation in place, moving around within our application becomes a lot easier.

Restricting the Application

All this login functionality would be wasted if a guest to our site had access to the same feature set enjoyed by our registered users—what would be the point of logging in?

Now that our login functionality is working, we can restrict certain parts of the application from use by anonymous guests and users who have not logged in.

Protecting the Form

The first action that will benefit from protection is the submission of stories. While we're adding this protection, we'll also check that when a new story is submitted, the application correctly saves the reference to the User who submitted it (as we defined in the relationship between a User and a Story).

The first step we need to take is to figure out how to intercept a request that comes from a user who's not currently logged in to our application. Once we've achieved this, we can direct the visitor to a login form instead of the story submission form. This sounds like a perfect job for a before filter, doesn't it?

We'll add our new filter code to the global ApplicationController class so that all of our controllers can benefit from this addition, since the filter is available to any of the controllers in our application.

The filter will be called login_required, which is suitably descriptive. As we're going to check from a few different places in our application whether or not a user is logged in, we'll extract this code into a separate controller method before we create our new filter. (Writing @current_user isn't exactly the most declarative thing in the world, anyway.)

Abstracting Code Using `helper_method`

The reason we're placing this functionality into a controller method (rather than creating a regular helper for it) is that the functionality it provides is useful to both controllers and views. However, regular helpers are available only to views, and controller methods are available only to controllers. We need some sort of magic bridge to make this controller method available to our views.

This magic bridge happens to be the helper_method statement, which makes regular controller methods available to views as if they were regular helper methods. We'll add this snippet to the protected area of our ApplicationController (in **app/controllers/application.rb**):

15-application.rb *(excerpt)*

```
class ApplicationController < ActionController::Base
  : controller code…
  protected

  def fetch_logged_in_user
    : method body…
  end
  def logged_in?
```

```
    ! @current_user.nil?
  end
  helper_method :logged_in?
end
```

Here, we've pulled our check of the current user's login status into a new method called `logged_in?`. Let's pause to examine something interesting about the single-line method body:

```
! @current_user.nil?
```

The exclamation mark reverses the actual result of the `nil?` statement. If the `@current_user` variable is `nil` (`nil?` returns true) our visitor is actually *not* logged in, so `logged_in?` needs to return false. With the additional call to `helper_method`, we can now use `logged_in?` throughout our application to replace any usage of `if @current_user`.

Requiring Users to Log In

While we're looking at our `ApplicationController`, let's add the `login_required` filter to it—this marks the first use of our new `logged_in?` helper method:

```
                                            16-application.rb (excerpt)

def login_required
  return true if logged_in?
  session[:return_to] = request.request_uri
  redirect_to new_session_path and return false
end
```

Let's break this code down. The first line of the filter exits the method with the value true if the user is already logged in:

```
return true if logged_in?
```

However, if the `logged_in?` helper method returns false, we need to:

1. Prepare to redirect the user to a location at which he or she can log in.

2. Remember where the user came from, so we can send the person back to that page once the login is complete.

To store the current URL, we grab it from the `request` object and add it to the user's session, so that we can retrieve it later:

```
session[:return_to] = request.request_uri
```

Next, we redirect the user to the `new_session_path`, which is the `new` action of `SessionsController`, and return false:

```
redirect_to new_session_path and return false
```

 Readable Code Equals Maintainable Code

The `and` keyword that's used here is in fact optional: the logic of this method would be identical if the `return` was placed on its own line. However, using `and` in this case adds to the readability of our code—and code that is more readable is more maintainable.

A return value of false is crucial here, because a filter that returns false halts the processing of any subsequent filters and exits the current controller method.

Right! Now we're armed with the protection facility, it's time to restrict access to the application's story submission capabilities to users who are logged in.

Restricting Access to Story Submission

While we don't want to let anonymous visitors submit new stories to our site, we want them to be able to view stories. This situation—restricting user access to certain specific actions—presents the perfect opportunity to use a filter condition.

Introducing Filter Conditions

A **filter condition** is simply a parameter that's passed to a filter, and specifies how the filter is applied. The parameter can control whether the filter is applied to either:

▪ every method *except* those listed
▪ *only* the actions listed

In this case, the *:only* parameter is the best way for us to limit the filter to a pair of actions, new and create. Both of these actions are needed to log in a user—new to display the actual form, and create being the action to which the form is submitted.

Let's apply the login_required filter to the top of our StoriesController class, which is located at **app/controllers/stories_controller.rb**. The *:only* parameter accepts a symbol (or array of symbols) that represents the methods to which it should be applied.

17-stories_controller.rb *(excerpt)*

```
class StoriesController < ApplicationController
  before_filter :login_required, :only => [ :new, :create ]
  : controller code…
end
```

There, that was easy! However, we've yet to make use of that *:return_to* URL that we stored in the user's session on the previous page. Let's put it to work next.

Redirecting the User

The part of our application that redirects users after they've successfully logged in is the create method of the SessionsController class, which is located in **app/controllers/sessions_controller.rb**.

Let's modify the redirection code to specify the location to which a user is redirected based on whether or not the user's session actually contains a *:return_to* URL. The changes that you'll need to make are listed in bold:

18-sessions_controller.rb *(excerpt)*

```
def create
  @current_user = User.find_by_login_and_password(
    params[:login], params[:password])

  if @current_user
    session[:user_id] = @current_user.id
    if session[:return_to]
      redirect_to session[:return_to]
      session[:return_to] = nil
```

```
    else
      redirect_to stories_path
    end
  else
    render :action => 'new'
  end
end
```

The aspect of this code that's really worth a mention is the fact that we reset the `:return_to` URL to `nil` after a successful redirect—there's no point in carrying around old baggage.

Now, fire up your web browser and execute the following steps to test out this new feature:

1. Log out of the application, if you're currently logged in.

2. Click the **Submit a new story!** link, and confirm in your browser's address bar that you're redirected to /session/new.

3. Log in using the login form, and verify that you're redirected back to the story submission form.

All good? Great!

Associating Stories with Users

The last enhancement that we'll add in this chapter is to associate a story with the ID of the user who submitted it. This will give us a record of who submitted what to Shovell.

Storing the Submitter

As we established the association between stories and user `ids` at the beginning of this chapter, we simply need to tell Rails *what* we want to store. Change the first line of the `create` action of the `StoriesController`, located at **app/controllers/stories_controller.rb**:

```
                                            19-stories_controller.rb (excerpt)

def create
  @story = @current_user.stories.build params[:story]
  ⋮
end
```

Storing the submitter is as simple as that! We know that the currently logged-in user is stored in @current_user, because we set it using the fetch_logged_in_user before filter. We're using the declared stories association (or, more specifically, its build method) to get us a Story object that comes preset with the id of the current user.

To illustrate, here's another example of this in action, performed straight in the Rails console (ruby script/console):

```
$ ruby script/console
>> u = User.find(:first)
=> #<User id: 1, …>
>> s = u.stories.build
=> #<Story id: nil, …>
>> s.user_id
=> 1
```

As you can see, the story that is *built* using the build method is completely unsaved. Yet it has a value set for its user_id attribute that is identical to the id of the User object that we created.

But of what use is storing information if we're not going to display it somewhere? You guessed it—displaying the submitter's details is our final task.

Displaying the Submitter

Lastly, we'll modify each story's display page to show the name of the user who submitted it. This page corresponds to the show action of our StoriesController class, the template for which is located at **app/views/stories/show.html.erb**:

```
                                                          20-show.html.erb (excerpt)

<ul id="vote_history">
  ⋮ vote history list items…
</ul>
<p class="submitted_by">
  Submitted by:
  <span><%= @story.user.login %></span>
</p>
<p>
  <%= link_to @story.link, @story.link %>
</p>
```

Here we're using `@story.user` to fetch the user object that's associated with the currently displayed story. We then display the value of the user's `login` attribute to produce the result shown in Figure 8.11.

Figure 8.11. The name of a story's submitter displays with the story

 ### Data Integrity in Development

One of the downsides of using an iterative approach to development is that our data is not necessarily complete at each stage of the development process. For example, unless you've specifically added `user_id` values to every `Story` object

in your database, you're probably seeing the odd page error. You could use either of these approaches to rectify this issue:

1. Manually add the missing values to your objects from the Rails console, remembering to use the **save** method so that the value is stored permanently.

2. Delete all data in your database (via the Rails console), and begin to add your data from scratch via the application.

We need only two or three objects at this stage of development, so neither of these options should be too onerous for you.

We've accomplished quite a lot in this chapter, both in theory and in code. Being professional Rails coders, our next step is to add tests for all of these cool features.

Testing User Authentication

To develop our testing suite, we'll create unit tests to cover changes to the application's model, followed by functional tests for each of our controllers.

Testing the Model

We haven't extended our models much in this chapter, so our unit tests will be fairly straightforward. Basically, all we've done is:

- create a new model (User)
- add a relationship between the User and Story model
- add a relationship between the User and Vote model

Before we can write any tests, though, we need to make sure that our test data is up to date.

Preparing the Fixtures

The User model didn't come with very meaningful fixture data, so let's address that now. Replace the contents of the model's fixture file (located at **test/fixtures/users.yml**) with the following data:

```
                                                                21-users.yml
patrick:
  login: patrick
  password: sekrit
  name: Patrick Lenz
  email: patrick@limited-overload.de
john:
  login: john
  password: gh752px
  name: John Doe
  email: john@doe.com
```

To test the associations between the three models properly, we'll also need to modify the fixtures for both our `Story` and `Vote` models. Only a small change is required: the addition of some data for the `user_id` attribute that we inserted at the start of this chapter.

Make the following changes in **test/fixtures/stories.yml**:

```
                                                    22-stories.yml (excerpt)
one:
  ⋮ YAML data…
  user: patrick
two:
  ⋮ YAML data…
  user: patrick
```

And make these alterations in **test/fixtures/votes.yml**:

```
                                                      23-votes.yml (excerpt)
one:
  ⋮ YAML data…
  user: patrick
two:
  ⋮ YAML data…
  user: john
```

Now that our fixtures contain appropriate data, we can start writing some unit tests.

Testing a User's Relationship to a Story

The unit tests for our User belong in **test/unit/user_test.rb**. First, we'll test the relationship between a User and a Story. Make the following changes to this file:

24-user_test.rb (excerpt)

```
class UserTest < ActiveSupport::TestCase
  def test_should_have_a_stories_association
    assert_equal 2, users(:patrick).stories.size
    assert_equal stories(:one), users(:patrick).stories.first
  end
end
```

We use two assertions to test the association between the Story and User models. The first assertion confirms that the total number of Story objects associated with the user patrick is indeed 2:

```
    assert_equal 2, users(:patrick).stories.size
```

The second assertion identifies whether or not the first Story associated with patrick is the first Story object in our fixture file:

```
    assert_equal stories(:one), users(:patrick).stories.first
```

With this test in place, let's add a test for the inverse of this relationship.

Testing a Story's Relationship to a User

By now, you're no doubt very familiar with the directory and file naming conventions we're using. The complementary unit test for the relationship between a User and a Story tests the Story's relationship to a User, and belongs in **test/unit/story_test.rb**. Make the following changes to this file:

25-story_test.rb (excerpt)

```
class StoryTest < ActiveSupport::TestCase
  ⋮ test methods…
  def test_should_be_associated_with_user
```

```
      assert_equal users(:patrick), stories(:one).user
    end
end
```

The assertion we've written here simply confirms that the user associated with the first story is the user we expect, based on our fixture data (that is, `patrick`):

```
assert_equal users(:patrick), stories(:one).user
```

Let's add some similar tests for the other relationship that our `User` model has: its relationship with a `Vote`.

Testing a `User`'s Relationship to a `Vote`

While we haven't yet added anything to our application's user interface to store or display the details of users associated with votes, we've put the infrastructure in place to do so. For this reason, we can test the relationship between a `User` and a `Vote` using a very similar approach to that we took with the unit tests we created for the relationship between a `Story` and a `User`.

To test a `User`'s relationship to a `Vote`, add the following test to **test/unit/user_test.rb**:

26-user_test.rb (excerpt)

```
def test_should_have_a_votes_association
  assert_equal 1, users(:patrick).votes.size
  assert_equal votes(:two), users(:john).votes.first
end
```

The first assertion compares the number of `Vote` objects associated with a test user with the number of votes that the same user was assigned in our fixture data:

```
assert_equal 1, users(:patrick).votes.size
```

The second assertion makes sure that the first `Vote` object associated with the user john matches our fixture data:

```
assert_equal votes(:two), users(:john).votes.first
```

Excellent! Only one more unit test to write: a test for the inverse of this relationship.

Testing a **Vote**'s Relationship to a **User**

The test that confirms a Vote's relationship to a User belongs in **test/unit/vote_test.rb**. Add the following test to this file:

27-vote_test.rb (excerpt)

```
class VoteTest < ActiveSupport::TestCase
  : test methods...
  def test_should_be_associated_with_user
    assert_equal users(:john), votes(:two).user
  end
end
```

This last test confirms that the user associated with the second vote of a story is indeed the second user who voted for the story, as defined by our fixture data.

Keeping the Test Schema Up to Date

You may be wondering how migrations are applied to the test database on which we're running our tests—as you'll recall, this database is quite separate from the development database to which our migrations are applied.

Rails is smart enough to figure out that testing should occur on a database with a structure that's identical to the one used for development. So Rails clones the structure of your development database, and applies it to the test database every time you execute your unit or functional tests.

Should you ever need to complete this cloning process manually, use this rake task:

```
$ rake db:test:clone_structure
```

Running the Unit Tests

We can now run our updated suite of unit tests using the following code, the results of which are shown in Figure 8.12:

```
$ rake test:units
```

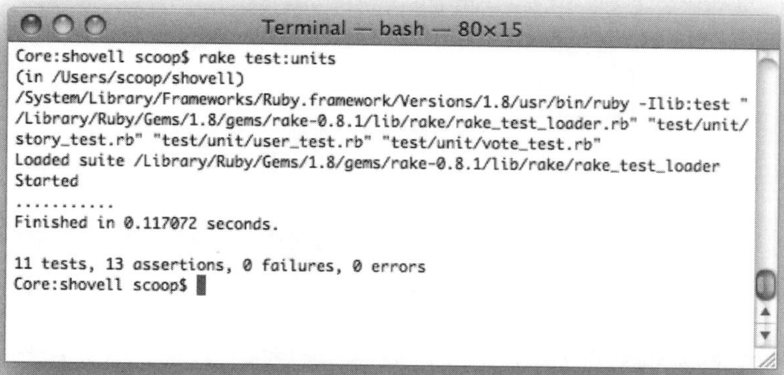

```
Core:shovell scoop$ rake test:units
(in /Users/scoop/shovell)
/System/Library/Frameworks/Ruby.framework/Versions/1.8/usr/bin/ruby -Ilib:test "
/Library/Ruby/Gems/1.8/gems/rake-0.8.1/lib/rake/rake_test_loader.rb" "test/unit/
story_test.rb" "test/unit/user_test.rb" "test/unit/vote_test.rb"
Loaded suite /Library/Ruby/Gems/1.8/gems/rake-0.8.1/lib/rake/rake_test_loader
Started
...........
Finished in 0.117072 seconds.

11 tests, 13 assertions, 0 failures, 0 errors
Core:shovell scoop$
```

Figure 8.12. Results expected from execution of the unit tests

Testing the Controllers

The majority of the functional code that we wrote in this chapter was in the
SessionsController, although we also made a few changes to the
StoriesController. Consequently, we have quite a few tests to write to ensure that
all of this new functionality is covered.

Testing the Display of the Login Form

The first test we'll add to our functional test file (**test/functional/sessions_control-
ler_test.rb**) is a simple HTTP GET operation that looks for the display of our login
form:

28-sessions_controller_test.rb (excerpt)

```ruby
class SessionsControllerTest < ActionController::TestCase
  def test_should_show_login_form
    get :new
    assert_response :success
    assert_template 'new'
    assert_select 'form p', 4
  end
end
```

There's not too much here that we haven't encountered before. The test asserts that:

- The page request was successful.
- The page is rendered with the template we expect.
- A form tag is contained in the result, with four <p> tags nested below it.

Testing a Successful Login

The following test, to be added to the same file, will attempt an actual login:

29-sessions_controller_test.rb (excerpt)

```ruby
def test_should_perform_user_login
  post :create, :login => 'patrick', :password => 'sekrit'
  assert_redirected_to stories_path
  assert_equal users(:patrick).id, session[:user_id]
  assert_equal users(:patrick), assigns(:current_user)
end
```

Let's look at each line of this test in more detail.

As was the case when we tested the submission of stories, here we need to pass additional arguments to the `create` action—values for the `login` and `password` parameters:

```ruby
post :create, :login => 'patrick', :password => 'sekrit'
```

The values we've used here match the values in our **users.yml** fixture file; if you added your own user to that file, you'll need to change this test accordingly.

If you think about how our `create` method works, you'll recall that we redirect users after they've logged in successfully. However, the URL to which a user is redirected varies depending on whether or not the user's session contains a URL. In this test, the user's session is empty, so we expect the user to be sent to the /`stories` page. The `assert_redirected_to` method comes in handy here:

```ruby
assert_redirected_to stories_path
```

Lastly, a successful login means that:

- The `id` of the user will be stored in the user's session.
- The instance variable `@current_user` will be set.

Within the test, we have access to the session of the hypothetical user who just logged in, so we can compare both the session value and the instance variable with the corresponding details that we set for the user in our fixture data:

```
assert_equal users(:patrick).id, session[:user_id]
assert_equal users(:patrick), assigns(:current_user)
```

In a perfect world, this would be the last of the tests that we need to write. However, in the *real* world, not every login attempt is successful.

Testing a Failed Login

Login attempts fail for various reasons—users may type their passwords incorrectly, or try to guess someone else's login details. When a login attempt fails, the application should not reveal any content that's intended for users who have logged in. As such, login failures need to be tested too!

Here's the test:

30-sessions_controller_test.rb (excerpt)

```
def test_should_fail_user_login
  post :create, :login => 'no such', :password => 'user'
  assert_response :success
  assert_template 'new'
  assert_nil session[:user_id]
end
```

If a user tries to log in to our application using a non-existent user name, the login form should redisplay. Our first assertion confirms that the page loads correctly, while the second assertion verifies that the page uses the new template:

```
assert_response :success
assert_template 'new'
```

The last assertion checks the `user_id` value that's stored in the user's session, to make sure it's `nil`:

```
assert_nil session[:user_id]
```

Okay, we've tested all our code that relates to our login procedures. But what happens *after* a user logs in?

Testing Redirection After Login

To trial the redirection of a user who logs in to his or her original destination, we'll add a test that populates the *return_to* value within the user's session before he or she logs in:

31-sessions_controller_test.rb (excerpt)

```
def test_should_redirect_after_login_with_return_url
  post :create, { :login => 'patrick', :password => 'sekrit' },
       :return_to => '/stories/new'
  assert_redirected_to '/stories/new'
end
```

This test is identical to the regular login test that we wrote earlier in the section called "Testing a Successful Login"—aside from the fact that we explicitly test for redirection to the story submission URL.

Testing a Logout

The last part of the SessionsController that we need to test is the destroy action. To emulate a user logging out, we actually need to create something that resembles an integration test. Why? Because before we can log out, we need to log in:

32-sessions_controller_test.rb (excerpt)

```
def test_should_logout_and_clear_session
  post :create, :login => 'patrick', :password => 'sekrit'
  assert_not_nil assigns(:current_user)
  assert_not_nil session[:user_id]

  delete :destroy
  assert_response :success
  assert_template 'destroy'
  assert_select 'h2', 'Logout successful'
```

```
      assert_nil assigns(:current_user)
      assert_nil session[:user_id]
   end
```

This test is longer than most of our previous tests, but with the number of tests that you have under your belt at this stage, you should be able to comprehend each line without much trouble.

First, we ensure that variables such as the @current_user instance variable and the user_id stored in the session are populated before the user logs out:

```
      assert_not_nil assigns(:current_user)
      assert_not_nil session[:user_id]
```

If we don't take this step, we can't guarantee that the destroy action is really doing its job.

The crux of this test lies in its last two lines:

```
      assert_nil session[:user_id]
      assert_nil assigns(:current_user)
```

Here we're confirming that the all-important variables that we populated when the user logged in are set to nil once the user has logged out.

Whew, that was quite a number of tests! We're not done with functional testing just yet, though. You may like to fortify yourself with a strong coffee before tackling the rest of the functional tests, in which we'll be testing the changes we've made to our StoriesController and ApplicationController classes.

Testing the Display of the Story Submitter

The following test checks that the name of the user who submitted a story is displayed correctly on a story's page. Add it to **test/functional/stories_controller_test.rb**:

```
                                    33-stories_controller_test.rb (excerpt)

class StoriesControllerTest < ActionController::TestCase
   : test methods…
   def test_should_show_story_submitter
     get :show, :id => stories(:one)
     assert_select 'p.submitted_by span', 'patrick'
   end
end
```

We've seen all this before—confirming that an element that contains our submitter's name is present is simply a matter of scanning the HTML code for a p element of class submitted_by, which contains the name of the submitter inside a span.

Testing the Display of Global Elements

To test the global elements that we added to the **application.html.erb** layout file, we'll add two tests. For the sake of convenience, both tests will utilize the index action of our StoriesController:

```
                                    34-stories_controller_test.rb (excerpt)

def test_should_indicate_not_logged_in
  get :index
  assert_select 'div#login_logout em', 'Not logged in.'
end

def test_should_show_navigation_menu
  get :index
  assert_select 'ul#navigation li', 2
end
```

We've covered these assert_select statements several times already, so I won't bore you by going through them again. Instead, let's move on to test that our Shovell application displays the name of the logged-in user at the top of every page.

Testing Display of the Username

The div element in the top-right corner of the browser window displays the name of the user who's currently logged in. We've checked the contents of this element when a user *hasn't* logged in; we still need to add a test to check whether the login has been successful.

Before we do so, though, let's add two methods that will make the authoring of this test (and others related to it) a whole lot easier. Since it's likely that we need access to this functionality in more than one place, we'll put these new methods inside the file **test/test_helper.rb**. This file is to tests what `ApplicationController` is to our controllers; every method added to that file is available to all of our test cases.

35-test_helper.rb (excerpt)

```
class Test::Unit::TestCase
  ⋮ class body…
  def get_with_user(action, parameters = nil, session = nil,
    flash = nil)
    get action, parameters, :user_id => users(:patrick).id
  end
  def post_with_user(action, parameters = nil, session = nil,
    flash = nil)
    post action, parameters, :user_id => users(:patrick).id
  end
end
```

As you can see above, the utility methods wrap `get` or `post` calls with a session container that contains the `id` of a logged-in user. Using this approach, we can test an action that was previously only available to users who were logged in, just by calling `get_with_user` or `post_with_user`. Using these methods will eliminate the need to worry about parameters each time we call `get` or `post`.

These utility methods take the same arguments as the original `get` and `post` methods provided by Rails, so they replace our original methods seamlessly. It is, of course, possible to make these utilities much more sophisticated than we've done here as well as add methods to cover the additional `put` and `delete` methods, but they'll serve us well for now.

Let's see them in action! Before that little detour, we were on the way to writing a test that confirms the contents of the `login_logout` div. These contents should include a **(Logout)** link as well as the user's name, which is set by our before filter, `fetch_logged_in_user`:

```
                                        36-stories_controller_test.rb (excerpt)

def test_should_indicate_logged_in_user
  get_with_user :index
  assert_equal users(:patrick), assigns(:current_user)
  assert_select 'div#login_logout em a', '(Logout)'
end
```

By making use of our new utility method get_with_user to simulate a logged-in user, requesting the index action of our StoriesController class is a no-brainer:

```
  get_with_user :index
```

Once we've gained access to the index page, it's easy to use some assertions (in which we're now absolutely proficient!) to confirm that the contents of the div are as we expect.

Testing Redirection After Logout

Our next few tests will cover the changes that we made to the new action of our StoriesController.

First, we'll check that a user who isn't logged in is correctly redirected to the login page if he or she tries to access our story submission form:

```
                                        37-stories_controller_test.rb (excerpt)

def test_should_redirect_if_not_logged_in
  get :new
  assert_response :redirect
  assert_redirected_to new_session_path
end
```

This is a fairly straightforward test—the `get` statement tries to request the story submission form without logging in first:

```
get :new
```

The remainder of the test confirms that the request results in the user being redirected to the `new` action of our `SessionsController`:

```
assert_response :redirect
assert_redirected_to new_session_path
```

Our test suite is certainly expanding. We have just two more tests to write in this chapter!

Testing Story Submission

If you've been particularly eager, and tried executing your functional test suite prematurely, you'll have noticed that a few tests that worked previously now fail. These failures occur because we modified our story submission form; it requires that a `user_id` is present in the session before a page request can be successful. Our old tests didn't account for this change, so they now fail.

We need to modify the four tests that are affected, so that each of them includes a user `id` in the session. At this point, it should become obvious that it was well worth the effort for us to create the `get_with_user` and `post_with_user` utility methods:

```
                                    38-stories_controller_test.rb (excerpt)
class StoriesControllerTest < ActionController::TestCase
  : class methods...
  def test_should_show_new
    get_with_user :new
    : method body...
  end

  def test_should_show_new_form
    get_with_user :new
    : method body...
  end

  def test_should_add_story
    post_with_user :create, :story => {
```

```
      ⋮ story attributes…
    }
    ⋮ method body…
  end
  def test_should_reject_missing_story_attribute
    post_with_user :create, :story => {
      ⋮ story attributes…
    }
    ⋮ method body…
  end
  ⋮ class methods…
end
```

As you can see, the changes are very small—the method that performs the request in each of the tests is modified from `get` and `post` to `get_with_user` and `post_with_user`, respectively.

Testing Storage of the Submitter

The last test we'll add checks that the user who's currently logged in is correctly associated with any stories that he or she submits:

39-stories_controller_test.rb (excerpt)

```
def test_should_store_user_with_story
  post_with_user :create, :story => {
    :name => 'story with user',
    :link => 'http://www.story-with-user.com/'
  }
  assert_equal users(:patrick), assigns(:story).user
end
```

Excellent. If you've made it this far, you're probably itching to see the results of executing our rapidly expanding test suite.

Running the Full Test Suite

Run the full test suite with our trusty `rake` tool. If everything has gone well, you should see results similar to Figure 8.13:

```
$ rake test
```

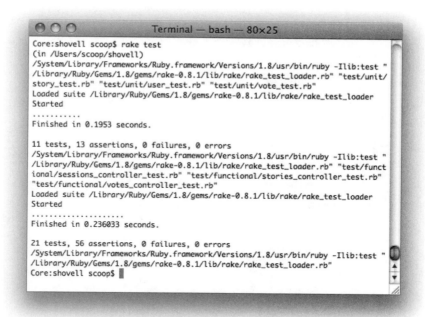

Figure 8.13. Running the test suite

If any of your tests failed, the error message that's displayed should help you to determine where things went wrong. The error will direct you to the location of the erroneous class and method, and the exact line number within that method. And before you start pulling your hair out, remember that you can double-check your code against the code archive for this book—it went through considerable testing before release, so you can count on the code in it to work!

Even more rewarding than seeing the number of tests and assertions that our test suite now covers is to take a look at the output of the `stats` task. This command displays a number of statistics relating to the architecture of our application, including the ratio of lines of application code to lines of test code. We've been extremely busy writing tests in this chapter, so let's see the results:

```
$ rake stats
```

My application reports a ratio of 1:1.8, as Figure 8.14 indicates.

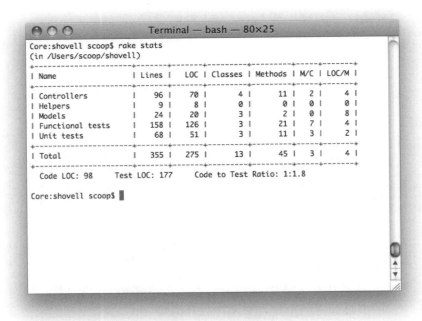

```
  ● ● ●           Terminal — bash — 80×25
Core:shovell scoop$ rake stats
(in /Users/scoop/shovell)
+----------------+-------+------+---------+---------+-----+-------+
| Name           | Lines |  LOC | Classes | Methods | M/C | LOC/M |
+----------------+-------+------+---------+---------+-----+-------+
| Controllers    |    96 |   70 |       4 |      11 |   2 |     4 |
| Helpers        |     9 |    8 |       0 |       0 |   0 |     0 |
| Models         |    24 |   20 |       3 |       2 |   0 |     8 |
| Functional tests |  158 |  126 |       3 |      21 |   7 |     4 |
| Unit tests     |    68 |   51 |       3 |      11 |   3 |     2 |
+----------------+-------+------+---------+---------+-----+-------+
| Total          |   355 |  275 |      13 |      45 |   3 |     4 |
+----------------+-------+------+---------+---------+-----+-------+
  Code LOC: 98    Test LOC: 177    Code to Test Ratio: 1:1.8

Core:shovell scoop$ █
```

Figure 8.14. The current test-to-code ratio

Wow! That means we've written almost twice the amount of code to test our application than we've written for Shovell itself. This is a good thing: it means that we can be confident that our application is of high quality!

Summary

In this chapter, we explored an approach for sectioning off the parts of a Rails application, so that some features are available to everyone and others are available only to users who have logged in.

First, we discussed some theory about sessions and cookies. We then created a new model—the User—and built a login form that allows users to log in to Shovell. We stored the login functionality in a new SessionsController class, which made extensive use of the session container. The end result was that we were able to restrict access to the story submission form to users who were logged in, and direct other visitors to the login form. And to top it all off, we verified that the changes to our code are free of bugs by writing a number of tests.

The next chapter, in which we'll add the last of the features to our Shovell application, will cover more complex `ActiveRecord` associations. Though we're moving into more advanced territory, we'll keep moving through each task step by step, so don't be nervous. Let's add the finishing touches to Shovell!

Advanced Topics

As we enter the final section of this book, we'll implement the last of the features that we listed back in Chapter 1, in preparation for Shovell's much-anticipated first release.

Along the way, we'll cover some of the more advanced topics that are involved in developing web applications with Ruby on Rails, such as writing your own helpers, using callbacks, and creating complex associations.

Promoting Popular Stories

To start this chapter, we'll make a change to the way our users view our application. We'll separate the display of our stories into two pages: one for stories with a score *above* a certain threshold, and one for stories with a score *below* that threshold. This will encourage readers to "shove" stories to the front page by voting for them. This functionality will replace the story randomizer that currently appears on the `index` page of our `StoriesController`—it's getting a little boring and doesn't really meet the needs of our application.

However, before we can start hacking away at these new pages, we need to refine our existing models. In particular, we need an easy way to select stories on the basis of their voting scores.

Using a Counter Cache

We've already seen how we can count the number of votes associated with a given story by calling the `size` method on the associated `Vote` object:

```
>> Story.find(:first).votes.size
=> 3
```

Behind the scenes, this snippet performs two separate SQL queries. The first query fetches the first story from the `stories` table; the second query counts the number of `Votes` whose `story_id` attributes are equal to the `id` of the `Story` object in question.

This approach to counting records isn't usually a problem in small applications that deal with only a handful of records. However, when an application needs to deal with several thousand records or more, these double queries can significantly impede the application's performance.

One option for tackling this issue is to use some more advanced SQL commands, such as `JOIN` and `GROUP BY`. However, like you, I don't really enjoy writing SQL queries. Instead, I'll introduce you to another funky Rails feature: the counter cache.

Introducing the Counter Cache

The **counter cache** is an optional feature of `ActiveRecord` associations, and it makes counting records fast and easy. The use of the word "counter" here is as in "bean counter," not as in "counter-terrorism." The name "counter cache" is intended to reflect the caching of a value which counts records. You can enable the counter cache by including the parameter `:counter_cache => true` when defining a `belongs_to` association.

From a performance point of view, the counter cache is superior to an SQL-based solution. When we're using SQL, the number of records for an object associated with the current object needs to be computed by the database every time that object is requested. The counter cache, on the other hand, stores the number of records of each associated object in its own column in the database. This value can be retrieved as often as is needed, without requiring potentially expensive computation to take place.

The Counter Cache Doesn't Count!

The counter cache doesn't actually go through the database to calculate the number of associated records every time an object is added or removed, effective from the point at which it was turned on. Instead, it increases the counter for every object that's added to the association, and decreases it for every object that's removed from the association, from the point at which it's enabled.

As the counter cache needs to be stored somewhere, we'll create room for it in our Story model with the help of a migration.

Making Room for the Cache

We'll generate a new migration template using the generate script:

```
$ ruby script/generate migration AddCounterCacheToStories
➥    votes_count:integer
```

Figure 9.1 shows the results of this task.

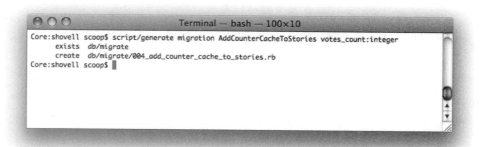

Figure 9.1. Generating a migration to add the counter cache

As expected, our new migration template is stored in the file **db/migrate/004_add_counter_cache_to_stories.rb**. This migration will be used to add a new column to the stories table; the column will store a value that represents the number of Vote objects associated with each Story. The name of the column should match the method that we would normally call to retrieve the object count, so we'll call it `votes_count`. Modify the migration file so it looks like this:

```
                                              01-004_add_counter_cache_to_stories.rb
class AddCounterCacheToStories < ActiveRecord::Migration
  def self.up
    add_column :stories, :votes_count, :integer, :default => 0
    Story.find(:all).each do |s|
      s.update_attribute :votes_count, s.votes.length
    end
  end
  def self.down
    remove_column :stories, :votes_count
  end
end
```

Let me explain what's going on here. Columns which store the counter cache need a default value of 0 in order to operate properly. This default value can be provided to `add_column` using the `:default` argument, as we've done in the first line of our `self.up` method:

```
add_column :stories, :votes_count, :integer, :default => 0
```

In the past, we've used migrations to make schema changes, but migrations can also be used to migrate data. As I mentioned earlier in this chapter, the number of objects associated with the model using the counter cache is never actually calculated by Rails—values are just incremented and decremented as records are modified. Consequently, the next line in our migration loops through the `Story` objects in the database, and manually calculates each `Story`'s initial voting score:

```
Story.find(:all).each do |s|
  s.update_attribute :votes_count, s.votes.length
end
```

`Story.find(:all)` returns an array of all stories in the database. We then use the `each` method to pass each of the `Story` objects, one after another, to the block of Ruby code that follows. The block calculates the voting score for the current story (which is held in the variable `s`) by calling the `length` method on the `votes` association. In effect, this is the same as counting all of the `Vote` objects associated with the current `Story`. The result of the `votes.length` calculation is then stored in the newly added `votes_count` attribute of the current `Story`, using the `update_attrib-ute` method.

As usual, we reverse the changes that we made in `self.up` in the `self.down` method:

```
def self.down
  remove_column :stories, :votes_count
end
```

Right, let's make use of this migration.

Applying the Migration

Go ahead and apply this migration using the `rake` tool:

```
$ rake db:migrate
```

Once that's completed, there's just one more small change we need to make to ensure that our association between a `Vote` and a `Story` uses the counter cache we've just set up. Change the `belongs_to` association in **app/models/vote.rb** to the following:

02-vote.rb (excerpt)

```
belongs_to :story, :counter_cache => true
```

It should be noted that Rails will, from this point forward, automatically refer to the value stored in the `votes_count` column, even if we actually call `votes.size`. Because of this behavior, none of our existing code in our project needs to change.

Excellent. Let's get that new front page happening!

Updating the RJS Template

One side-effect of using a counter cache is that the cached values are not refreshed when a new object is created in a collection—for example, when we create new `Vote` objects via Ajax and then immediately access the cached value in `votes_count` (indirectly, via the `votes.size` call). This is easily rectified by forcing a reload of the object between casting the vote and displaying the vote count. Modify the first line of the **app/views/votes/create.js.rjs** template file like so:

```
                                           03-create.js.rjs (excerpt)
page.replace_html 'vote_score',
    "Score: #{@story.reload.votes.size}"
```

Implementing the Front Page

The core concept of social news sites like Digg is that they're user-moderated. Stories that have yet to receive a certain number of votes don't appear on the site's front page—instead, they reside in a "voting area," where they can be viewed and voted upon by the site's users.

The story promotion system that Digg uses is actually rather complicated. It takes into account a range of factors other than the number of votes a story receives, including the amount of activity the site was experiencing at the time the vote was cast, and the rate at which a story receives votes. However, we'll implement a much simpler algorithm for Shovell: stories with a voting score above a certain threshold will appear on the front page, while stories with a score below that threshold will be displayed on the voting page, ready to be "shoved."

First, we'll make all the changes required to get our front page running smoothly, utilizing standard templates and partials. We can then make use of these templates to implement our voting bin.

Modifying the Controller

The first change that we'll make is to our **StoriesController**. We need to replace the current **index** action (which displays a random story) with one that retrieves the list of stories which have received enough votes to appear on the front page. Modify the **index** method of the **StoriesController** class located in **app/controllers/stories_controller.rb** so that it looks like this:

```
                                       04-stories_controller.rb (excerpt)
def index
  @stories = Story.find :all,
      :order => 'id DESC',
      :conditions => 'votes_count >= 5'
end
```

Let's take a look at this code.

`Story.find :all`, as you already know, fetches from the database all stories that match an optional criterion. We're specifying that our records be ordered by descending `id` here, which will ensure that the newest stories appear at the top of the results, and older ones show at the bottom.

To implement the voting threshold, we've specified a condition that the total `votes_count` must be greater than or equal to five, using the counter cache that we created in the previous section. The result of the `find` operation will then be stored in the `@stories` instance variable.

Modifying the View

Now that we've retired the story randomizer, we also have to rip apart the **index.html.erb** template, which was formerly responsible for rendering a single story link. Our new template will render a collection of stories, each displaying its current voting score and the name of the user who submitted it.

Modify the corresponding index template (located at **app/views/stories/index.html.erb**) so that it looks like this:

```
05-index.html.erb
<h2>
  <%= "Showing #{ pluralize(@stories.size, 'story') }" %>
</h2>
<%= render :partial => 'story', :collection => @stories %>
```

The first line of ERb code outputs the number of stories being displayed:

```
<%= "Showing #{ pluralize(@stories.size, 'story') }" %>
```

To display this value, we're making use of the `pluralize` helper provided by Rails. `pluralize` displays the noun which is passed in as an argument, either in singular or in plural form. If there's only one story to show, the header will read **Showing 1 story**; in all other cases it will read **Showing x stories**, where x is the number of stories available.

Most of the time, Rails is smart enough to correctly pluralize the most common English nouns automatically. If this doesn't work for some reason, you have the option of passing both singular *and* plural forms, like so:[1]

```erb
<%= "Showing #{ pluralize(@stories.size, 'story', 'stories') }"%>
```

To render each story in the collection we retrieved, we're using a partial—something we first encountered when displaying voting history back in Chapter 7:

```erb
<%= render :partial => 'story', :collection => @stories %>
```

As this is the advanced topics chapter, here's another tip. The above line can be abbreviated as follows:

```erb
<%= render :partial => @stories %>
```

How would this work? Given a call like this, Rails looks at the type of object you pass in by checking the class of the first object in the array, which happens to be a `Story` object. It then assumes a straight mapping between models and controllers and looks for a partial template in **app/views/stories/_story.html.erb**. Had we passed in a collection of votes, as we did back in the section called "Adding Voting History" in Chapter 7, Rails would look for a template in **app/views/votes/_vote.html.erb**. See the pattern?

The next item on our list is the creation of the partial.

Creating the Partial

Create the file **app/views/stories/_story.html.erb**, and edit it to appear as follows:

06-_story.html.erb (excerpt)

```erb
<% div_for(story) do %>
  <h3><%= link_to story.name, story %></h3>
  <p>
    Submitted by: <%= story.user.login %> |
```

---

[1] If you need to "train" Rails to correctly pluralize a noun in more than one spot, it may be worth adding your own pluralization rules to the Rails Inflector. See the **config/initializers/inflections.rb** for an example.

```
      Score: <%= story.votes_count %>
    </p>
<% end %>
```

This partial is responsible for displaying the core facts of a story in the listings on the application's front page (and, as you'll see later, in the voting bin). It's a fairly straightforward template that you should have no trouble understanding. The only new thing is the use of the `div_for` helper, which nicely wraps our story in `<div>` tags and automatically assigns a `class` of `story` and an element `id` of `story_id`. Both values are directly derived from the object being passed to the helper. For example, passing in an object of class `Story` and an `id` of 2, `div_for` would provide us with a tag as follows:

```
<div id="story_2" class="story">
  ⋮ HTML…
</div>
```

Apart from the `<div>` tag, the title of the story is displayed in an h3 element, which links directly to the story page using the `link_to` helper, and the original submitter of the story and current voting score are displayed underneath.

We'll now use the assigned element `class` of `story` to apply some CSS styling.

Styling the Front Page

Now that we have some new elements on the front page, let's add style rules for those elements to our style sheet, which is located at **public/stylesheets/style.css**:

07-style.css (excerpt)

```
.story {
  float: left;
  width: 50%;
}

.story h3 { margin-bottom: 0; }
.story p  { color: #666; }
```

While we're giving our front page an overhaul, let's also get rid of the default Rails welcome page that's displayed when a user accesses http://localhost:3000/, and make our new front page the default page instead.

Setting the Default Page

To set the default page, we once again need to alter Rails's routing configuration, which is located in the file **config/routes.rb**. If you look closely, you'll notice a commented line like this (if you deleted it earlier, don't worry—you can just type out the line you need in a moment):

```
# map.root :controller => "welcome"
```

By removing the # character and making a slight change to the route, we can set the destination for requests for the address http://localhost:3000/ to be the `index` action for our `StoriesController`:

08-routes.rb (excerpt)

```
map.root :controller => "stories"
```

Before you jump into your browser to test this new route, you should be aware of one small caveat: the default Rails welcome page is a simple HTML page (it contains no ERb code at all). It lives at **public/index.html**, and when present, it will be displayed in favor of any other action configured in the Rails routing configuration file. So, in order to display our story index, this file has to be removed—go ahead and delete it now.

Okay, let's take a peek at our new front page (after making sure our web server is running); mine's shown in Figure 9.2. Depending on how many votes you've given your stories, you may or may not see any stories listed.

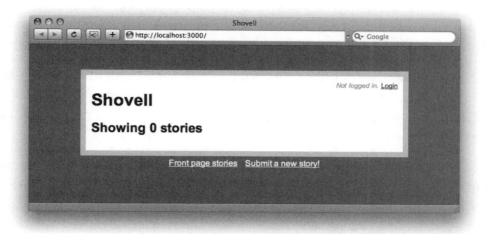

Figure 9.2. The all new (but empty) front page

If, like me, your front page is looking rather empty, you're probably keen to get voting! Let's quickly cover the implementation of the voting bin, so you can use it to start voting on stories in the queue.

Implementing the Voting Bin

To create a voting bin, create a new method called `bin` in the file **/app/controllers/stories_controller.rb**, like so:

```
09-stories_controller.rb (excerpt)

class StoriesController < ApplicationController
  : controller code...
  def bin
    @stories = Story.find :all,
        :order => 'id DESC',
        :conditions => 'votes_count < 5'
    render :action => 'index'
  end
end
```

Most of that code probably looks straightforward enough—but what about that `render` call that's hiding in there?

Well, before I explain that line of code, let me point something out to you, in case you haven't spotted it already: this code is almost identical to the code we wrote for our `index` action—it just applies a different condition to the collection of stories.

That fact should trigger the realization that this is a good opportunity to reuse some code. Let's extract most of the code that's used in these two controller methods (`index` and `bin`) and place it in a protected controller method called `fetch_stories`, which we'll then use from both locations within our code.

As we discussed earlier, protected methods are only accessible from within a class and its subclasses; they're not accessible from anywhere outside the class. If we were to make `fetch_stories` a publicly accessible method, it would be exposed via the URL http://localhost:3000/stories/fetch_stories, which is certainly not what we want!

Here's that extracted method:

```
def fetch_stories(conditions)
  @stories = Story.find :all,
        :order => 'id DESC',
        :conditions => conditions
end
```

As the only part that differs between the `index` and `bin` actions is the condition, we'll allow the condition to be passed to the new protected method as an argument.

Our `StoriesController` should now look a bit like this (only the code relevant to this section is shown):

```
                                          10-stories_controller.rb (excerpt)
class StoriesController < ApplicationController
  ⋮ controller code…
  def index
    fetch_stories 'votes_count >= 5'
  end

  def bin
    fetch_stories 'votes_count < 5'
    render :action => 'index'
  end
```

```
  ⋮ controller code…
  protected
  def fetch_stories(conditions)
    @stories = Story.find :all,
        :order => 'id DESC',
        :conditions => conditions
  end
end
```

Now, back to that peculiar `render` call in the `bin` action:

```
render :action => 'index'
```

I mentioned earlier that the two actions we have for listing stories (`index` and `bin`) are almost identical; well, another thing that they have in common is the template that they use. The above line of code makes sure of that. It specifies that the view template for the `index` action should also be used by the `bin` action. As such, we're rendering the exact same template for a slightly different set of stories.

Before we go ahead and give our two pages sufficient visual distinction—they need headings that read something like **Showing 3 upcoming stories** or **Showing 7 front-page stories** so our users won't have a difficult time determining which page of the application they're looking at—let's quickly digress to add yet another little bit to our routing configuration to make it easy to refer to our voting bin when we want to link to it.

Adding Custom Actions to RESTful Routes

RESTful routes, as you may remember from the section called "Mapping a New Resource" in Chapter 6, gives us a defined set of routes and route generation helpers to refer to these routes (or URLs). In the last section, we implemented a new controller action that isn't contained in that set of default routes, so we have to tell Rails a little about what we'd like to do with this new action, how users will reach it, and how we want to refer to it.

Back in **config/routes.rb**, here's the line that gives us all the RESTful goodness for doing regular operations on stories as well as its votes:

```
map.resources :stories, :has_many => :votes
```

You may be able to tell from our use of helpers like `stories_path` and `story_path` in the past couple of chapters that there are routes which operate on the stories in general (without referring to a specific one by `id`, such as `stories_path`, for instance) and those that operate specifically on a story (for example, `story_path`), which need an actual story object to be passed in to operate properly.

We need to talk about this distinction in order to be able to add a custom action to our set of defined routes at the right spot. Since our `index` and `bin` actions are so similar in function, we can safely presume that `bin` would be another action that will operate on the entire collection of stories, since it displays an arbitrary set of stories based on their votes count.

To include a new custom route which operates on a collection of objects, add the following to the routing configuration file:

11-routes.rb *(excerpt)*

```
map.resources :stories, :has_many => :votes, :collection =>
    { :bin => :get }
```

In addition to the name of the custom action, Rails wants us to tell it the actual HTTP method used to talk to this action, which in this case is GET. By changing our routing configuration in this way, we obtain a newly defined helper method: `bin_stories_path`, which refers to the stories in our submission bin. We'll use this helper in a moment, when we modify the site navigation menu to include a link to this bin.

Next up, though, we'll deal with the missing distinction between our two story-listing pages by adding distinct headings to the `index.html.erb` template with a little assistance from some `ActionView` helpers.

Abstracting Presentation Logic

In this section, we'll look at a way to abstract any presentation logic that you find yourself adding to your view templates. First, let's discuss why we need to bother extracting Ruby code from our views even though view templates may appear to be the easiest place to implement presentation logic.

Avoiding Presentation Logic Spaghetti

Recall that our intention is to display in the index template a heading that's appropriate, depending on whether the list of stories being displayed contains front-page stories or upcoming stories.

Of course, we could implement this functionality by adding the logic directly to the **app/views/stories/index.html.erb** template (don't do this just yet!):

```erb
<h2>
  <% if controller.action_name == 'index' %>
    <%= "Showing #{ pluralize(@stories.size,
         'front page story') }"%>
  <% else %>
    <%= "Showing #{ pluralize(@stories.size, 'upcoming story') }" %>
  <% end %>
</h2>
```

However, you'll notice that this solution entails a fair amount of duplication—all we're changing in the `else` block is a single word! Additionally, the fact that in view templates Ruby code is always wrapped in ERb tags (`<% %>` and `<%= %>`) means that these templates can sometimes begin to look like a dish of spaghetti, containing chained method calls, nested levels of parentheses, `if` clauses, and other complexities.

When your own code starts to look like spaghetti, it may be time to consider extracting some of that code into an `ActionView` helper.

Introducing `ActionView` Helpers

As you've heard countless times now, a view should contain presentational code only. In order to adhere to the MVC paradigm as strictly as possible, you should aim to place all logic outside the views: in a controller (for application logic) or a model (for business logic). There's a third option for any presentation-related logic that doesn't quite belong in a controller or a model: the **ActionView helper**.

We talked about making helper methods available to views in the section called "Protecting the Form" in Chapter 8, when we implemented the `logged_in?` method. However, back then, we implemented this functionality as a protected controller method, which was then made available to our views using the `helper_method` statement.

Native `ActionView` helpers differ from protected helper methods in that they're *not* available to controllers—hence the name. An `ActionView` helper is a function that helps to reduce the clutter in your view templates.

Writing an `ActionView` Helper

`ActionView` helpers are available in two basic forms.

The first is the global helper, which is stored in the file **app/helpers/application_helper.rb**. You can think of a global `ActionView` helper as being the "view" equivalent to the `ApplicationController` class in the "controller" world. Any helper that you add to this file will be available from every view of every controller.

The second form of `ActionView` helper is one that's specific to the views of a particular controller. We'll use this approach for our `ActionView` helper—we'll create a new helper method for our `StoriesController` in the file **app/helpers/stories_helper.rb**. That way, it will be clear that it's related to `StoriesController`.

By default, Rails' `ApplicationController` contains the line `helper :all`, which makes available all helper methods to all the controllers, all the time. But even if it doesn't make a difference, access-wise, whether you place a helper method into **application_helper.rb** or **stories_helper.rb**, you'd end up with a really cluttered global helper file very quickly. Instead, stick to the habit of grouping our helpers by the area they affect. In this case, we're talking about a headline for the story listings, so it really belongs in the **stories_helper.rb** file.

Here's the helper method you'll need to add:

```
                                                    12-stories_helper.rb
module StoriesHelper
  def story_list_heading
    story_type = case controller.action_name
        when 'index': 'front-page story'
        when 'bin': 'upcoming story'
      end
    "Showing #{ pluralize(@stories.size, story_type) }"
  end
end
```

Let's step through this code. The first thing it does is populate a variable `story_type` using a Ruby `case` statement:

```
story_type = case controller.action_name
    when 'index': 'front-page story'
    when 'bin': 'upcoming story'
  end
```

This statement compares the value of `controller.action_name` (which contains the text value of the controller action that's being executed, exactly as it appears in the URL) with a couple of predefined values (namely, the values `'index'` and `'bin'`).

Next, we display the same **Showing** ... string with the `pluralize` helper that we used in our previous attempt at writing this view:

```
"Showing #{ pluralize(@stories.size, story_type) }"
```

However, this time, we're passing `story_type` as the part of the string that's being pluralized. This string is either set to `front-page story` or `upcoming story`.[2] While this isn't necessarily a shorter solution than the previous one, it certainly removes a lot of clutter from our view, which we can now reduce to a single line!

13-index.html.erb

```
<h2><%= story_list_heading %></h2>
<%= render :partial => @stories %>
```

Now we just need to add our voting bin page to the navigation menu in the footer of each page, and we're done!

Expanding the Navigation Menu

To add a link to our navigation menu, we simply add another list item to the unordered list at the bottom of the application layout. The layout is stored in **app/views/layouts/application.html.erb**:

---

[2] If we wanted to be extra-pedantic about reducing code duplication, we could even extract the word "story" from that string, and simply set the `story_type` variable to "front page" or "upcoming." But you have to draw the line somewhere!

14-application.html.erb *(excerpt)*

```
<ul id="navigation">
  <li><%= link_to 'Front page stories', stories_path %></li>
  <li><%= link_to 'Upcoming stories', bin_stories_path %></li>
  <li><%= link_to 'Submit a new story!', new_story_path %></li>
</ul>
```

Excellent! Now we can finally give our changes a whirl. Point your browser to **http://localhost:3000/** and click the **Upcoming stories** link at the bottom of the page.

The resulting page, an example of which is depicted in Figure 9.3, should contain all the stories in your database that have a voting score below 5.

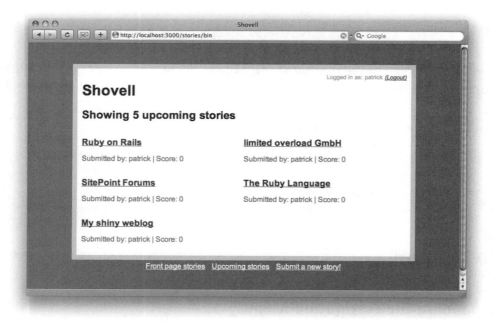

Figure 9.3. The story voting bin

Before you use this unique opportunity to promote the first story to Shovell's front page, we'll go ahead and require users to be logged in before they can vote. This will give us the ability to check a user's voting history later on.

Our application is looking much more like a story-sharing site. On to the next feature!

Requiring a Login to Vote

The next enhancement we'll make will ensure that users log in before they're able to vote. First, we need to modify VotesController so that the create method responds only to users who are logged in. We then need to store the id of the current user as part of the new vote.

The first step is to add a new before_filter in **app/controllers/votes_controller.rb**, like so:

15-votes_controller.rb *(excerpt)*

```ruby
class VotesController < ApplicationController
  before_filter :login_required
  : controller code…
end
```

Since the VotesController only contains a single action right now, we don't need to limit the before_filter by using the :except or :only options.

Now, it doesn't make much sense to display a feature to visitors if they can't make use of it. Let's add a little login teaser to the story page, to suggest that visitors can choose to log in if they want to vote for stories. Make the following changes to **app/views/stories/show.html.erb**:

16-show.html.erb *(excerpt)*

```erb
<% if logged_in? %>
<div id="vote_form">           :url => story_votes_path(@story) do %>
  <% form_remote_for [ @story, Vote.new ] do |f| %>
    <%= f.submit 'shove it' %>
  <% end %>                ⌐tag
</div>
<% else %>
  <p>
    <em>
      You would be able to vote for this story if you were
      <%= link_to 'logged in', new_session_path %>!
    </em>
  </p>
<% end %>
```

This *if* clause decides whether or not to display the **shove it** link to the visitor, depending on his or her login status. If the user isn't logged in, that person is presented with a teaser and a link to log in, as shown in Figure 9.4.

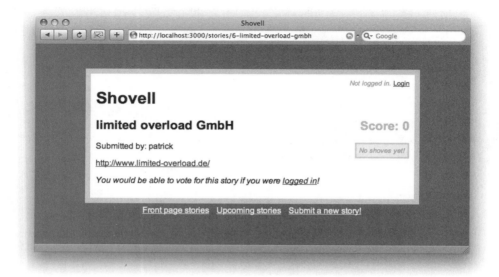

Figure 9.4. Hiding the voting link from visitors

To complete this feature addition, we need to modify the `create` action of our `VotesController` so that it stores the current user with each vote:

```
                                        17-votes_controller.rb (excerpt)
class VotesController < ApplicationController
  : controller code...
  def create                    [:story-id]
    @story = Story.find(params[:id])
    @story.votes.create(:user => @current_user)
    : method body...
  end
end
```

This new line saves the reference to the current user with each vote.

Excellent! Now it's time to create some additional stories and start submitting some votes, if you haven't done so already.

Visit the voting bin by selecting the **Upcoming stories** link from the navigation menu, and click on a story's title to visit the story page. From there, you can click the **shove it** link a few times until the story has five or more votes. Visit the front page, and you should see your story appear! The result of my serial voting is shown in Figure 9.5.

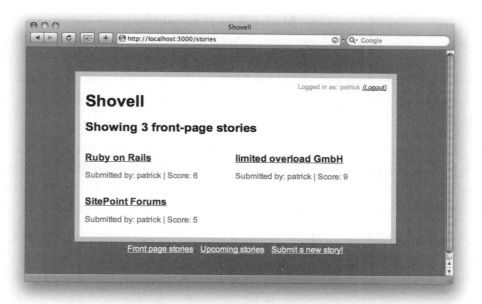

Figure 9.5. Viewing stories on the front page

That's another feature crossed off the list. Next!

Auto-voting for Newly Submitted Stories

The next step we'll take is to hop into the `Story` model and remedy a piece of functionality that will indisputably aid in the promotion of your stories to the front page. New stories will be automatically voted for by yourself as soon as you submit them. To implement this feature, I'll introduce you to a feature of Rails models that we haven't touched on yet: **callbacks**. Callbacks are little snippets of code that are triggered by model events—for example, they're triggered when a model is created, updated, or destroyed.

Introducing Model Callbacks

Callbacks in models can be called before or after certain actions, such as the creating, updating, or destroying of a model. The concept of a callback may sound similar to the filters we applied to our controllers in the section called "Introducing Filters" in Chapter 8—that's because they certainly *are* similar.

In fact, we've already encountered a callback in our application—it was used to apply the validation we implemented in the section called "Applying Validations" in Chapter 6. Internally, `ActiveRecord` calls validation methods before calling the `save` method that writes a model to the database. If the callback result allows the request to continue—meaning that the request has passed the defined validations—the save operation is executed.

The names of the available callback methods are fairly intuitive: `before_create`, `before_save`, and `before_delete` are called before the model in question is created, saved, and deleted, respectively. There are also a number of `after_` callbacks that, as expected, are called after the operation.

Like filters in controllers, callbacks in models are usually defined as protected methods. The callback resides in a model class, and is referred to by the class method via a symbol. Here's an example:

```
class Story < ActiveRecord::Base
  after_create :create_initial_vote
  ⋮ model code…
  protected
    def create_initial_vote
      ⋮ callback method…
    end
end
```

We'll use `after_create`, because we'd like to create votes for newly submitted stories only, and not for every update of an existing story (which would require the use of the `after_save` callback).

An Alternative Callback Syntax

In your experimentation with Rails, you may come across the following syntax for model callbacks. In this syntax, the code that's to be executed when an event occurs is defined as an instance method named after the callback:

```
class MyModel < ActiveRecord::Base
  def after_save
  : callback method…
  end
end
```

While this approach is technically correct, I prefer to define my callbacks using descriptive method names, and to refer to them using the `after_save` `:my_method` syntax instead.[3] This way, it's much easier to see what's going on, because you can glance at the header of the model class in which the callbacks are declared, then look at each of the callback methods separately.

The reason we're using `after_create` instead of `before_create` should be obvious: if we were to create the vote *before* the model itself had been saved to the database, we'd risk the model's failure to pass the validation checks and we'd have created a vote for an invalid record!

Adding a Callback

Let's add a callback to our `Story` model. Add the following code to the file **app/models/story.rb**:

```
                                                    18-story.rb (excerpt)

class Story < ActiveRecord::Base
  after_create :create_initial_vote
  : model code…
  protected
    def create_initial_vote
      votes.create :user => user
    end
end
```

---

[3] The `after_find` callback actually *needs* to be defined using this alternative syntax, due to performance implications associated with defining it using the preferred syntax.

Once again, just one line of Ruby code is sufficient to accomplish the task at hand. Let's dissect what this line actually does.

First, you'll notice that we're able to directly use two of the attributes of the story: the `votes` association and the `user` attribute. As long as a method doesn't carry variables of the same name, executing `votes` or `user` will refer to the methods of the story object. We know the submitter of the story is stored in `user`, so we can directly refer to that attribute in order to create the initial vote:

```
votes.create :user => user
```

Before we try out our newly implemented callback that creates the initial vote, let's add something that's been missing from our stories.

Adding a Description to Stories

In the next enhancement to our application, we'll add an extra attribute to our `Story` model: a `description` column which allows users to write a few paragraphs about their submissions.

Adding a Model Attribute

Since we're talking about adding an attribute, you may be assuming that there's a new migration ahead—and indeed there is. Let's generate the migration file which will store the code we'll use to add the description column:

```
$ ruby script/generate migration AddDescriptionToStories
➥    description:text
```

The contents of this migration (stored in **db/migrate/005_add_description_to_stories.rb**) are very straightforward, so they won't need a great deal of explanation:

19-005_add_description_to_stories.rb (excerpt)

```
class AddDescriptionToStories < ActiveRecord::Migration
  def self.up
    add_column :stories, :description, :text
  end

  def self.down
```

```
      remove_column :stories, :description
    end
end
```

As you can see, we're adding a single column to the `stories` table. We've specified that the new `description` column must be of type `text`, because a column of type `string` can only store up to 255 characters, and it's possible that story descriptions will exceed this limit.

The final step is to apply this migration using the `rake` task:

```
$ rake db:migrate
```

The output of this migration is shown in Figure 9.6.

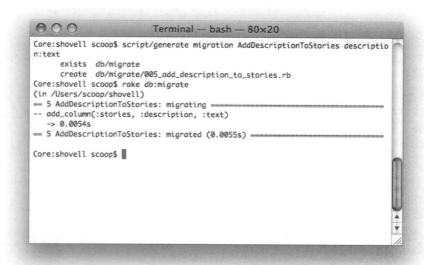

Figure 9.6. Adding and applying our fifth migration

Expanding the Submission Form

One last change we'll make before we test our initial vote creation code is to add another field to the story submission form (in the file **app/views/stories/new.html.erb**). This field will accept the description column that we just added:

20-new.html.erb (excerpt)

```erb
<% form_for @story do |f| %>
  ⋮ form HTML…
<p>
  description:<br />
  <%= f.text_area :description %>
</p>
<p><%= submit_tag %></p>
<% end %>
```

Figure 9.7 shows the form after we apply this change.

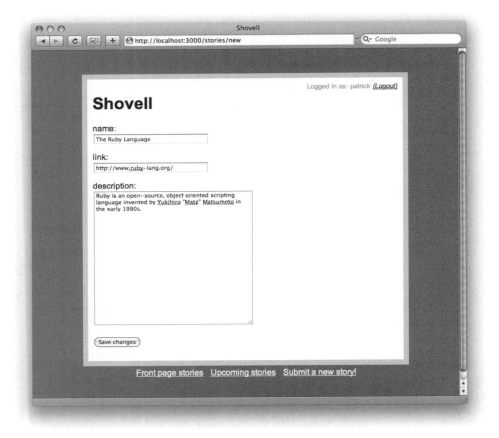

Figure 9.7. Allowing users to add a story description

To accommodate a larger story description—remember, we've given our users plenty of room by making the `description` column of type `text`—we're using a `textarea` instead of a one-line `input` field:

```
<%= f.text_area :description %>
```

We also need to display the story's description on the story's page, just above the `submitted_by` paragraph in the file **/app/views/stories/show.html.erb**:

21-show.html.erb (excerpt)

```
<ul id="vote_history">
: vote history…
</ul>
<p>
  <%= @story.description %>
</p>
<p class="submitted_by">
: submitted by…
</p>
```

Right! Let's hop over to our browser and submit a new story to see whether the automated submission of the first vote works as expected. And, sure enough, it does—as Figure 9.8 shows!

Figure 9.8. A story with an auto-generated permalink

Adding User Pages

In order to track the history of our site's usage on a per-user basis, we'll need to create a place where this information can be displayed.

We'll add a user page, which will list the six stories most recently submitted by the logged-in user and the six stories for which that person most recently voted. To select the most recently voted-for stories, we'll make use of another type of relationship: the join model.

Introducing the Join Model Relationship

A **join model** relationship is a relationship between two models, which relies upon a third—otherwise there's no direct relationship between the two models that are being linked.

In our Shovell application, an association only exists between our Story and User models when we're talking about who *submitted* each story—we don't currently have the ability to find out who *voted* for each story. This is where the join model comes into play: the Vote model is already associated with both the User and the Story models; with the addition of the has_many :through statement, the Vote can serve as the connecting element in this new relationship. This relationship is illustrated in Figure 9.9.

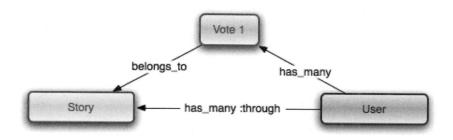

Figure 9.9. A join model relationship

The Vote model is the join model because it joins the User and the Story models.

Introducing the `has_many` `:through` Association

The code that implements a join model relationship is the line has_many :through. Let's use it to add a join model relationship to our User model. Open the file **app/models/user.rb** and make the changes in bold below:

```
                                                    22-user.rb (excerpt)

class User < ActiveRecord::Base
  has_many :stories
  has_many :votes
  has_many :stories_voted_on,
      :through => :votes,
      :source => :story
end
```

Normally, Rails is smart enough to figure out associated class names on its own, so long as the associations are given a name that matches the plural form of the class name (for instance, :stories). However, because our User model already has a has_many relationship (has_many :stories), we need to assign this new association a different name (:stories_voted_on). We also need to specify the model with which we're associating the users, which is exactly what the :source => :story argument does.

The code that defines this relationship as a join model relationship is the :through => :votes argument, which can be read as: "a User *has many* Stories *through* the Vote model."

With this association in place, we find that several new instance methods are available to every User object:

```
>> u = User.find(:first)
=> #<User id: 1, …>
>> u.stories_voted_on.size
=> 1
>> u.stories_voted_on.first
=> #<Story id: …>
```

As you can see, this association behaves like a regular has_many association, and if you were none the wiser, you'd never actually know that three models were involved in retrieving the associated data.

Adding Another Controller

Before we implement our user page, we need to generate another controller, since we haven't dealt with User objects so far.

By now, you should be ever so familiar with the procedure to generate a controller with the script/generate command, so I'll spare you the details. Enter the following command to create a new UsersController:

```
$ ruby script/generate controller Users show
```

Additionally, we'll add a resource declaration to the routing configuration stored in config/routes.rb, like so:

23-routes.rb (excerpt)

```
map.resources :users
```

must go above stories/votes mapped resources

The actual implementation of the show action in UsersController is as follows:

24-users_controller.rb (excerpt)

```ruby
class UsersController < ApplicationController
  def show
    @user = User.find(params[:id])
    @stories_submitted = @user.stories.find(:all,
        :limit => 6, :order => 'stories.id DESC')
    @stories_voted_on  = @user.stories_voted_on.find(:all,
        :limit => 6, :order => 'votes.id DESC')
  end
end
```

Let's look at this code. Remember that the `params` hash stores the various parts of the current URL, as defined in the application's routing configuration. To retrieve the requested user from the database, we're using the `find` method:

```ruby
@user = User.find(params[:id])
```

The data we're going to display on the user page is fetched by the associations that are available via the `User` object. We then populate a couple of instance variables using `find` calls with two options—first to sort the items in the desired order, and again to limit the number of items retrieved:

```ruby
@stories_submitted = @user.stories.find(:all,
    :limit => 6, :order => 'stories.id DESC')
@stories_voted_on  = @user.stories_voted_on.find(:all,
    :limit => 6, :order => 'votes.id DESC')
```

Since multiple tables are involved in retrieving the data we're interested in, we have to be a little more explicit with our ordering instructions. Here, we're using `stories.id` and `votes.id` in the order clause, respectively. The part before the period actually specifies the table that contains the `id` column to sort by. Since most (if not all) of our tables actually *have* an `id` column, this is a necessary evil.

The next task on our list is to create the view template for this page!

Creating the View

The view template for our user page has been generated (with fairly non-spectacular content) in **app/views/users/show.html.erb**. This template will use the instance vari-

ables that we created in our controller to display the recently submitted stories and
votes. It does so by rendering a collection of partials:

```
25-show.html.erb
<h2>Stories submitted by <%= @user.name %></h2>
<div id="stories_submitted">
  <%= render :partial => @stories_submitted %>
</div>
<h2>Stories voted for by <%= @user.name %></h2>
<div id="stories_voted_on">
  <%= render :partial => @stories_voted_on %>
</div>
```

The partial we're rendering with this code already exists. We're reusing the story
partial from StoriesController, which Rails will figure out to use because we're
passing in a collection of Story objects using the shorthand notation of the render
call:

```
<%= render :partial => @stories_submitted %>
```

Next, we'll add a link to the user page by linking the name of the submitter as it's
displayed on the story page (/app/views/stories/show.html.erb), like so:

```
26-show.html.erb (excerpt)
<p class="submitted_by">
  Submitted by:
  <span><%= link_to @story.user.login, @story.user %></span>
</p>
```

Now we'll make a small addition to our style sheet for the sake of some visually pleasing cosmetic treatment:

27-style.css (excerpt)

```css
.story p {
  color: #666;
  font-size: 0.8em;
}
h2 {
  clear: both;
  margin: 0;
  padding: 10px 0;
}
```

Lastly, we'll add the `login` of the user in question to the links generated for the user page by overriding the `to_param` method of `User`, just like we did with the `Story` class:

28-user.rb (excerpt)

```ruby
class User < ActiveRecord::Base
  : model code…
  def to_param
    "#{id}-#{login}"
  end
end
```

In practice, you should probably ensure that the `login` attribute doesn't contain non-alphanumeric characters. You can accomplish this little exercise with some help from the `validates_format_of` validation.

There we go! As Figure 9.10 shows, we now have a user page which makes use of our newly added `has_many :through` association to list both the stories that were submitted by a given user and the stories for which that person recently voted.

Figure 9.10. Example of a user page

Testing the New Functionality

As usual, we'll add test coverage by writing unit tests, then adding functional tests, for all of the enhancements we've made.

Testing the Model

We made a number of changes to our model in this chapter, including utilizing the counter cache and introducing the join model relationship. Let's write some unit tests for those changes now.

Testing Additions to the Counter Cache

The first change we made in this chapter was to modify the Story model so that it uses the counter cache to track the number of votes associated with any given Story. To test this feature, we have to pull a few tricks out of the box, as there are numerous conditions to take into account.

To begin with, let's add a test to the test case for the scenario in which a vote is cast. The test case is located in **test/unit/story_test.rb**:

```ruby
class StoryTest < ActiveSupport::TestCase
  ⋮ test methods…
  def test_should_increment_votes_counter_cache
    stories(:two).votes.create
    stories(:two).reload
    assert_equal 1, stories(:two).attributes['votes_count']
  end
end
```

There's a couple of methods we haven't encountered before, so let's dissect this code.

The purpose of this test is to verify that the cached votes count is properly incremented when a new vote is added. Therefore, the first step we need to take is to create a new vote:

```ruby
stories(:two).votes.create
```

The second line is where things get interesting—we're forcibly reloading the model from the database.

```ruby
stories(:two).reload
```

We do this because once a new vote has been added, the number of stories that are cached in each model's attributes is suddenly out of sync with the database.

If we were to check the log file when we come to run our tests later on, we'd find lines like the following:

```
UPDATE stories SET votes_count = votes_count + 1 WHERE (id = 2)
```

This is the SQL statement that Rails generates to update the counter cache. You'll notice that the statement doesn't bother to check the current value of votes_count—it just tells the database to increment votes_count by one. And with good reason!

You see, in a live application, many users may be using the site at the same time, and some of them might even be casting votes in parallel. The value of `votes_count` would be totally negated if the SQL for each vote submission relied upon its own copy of `votes_count` at the time the statement was executed.

As such, you need to reload the model if you ever require access to the current number of votes immediately after a new vote is added, just as we did in the RJS template earlier in this chapter. This situation isn't likely to occur very often; normally you'd redirect your user to a new page anyway. But when we're writing tests that simulate user behavior, it's important to be mindful of this issue.

There's also something special about the assertion in this test: instead of comparing the return value of the `votes_count` instance method, we access the "raw" attribute as it comes out of the database:

```
assert_equal 1, stories(:two).attributes['votes_count']
```

If we had used the instance method, we wouldn't have had to enable counter caching at all in order for our test to pass—`votes_count` would simply have issued a second database query to count the votes. By using the attribute itself, we're asserting that the counter cache is doing its job.

Testing Deletions from the Counter Cache

With that first test out the way, this second test, which covers the deletion of votes, should be fairly straightforward. Our application doesn't yet allow users to delete votes, but we'll include this test anyway, for the sake of completeness:

30-story_test.rb (excerpt)

```
class StoryTest < ActiveSupport::TestCase
  ⋮ test methods…
  def test_should_decrement_votes_counter_cache
    stories(:one).votes.first.destroy
    stories(:one).reload
    assert_equal 1, stories(:one).attributes['votes_count']
  end
end
```

This test is basically the opposite of the previous one. First, we destroy the first vote from the first story and then reload the model to reflect this change:

```
stories(:one).votes.first.destroy
stories(:one).reload
```

Finally, we compare the cached `votes_count` value to the value we expect it to have:

```
assert_equal 1, stories(:one).attributes['votes_count']
```

Preparing the Fixtures

As if those tests didn't already contain enough workarounds, we also need to set the initial `votes_count` value for each story in our fixture file. Like the "magical" auto-populating column names we first encountered in Chapter 7, the counter cache is not properly populated when fixtures are transferred to the database. Add the following values into the fixture file at **test/fixtures/stories.yml** to reflect the way in which the vote fixtures are associated with the story fixtures; while we're changing this file, we'll add an all-new story to our fixture data. We'll make use of this in the functional tests that we'll write later on:

```
                                            31-stories.yml (excerpt)
one:
  ⋮ YAML data…
  votes_count: 2
two:
  ⋮ YAML data…
  votes_count: 0
promoted:
  name: What is a Debugger?
  link: http://en.wikipedia.org/wiki/Debugger/
  user: john
  votes_count: 5
```

Testing the Creation of the Initial Vote

The next test covers the new functionality that we added to our model for the automatic creation of a vote when you submit a story:

```
                                              32-story_test.rb (excerpt)
class StoryTest < ActiveSupport::TestCase
  ⋮ test methods…
  def test_should_cast_vote_after_creating_story
    s = Story.create(
        :name => 'The 2008 Elections',
        :link => 'http://elections.com/',
        :user => users(:patrick)
    )
    assert_equal users(:patrick), s.votes.first.user
  end
end
```

You should be able to follow the twists and turns of this test quite easily. To test the creation of a vote after a story has been saved to the database, a new story is created (don't forget to pass in a user!):

```
s = Story.create(
    :name => 'The 2008 Elections',
    :link => 'http://elections.com/',
    :user => users(:patrick)
)
```

The assertion of this test confirms that the user of the first vote attached to the newly created story is indeed the user we passed in when we created the story in the first place:

```
assert_equal users(:patrick), s.votes.first.user
```

This confirms that there is at least a single vote and that the user has been properly inherited from the story.

Testing the Join Model Relationship

Lastly, we need to add a test to deal with the new has_many :through association that we added to our User model. Expand the test cases (located in **test/unit/user_test.rb**) as follows:

33-user_test.rb *(excerpt)*

```ruby
class UserTest < ActiveSupport::TestCase
  : test methods…
  def test_stories_voted_on_association
    assert_equal [ stories(:one) ],
        users(:patrick).stories_voted_on
  end
end
```

This test relies on fixture data. Therefore, we can assert immediately that the list of stories for which our test user voted is equal to the list that we expect:

```ruby
    assert_equal [ stories(:one) ],
        users(:patrick).stories_voted_on
```

Next, we've got some functional tests to write.

Testing the `StoriesController`

In this chapter, we've added to `StoriesController` quite a bit of functionality that needs testing. This is a little more complicated than in previous chapters, so the corresponding tests will also be more complex. Additionally, we've added a new `UsersContoller` with a relatively simple action, that also needs testing.

Testing the Rendering of Templates

We'll start by changing an existing test (`test_should_show_index`) and add one more basic tests to cover correct template rendering:

34-stories_controller_test.rb *(excerpt)*

```ruby
class StoriesControllerTest < ActionController::TestCase
  : test methods…
  def test_should_show_index
    get :index
    assert_response :success
    assert_template 'index'
    assert_not_nil assigns(:stories)
  end

  def test_should_show_bin
```

```
    get :bin
    assert_response :success
    assert_template 'index'
    assert_not_nil assigns(:stories)
  end
  : test methods…
end
```

Both tests are very similar in nature and neither exposes any new functionality. Each calls its respective action, checks that the request was responded to successfully, and confirms that the proper template is rendered (remember, we're using exactly the same template for both the index and bin actions). It also ensures the @stories instance variable doesn't wind up being nil.

Testing the Story Index Pages

As a next step, we're confirming that each of the story-listing actions (index and bin) picks the proper records from the database. One list shows only "promoted" stories, which have a voting score of at least 5; the other shows the remaining stories:

35-stories_controller_test.rb (excerpt)

```
def test_should_only_list_promoted_on_index
  get :index
  assert_equal [ stories(:promoted) ], assigns(:stories)
end

def test_should_only_list_unpromoted_in_bin
  get :bin
  assert_equal [ stories(:two), stories(:one) ],
    assigns(:stories)
end
```

In both of these tests, we compare the value that's assigned to the @stories instance variable (which is accessed by the assigns(:stories) construct) with our fixture data.

Testing the Routing Configuration

We also altered the routing configuration in this chapter; let's add a test to confirm that our changes are working properly:

```
                                          36-stories_controller_test.rb (excerpt)
def test_should_use_story_index_as_default
  assert_recognizes({ :controller => 'stories',
      :action => 'index' }, '/')
end
```

The `assert_recognizes` assertion confirms that a given request is translated into an expected set of parameters, mostly consisting of a controller and an action name:

```
assert_recognizes({ :controller => 'stories', :action => 'index' }, '/')
```

Our assertion here confirms that a request for "/" (the front page of our domain) is indeed routed to the `index` action of `StoriesController`.

Testing Page Headings

The next pair of tests deals with the view side of the `index` and `bin` actions and confirms that the header tag contains a proper heading, complete with the expected number of stories:

```
                                          37-stories_controller_test.rb (excerpt)
def test_should_show_story_on_index
  get :index
  assert_select 'h2', 'Showing 1 front-page story'
  assert_select 'div#content div.story', :count => 1
end

def test_should_show_stories_in_bin
  get :bin
  assert_select 'h2', 'Showing 2 upcoming stories'
  assert_select 'div#content div.story', :count => 2
end
```

The second `assert_select` assertion tests for an appropriate number of `div` elements with a `class` attribute of `story`. These `div`s come out of the **_story.html.erb** partial and, as such, we're looking for one `div` per story. Each story `div` is contained in the all-encompassing `div` that has an `id` of `content`.

Testing the Story Submission Form

We also added to the story submission form a new field that allows users to submit story descriptions. To test this functionality, change the existing `test_should_show_new_form` test to match the following:

```ruby
                                        38-stories_controller_test.rb (excerpt)

def test_should_show_new_form
  get_with_user :new
  assert_select 'form p', :count => 4
end
```

In this test, the `assert_select` call counts the number of p elements below the `<form>` tag, and checks the total against our expected number of 4—three form fields plus a **Submit** button.

Testing the Story Display Page

Since users who are not logged in no longer see the **shove it** button, we need to revise an existing test and add a new one:

```ruby
                                        39-stories_controller_test.rb (excerpt)

def test_should_show_story_vote_elements
  get_with_user :show, :id => stories(:one)
  : method body…
end

def test_should_not_show_vote_button_if_not_logged_in
  get :show, :id => stories(:one)
  assert_select 'div#vote_link', false
end
                    form
```

We pass *false* to `assert_select` to confirm that there are *no* elements on the page that match the given CSS selector.

Testing the Navigation Menu

We added an item to our navigation menu, so we need to increase the number of list items that we check for in the following test from two to three:

```
                                      40-stories_controller_test.rb (excerpt)
def test_should_show_navigation_menu
  get :index
  assert_select 'ul#navigation li', 3
end
```

Testing the Story Submitter Link Text

Lastly, let's change our existing test for the story submitter on the story page (`test_should_show_story_submitter`) to make sure that it now links to the story submitter's user page:

```
                                      41-stories_controller_test.rb (excerpt)
def test_should_show_story_submitter
  get :show, :id => stories(:one)
  assert_select 'p.submitted_by a', 'patrick'
end
```

Whew! That was quite a litany of tests. Let's now turn our attention to the tests of the other controllers that were affected by all the goings-on in this chapter.

Testing the `VotesController`

Since we've modified the voting procedure so as to be available for logged-in users only, we have to modify some existing tests as well as add a new one to cover storage of the user for every cast vote.

Testing Restricted Functionality

As we've made the vote action available only to users who have logged in, we need to revise those tests that request the `create` action of `VotesController` to log in to the application first. These revisions mostly involve modifying the `get` and `post` calls:

```
                                      42-votes_controller_test.rb (excerpt)
class VotesControllerTest < ActionController::TestCase
  : test methods…
  def test_should_accept_vote
```

```
  ⋮ method body…
    post_with_user :create, :story_id => stories(:two)
    assert ! assigns(:story).reload.votes.empty?
  end

  def test_should_render_rjs_after_vote_with_ajax
    xml_http_request :post_with_user, :create,
        :story_id => stories(:two)
    ⋮ method body…
  end

  def test_should_redirect_after_vote_with_http_post
    post_with_user :create, :story_id => stories(:two)
    ⋮ method body…
  end
  ⋮ test methods…
end
```

Testing User Voting History

Additionally, we'll add a test to confirm that the vote action indeed stores the current user with the submitted vote:

43-votes_controller_test.rb *(excerpt)*

```
def test_should_store_user_with_vote
  post_with_user :create, :story_id => stories(:two)
  assert_equal users(:patrick), assigns(:story).votes.last.user
end
```

Testing the `UsersController`

Without further ado, we'll add three tests to cover the functionality encapsulated within the user page we added to `UsersController`:

44-users_controller_test.rb *(excerpt)*

```
class UsersControllerTest < ActionController::TestCase
  def test_should_show_user
    get :show, :id => users(:patrick)
    assert_response :success
    assert_template 'show'
```

```
      assert_equal users(:patrick), assigns(:user)
    end

    def test_should_show_submitted_stories
      get :show, :id => users(:patrick)
      assert_select 'div#stories_submitted div.story', :count => 2
    end

    def test_should_show_stories_voted_on
      get :show, :id => users(:patrick)
      assert_select 'div#stories_voted_on div.story', :count => 1
    end
end
```

All three tests use basic assertions to confirm that the proper user is found by the show action, and that that user's story submissions and story votes are displayed properly on the page.

Running the Complete Test Suite

We've made a massive number of additions to our suite of tests in this chapter, so it should be especially rewarding to run the full suite now, using:

```
$ rake test
```

Figure 9.11 shows the results of all of our tests.

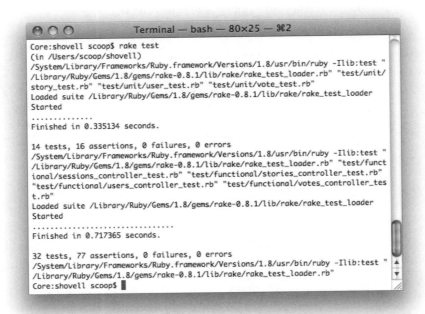

Figure 9.11. Running the test suite

Summary

Wow, what a journey! In this chapter, we've added a stack of features to Shovell, such as the display of popular story listings on the front page and the implementation of a voting bin containing stories that people can vote on.

Along the way, we learned that the counter cache offers an easy way to store the number of records associated with any given model, and we used `ActiveRecord` callbacks as a means to hook into certain events occurring on our models. We used a `after_create` callback to cast an initial vote for submitted stories, and we also tackled `ActionView` helpers to reduce clutter in our shared view.

Lastly, we covered an additional type of association: the join model relationship. It was used to implement a user page to show the story submissions and voting history of each registered user.

After numerous tests and assertions, we can attest that Shovell is in very good shape indeed. Of course, there are countless enhancements that we could make to our little application; some of the functionality that comes to mind includes:

- creating a form that allows new users to register
- sending an email to new users to inform them of their passwords
- encrypting user passwords in the database
- allowing users to comment on stories
- restricting users to vote for each story only once

I'm sure your mind is racing with ideas for a number of spectacular features that could set your application apart from the pack! While the addition of all of these features is more than we could possibly cover in this book, I've given you a solid grounding—both in theory and in practice—that you can build on to further develop Shovell on your own. Don't forget to keep expanding your test suite to include all the cool new features that you add!

In the next chapter, we'll take a quick look at the Rails plugin architecture, and use one of the existing plugins to expand Shovell's feature set—implementing tagging functionality for our story submissions.

Chapter 1

Rails Plugins

While this book is unable to cover all of the built-in functionality that ships with Rails—and there's plenty of functionality for you to discover and experiment with once you're beyond the last chapter—the plugins architecture of Rails warrants our attention.

What Is a Plugin?

A **plugin** is a component that you can add to your application to extend its functionality. While you can certainly write your own plugins,[1] we'll limit our discussion here to using existing plugins. Plugins have been developed for various parts of the Rails framework, and add functionality in a range of areas, including:

- extensions to `ActiveRecord` functionality
- helper methods
- new template engines (for coding a view using an alternate templating language)

---

[1] http://wiki.rubyonrails.com/rails/pages/HowTosPlugins/

The original list of plugins is located in the Rails wiki; each entry simply links to the plugin code that various people have contributed and published.[2] Other useful plugin directories can be found at RailsLodge[3] and Agile Web Development.[4]

Plugins are installed using a command line script that's available in the **script** subdirectory of every Rails application. By default, this script will only install the plugins contained in the official Rails repository. To install a plugin from a different location, you must know the exact URL from which the plugin is available—information that's usually provided by the plugin developer.

Let's explore what the `plugin` script can do for us.

Invoke the script from the command line, without arguments, so that we can view its usage instructions:

```
$ ruby script/plugin
```

You should be presented with a set of usage instructions that numbers several pages, and even includes examples. An excerpt of this output can be seen in Figure 10.1.

Using the `plugin` script, plugins can be installed, removed, and even updated, should a newer version than the one you originally installed become available. The other commands listed in Figure 10.1 relate to adding, listing, and removing additional plugin repositories; we won't cover them in this book.

Plugins you've installed for your application usually reside in the `vendor/plugins` folder within your application's root folder. Each plugin resides in its own subdirectory, where it will be automatically found and loaded by Rails. The upshot of this is that you don't need to instruct Rails to "load plugin A from location B."

Every Rails plugin ships with a **README** file that contains instructions for using the plugin. Many plugins also ship with test cases that assert their proper functioning.

Okay, enough theory! Let's go ahead and install our first plugin.

---

[2] http://wiki.rubyonrails.org/rails/pages/Plugins
[3] http://www.railslodge.com/
[4] http://agilewebdevelopment.com/plugins/

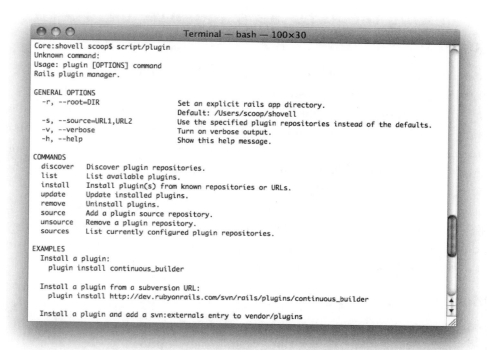

Figure 10.1. Usage instructions for `script/plugin`

Adding Tagging to Shovell

The Web 2.0 ideal not only encourages the (mindful) use of Ajax functionality, it almost dictates that a web application *must* have "tagging" to be classified as a Web 2.0 application. And Shovell is no exception!

Tagging is the process by which content creators attach simple, textual labels to their data, be it a photo, a link, a story, or a restaurant review. These tags vary widely in their nature—they may be location-related, content-related, and so on. The result is that everyone seems to have a unique system for tagging data.

Tags are definitely more flexible than a simple category tree—they allow you to assign as many or as few tags as you like to any item of data. The convention that has evolved around this functionality is for the user to enter tags for a content item into a text field. Multiple tags should be separated by a space or a comma.

Introducing the `acts_as_taggable_on_steroids` Plugin

Instead of reinventing the wheel and implementing our own tagging system for Shovell, we'll use one of the available Rails plugins for this job: `acts_as_taggable_on_steroids`. You may be wondering what kind of name the developer originally chose for his plugin. At some point David Heinemeier Hansson himself actually developed a plugin named `acts_as_taggable` as a proof of concept for some then-new features for Rails. It wasn't really intended for production use and has since been deprecated. But, tagging being such an essential component of today's web sites with user-generated content, Jonathan Viney, a Rails core contributor and all-round guru, picked up where Heinemeier Hansson left off and created his work under the name of `acts_as_taggable_on_steroids`. With that bit of family history out of the way, let's have a look at what this plugin can do for us.

What `acts_as_taggable_on_steroids` Does

As this isn't the most obvious name for a plugin, allow me to explain a little bit about the background of the `acts_as_*` naming convention.

In Rails' own plugin repository can be found a number of **acts**, which are functional extensions to an `ActiveRecord` model. These acts equip models with certain functionality that usually can be enabled using a single line of code.

As this functionality typically enables models to "act as something else," the convention of calling these functional additions "acts" arose, and the code that enables the functionality `acts_as_something` shortly followed.

At the time of writing, three related acts are available from Rails' own plugin repository: `acts_as_list`, `acts_as_tree`, and `acts_as_nested_set`. While some are more complex than others, each of these acts applies a hierarchy to a set of model objects. In the case of `acts_as_list`, objects are positioned in a flat list; with `acts_as_nested_set`, the resulting hierarchy is a sophisticated tree system, such as that used in a threaded forum, for example.

But what about `acts_as_taggable_on_steroids`? As the name suggests, this plugin provides a simple yet effective means by which you can make your models taggable. It ships with its own `ActiveRecord` model class called `Tag`, as well as functionality for parsing a list of tags divided by spaces into separate model objects of class `Tag`.

Of course, before we can play with this plugin, we'll need to install it.

Installing the `acts_as_taggable_on_steroids` Plugin

To install the plugin, change directory to the application root folder, and, on one line, execute the following command:

```
$ ruby script/plugin install http://svn.viney.net.nz/
➡things/rails/plugins/acts_as_taggable_on_steroids/
```

You'll see all the files that were added to your **vendor/plugins/** directory in the output of the `plugin` script. The files that make up the acts_as_taggable_on_steroids plugin are placed in a folder which has the same name as the plugin, as Figure 10.2 shows.

As I mentioned, you don't have to load this plugin explicitly, so here's where the installation instructions end!

git://github.com/jviney/acts-as-taggable_on-steroids-git

(install git first)

Figure 10.2. Installing the `acts_as_taggable_on_steroids` plugin

Creating a Migration for the Plugin

Our plan is to allow users of our application to add tags to stories submitted to
Shovell, so we'll need to make our `Story` model taggable. Both the tags themselves
and the relationships between tags and stories need to be stored somewhere; you
guessed it, we need to use a migration to create new tables. And while this plugin
makes use of a new model (the `Tag` model provided by the `acts_as_tag-
gable_on_steroids` plugin), the model wasn't created by the `generate` script, so
we don't yet have a migration to go with it. Luckily, the plugin does come with a
convenient generator method to create a fitting migration:

```
$ ruby script/generate acts_as_taggable_migration
```

The `acts_as_taggable_on_steroids` plugin uses two tables:

▪ The `tags` table stores the `Tag` model, which is just a regular `ActiveRecord` model. This table contains one entry for each tag. So, for example, if you tagged two or more `Story` models with the tag `ruby`, only one `Tag` object (`ruby`) would be stored in the database. This approach makes it easy for our application's users to find content: if a user was interested in finding stories about Ruby, he or she could browse through all of the stories to which the `ruby` tag was applied.

▪ The `taggings` table stores the actual mappings between the `Tag` model and those models that make use of the `acts_as_taggable_on_steroids` functionality.

Following is the migration code that was generated for us. It is actually ready to use as is, and is stored in **db/migrate/006_acts_as_taggable_migration.rb** file:

```
                                              01-006_acts_as_taggable_migration.rb
class ActsAsTaggableMigration < ActiveRecord::Migration
  def self.up
    create_table :tags do |t|
      t.column :name, :string
    end

    create_table :taggings do |t|
      t.column :tag_id, :integer
      t.column :taggable_id, :integer

      # You should make sure that the column created is
      # long enough to store the required class names.
      t.column :taggable_type, :string

      t.column :created_at, :datetime
    end

    add_index :taggings, :tag_id
    add_index :taggings, [:taggable_id, :taggable_type]
  end

  def self.down
    drop_table :taggings
    drop_table :tags
  end
end
```

The above migration starts out simply enough. It creates the `tags` table that contains just one column: `name` (in addition to the `id` column belonging to every table).

While it may appear simple on the surface, the `taggings` table is a little more complex than a mere list of objects and their tags. As I mentioned, it's possible to make more than one model in your application taggable. However, the mappings between the `Tag` model and those models to which tagging functionality has been added use a single table.

`acts_as_taggable_on_steroids` uses each of the columns created in the `taggable` table as follows:

- `tag_id` stores the `id` of the `Tag` model.

- `taggable_id` stores the `id` of the object that is *being tagged* (for example, the `id` of a `Story`).

- `taggable_type` stores the class of the object that is being tagged (for example, `Story`).

Before we can give our `Story` model a little `acts_as_taggable_on_steroids` goodness, we need to apply the migration that we just generated:

```
$ rake db:migrate
```

Figure 10.3 shows the outputs that result when this migration is created, and then applied.

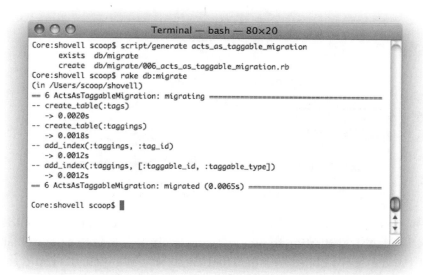

Figure 10.3. Adding and applying the `acts_as_taggable_on_steroids` migration

Great! Now we can make our `Story` model taggable. But what's really going on here?

Understanding Polymorphic Associations

We've looked at the underlying tables utilized by the `acts_as_taggable_on_steroids` plugin, and we know which columns are used to store what. But what kind of association is this?

It's not a one-to-many relationship, because one tag may be applied to many items *and* one item may have many tags. It's a kind of bidirectional, one-to-many relationship. While Rails developers have always used the `has_and_belongs_to_many` (sometimes abbreviated to "habtm") relationship to express this kind of functionality, Rails features a type of relationship that's better suited for this situation. This relationship is called a **polymorphic association**.

In a polymorphic association, a model is associated with objects of more than one model class, as Figure 10.4 illustrates. In order to store this relationship in the database accurately, the object's class name *and* its ID need to be stored. Take a peek at the migration that we just created, and you'll see that this is exactly what's achieved by the schema it creates.

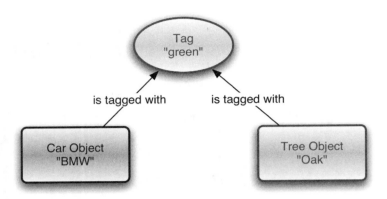

Figure 10.4. Two models are assigned the same tag

If the schema didn't save both the class name and ID of the object, we could potentially be faced with a situation in which a tag was applied to both a User object with an id of 1 and a Story object *that also* had an id of 1. What chaos would result!

Fortunately, Rails handles most of the details that implement this relationship automatically and transparently for you.

Making a Model Taggable

To use acts_as_taggable_on_steroids, modify the Story class definition located in **app/models/story.rb** as follows:

```
                                                        02-story.rb (excerpt)

class Story < ActiveRecord::Base
  acts_as_taggable
  ⋮ Story model...
end
```

Yes, that *is* it! With the plugin in place, it takes just 16 characters to make a model taggable. Please note that the function name is still acts_as_taggable as opposed to the plugin name, which is acts_as_taggable_on_steroids.

Next, we'll hop into the Rails console to play with our Story model's new functionality. The acts_as_taggable_on_steroids plugin has added a variety of extra methods to our model. Let's take a look at some of them.

First, retrieve a story from the database:

```
>> s = Story.find(:first)
=> #<Story id: 2, name: "SitePoint Forums", …>
```

We can look at the tags already assigned to this story by using the `tag_list` instance method:

```
>> s.tag_list
=> []
```

By simply assigning a new value to the `tag_list` attribute, we have the ability to tag an object. In its simplest form, this value can be a comma-separated list of tags to apply:

```
>> s.tag_list = 'sitepoint, forum, community'
=> "sitepoint, forum, community"
```

When the model is then saved to the database, we can use the `tag_list` method again to fetch an array of tags assigned to the model:

```
>> s.save
=> true
>> s.tag_list
=> ["sitepoint", "forum", "community"]
```

The `tag_list` method is in fact a shortcut to the association data, which is available through the `tags` instance method. This method provides access to an array of the `Tag` objects with which this particular story is associated:

```
>> s.tags.size
=> 3
```

As I mentioned earlier in the chapter, we can also use methods of the `Tag` class to retrieve a list of stories that are tagged with a particular word. Below, we load up an existing tag (which we've just created through the assignment of a comma-separated list of tags to the `tag_list` attribute of the `Story` model) using a standard `ActiveRecord` dynamic finder method:

```
>> t = Tag.find_by_name("sitepoint")
=> #<Tag id: 1, name: "sitepoint">
```

Each `Tag` instance collects a list of all the objects to which it has been assigned—information that's available through the `taggings` instance method. Let's request the size of the array:

```
>> t.taggings.size
=> 1
```

Based on the value returned by the `size` method, we can hazard a guess that the object available in this array is the `Story` object that we tagged earlier. Let's use the `first` method to be sure:

```
>> t.taggings.first
=> #<Tagging id: 1, tag_id: 1, taggable_id: 2,
taggable_type: "Story", …>
```

Yes, we were right!

The objects contained in this `taggings` array are the fully functional model objects of class `Tagging`. This is sort of the intermediate model between the `Tag` and the object *being tagged*, such as a `Story` object. If we want to access the actual tagged model, we have to go through yet another association that the `acts_as_taggable_on_steroids` plugin defined for us: `taggable`.

```
>> t.taggings.first.taggable
=> #<Story id: 2, name: "SitePoint Forums", …>
```

This property retrieved for us the actual story object we applied the tag to. We're now free to invoke the same methods and access the same attributes that we would when dealing straight with a `Story` object. Let's request the name of the story that we've tagged with the `sitepoint` tag:

```
>> t.taggings.first.taggable.name
=> "SitePoint Forums"
```

Straightforward stuff, no? Although I've got to admit that that's a lot of chained method calls there. Didn't we learn about a new type of association that connects a model *through* another model in the last chapter? Feel free to implement that on your own!

One last thing—because it's conceivable that a tag may be applied to more than one type of model, each model is equipped with a new dynamic finder which fetches only objects of that object's class that have been assigned a certain tag. That dynamic finder is `find_tagged_with`:

```
>> s = Story.find_tagged_with("sitepoint")
=> [#<Story id: 2, name: "SitePoint Forums", …>]
>> s.size
=> 1
>> s.first.name
=> "SitePoint Forums"
```

Okay, enough with the console! Let's give users the ability to tag stories through our application's web interface.

Enabling Tag Submission

Before we get all fancy about *displaying* tags all over our site, we need to add a way for users to *submit* tags with a new story. Let's add a new form field to the story submission form.

Modifying the View

To add the form field, modify the submission form that's located in the file **app/views/stories/new.html.erb**:

03-new.html.erb (excerpt)

```
<% form_for @story do |f| %>
  : form HTML…
  <p>
    tags:<br />
    <%= f.text_field :tag_list %>
  </p>
  <p><%= submit_tag %></p>
<% end %>
```

Users will be separating each tag with a comma, so a simple text field for tag entry will do the job nicely:

```
<%= f.text_field :tag_list %>
```

The only mind-bending thing about this line is the use of a regular `text_field` method. This would have us believe that our `Story` object somehow gained a database column for `tag_list`, which it most certainly did not. In fact, this is exactly why the `acts_as_taggable_on_steroids` uses a pragmatic approach for the implementation of tagging for specific objects. It simply provides the `tag_list` and `tag_list=` methods for objects of classes which have been tag-enabled with `acts_as_taggable` that closely resemble what `ActiveRecord` provides us with for regular, database-backed attributes. Behind the scenes, the plugin intercepts what's being set for this attribute and transparently handles creation of new `Tag` objects and `Taggings` relationships. Cool, huh?

Modifying the Controller

To assign the submitted tags to the new story, you probably expected to have to modify the `create` action of the `StoriesController` class. Well, it turns out you don't! As outlined in the previous section, `tag_list` is being treated as yet another attribute. And we didn't have to modify any controller code when we added the `description` attribute back in the last chapter.

Right, our users can submit tags with their stories! Let's display them then, shall we?

Enabling Tag Display

We want our tags to appear in a few places. First of all, they need to be visible on the story page itself. It would also be nice to see them in the story listings on the front page, and on the page showing stories in the voting bin.

Modifying the View

To display the assigned tags on the story page, modify the `show` template, located at **app/views/stories/show.html.erb**. Add the following code between the containers of the story link and the voting form (`vote_form`):

04-show.html.erb (excerpt)

```
<% unless @story.tag_list.empty? %>
  <p class="tags">
    <strong>Tags:</strong>
```

```
      <%= @story.tag_list %>
    </p>
<% end %>
```

Once again, if a story has an empty list of tags, we don't bother to list them, so we wrap the logic in an `unless` clause:

```
<% unless @story.tag_list.empty? %>
  : tag HTML…
<% end %>
```

If tags *are* associated with a story, we go ahead and simply render the list of tags for now:

```
    <%= @story.tag_list %>
```

Updating the `story` Partial

Last of all, we display tags for each story that appears in the story listings on the front page and in the voting bin. To add this information to the display, we'll modify the **app/views/stories/_story.html.erb** partial like so:

```
                                                    05-_story.html.erb (excerpt)
<% div_for(story) do %>
  <h3><%= link_to story.name, story %></h3>
  <p>
    Submitted by: <%= story.user.login %> |
    Score: <%= story.votes_count %><br />
    Tags: <%= story.tag_list %>
  </p>
<% end %>
```

This code also prints a simple, comma-separated list of the tags assigned to a story using the `tag_list` instance method.

Assigning Our First Tags

With a solid foundation in place for the assignment and display of tags in the application, you can now start experimenting with this exciting new piece of functionality. Submit a new story from your browser using the story submission form, and this time include a few tags, as I've done in Figure 10.5. If your web server is still running from the previous chapter, you may need to restart it before it will recognize the new plugin.

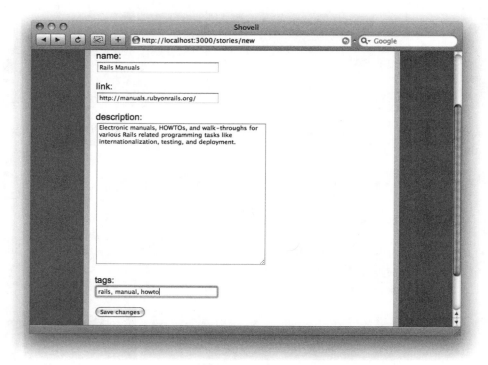

Figure 10.5. Submitting a story with tags

When you view the front page, the upcoming page, or the individual story listings, you should see the tags that you submitted display nicely below your story, as in Figure 10.6.

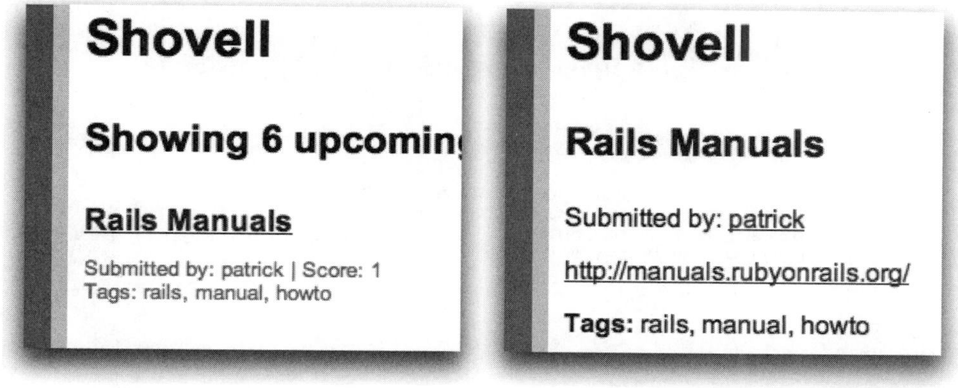

Figure 10.6. Tags displaying for the new story

Everything looks good! However, we'd like to link those tags to a page showing all stories that have this tag in common. Let's do this next.

Viewing Stories by Tag

At this stage, we're taxing ourselves with having to create a separate controller to implement the view-by-tag feature, since that will work nicely with the RESTful approach we're taking to Shovell's development. However, as you've made it to the final third of the book, creating a new controller shouldn't impose too much on your Rails development skills.

Creating the Controller

Our new controller is supposed to deal with objects of class `Tag`, so `TagsController` seems to be an excellent fit. Create it as follows:

```
$ ruby script/generate controller Tags show
```

The result of this operation should look similar to Figure 10.7.

Figure 10.7. Generating the `TagsController`

To actually make our new controller adhere to RESTful principles, we need another entry in **config/routes.rb**:

06-routes.rb *(excerpt)*

```
ActionController::Routing::Routes.draw do |map|
  map.resources :tags
  : other routes…
end
```

Now go ahead and open **app/controllers/tags_controller.rb**, and adjust the show action to look like this:

07-tags_controller.rb *(excerpt)*

```
class TagsController < ApplicationController
  def show
    @stories = Story.find_tagged_with(params[:id])
  end
end
```

There's nothing too fancy here; we simply retrieve all of the stories that are tagged with a particular tag using a method that we played with in the `console` script earlier in this chapter—`find_tagged_with`:

```
@stories = Story.find_tagged_with(params[:id])
```

The last task this page requires of us is the creation of an appropriate heading to distinguish it from our other story lists.

Filling in the View Template

The view template for the `show` action is really very simple. In fact, we could almost reuse the **app/views/stories/index.html.erb** template, but it is kind of awkward to reuse action templates between two separate controllers, so we'll decide against it. What we will do, however, is reuse the partial to render a list of stories.

To do so, open **app/views/tags/show.html.erb** and adjust it as follows:

08-show.html.erb *(excerpt)*

```
<h2>Stories tagged with <%= params[:id] %></h2>
<%= render :partial => @stories %>
```

This ends up being similar to the aforementioned `index` template, but still retains the flexibility to drag in additional models that we can equip with tagging functionality in the future.

Displaying Tagged Stories

Although we know what kind of tag we've used in our story submissions and thus could simply construct a URL to a tag page on our own, we want to enable our users to click on each of the tags displayed in the story listings to reach the respective page listing all stories with that tag.

To do this, we'll change the **app/views/stories/show.html.erb** template slightly to render a partial instead:

```
                                            09-show.html.erb (excerpt)

<% unless @story.tag_list.empty? %>
  <p class="tags">
    <strong>Tags:</strong>
    <%= render :partial => @story.tags %>
  </p>
<% end %>
```

If you recall the shorthand syntax we first met a couple of chapters ago, this render call will actually go to search for a partial in **app/views/tags/_tag.html.erb**, so let's create that partial now.

Creating a `tag` Partial

To render a collection of tags assigned to a story, we need a `tag` partial. Create the file **app/views/tags/_tag.html.erb**, and edit the contents to contain the following single line:

```
                                            10-_tag.html.erb (excerpt)

  <%= link_to tag, tag_path(:id => tag.name) %>
```

This `link_to` call departs slightly from the oh-so-comfortable, convention-laden form that we've grown to love. The reason is that we actually want the URL for our tag pages to look like this:

```
http://localhost:3000/tags/sitepoint
```

While we could certainly go ahead and modify the `to_param` method of the `Tag` class, this would require changing the contents of the `acts_as_taggable_on_ster-oids` plugin. Although this is certainly possible, it's best discouraged—a future update to the plugin could break our changes. This is the reason why I opted to construct the URL by explicitly assigning the `name` value of the tag to the `id` part of the URL.

Updating the Style Sheet

To give our tag links a little room to breathe on the page, let's add the following snippet of CSS to our style sheet, located at **public/stylesheets/style.css**:

```
                                        11-style.css (excerpt)
.tags a { padding: 0 3px; }
```

Excellent. Let's see how it's all looking now, shall we? Loading up a page of a story that has tags assigned should look similar to Figure 10.8.

Figure 10.8. A tagged story with links

Clicking on any of the provided tags should reveal a list of stories that share this tag, an example of which can be found in Figure 10.9. Lovely!

Figure 10.9. Listing all stories tagged with "rails"

Testing the Tagging Functionality

Some plugins come bundled with complete test coverage; others do not. The original `acts_as_taggable` was quite bare bones in that regard. The makeover, however, is indeed *on steroids* with its extensive test coverage. Still, it's good practice to add tests to your test suite to ensure that you're testing *your usage* of the plugin, which definitely isn't covered by the standard test suite for the plugin.

Testing the Model

To test the tagging functionality that our `Story` model has inherited, we're going to add two more unit tests to the `StoryTest` test case.

Testing the Assignment of Tags

The first test we'll add to the **/test/unit/story_test.rb** file is as follows:

```
                                              12-story_test.rb (excerpt)

class StoryTest < ActiveSupport::TestCase
  ⋮ test methods...
  def test_should_act_as_taggable
```

```
    stories(:one).tag_list = 'blog, ruby'
    stories(:one).save
    assert_equal 2, stories(:one).tags.size
    assert_equal [ 'blog', 'ruby' ], stories(:one).tag_list
  end
end
```

This test uses the `tag_list` attribute accessor to apply two tags to one of the stories in our fixture data:

```
    stories(:one).tag_list = 'blog, ruby'
```

To reflect the newly added tags, we need to save the object in question:

```
    stories(:one).save
```

The two assertions in this test confirm that the number of tags assigned to the story meets expectations, and that the list of tags returned by the `tag_list` method contains the correct tags, in the form of an array:

```
    assert_equal 2, stories(:one).tags.size
    assert_equal [ 'blog', 'ruby' ], stories(:one).tag_list
```

Testing the Finding of a Story by Tag

The next unit test we need to add for our `Story` model is as follows:

13-story_test.rb (excerpt)

```
def test_should_find_tagged_with
  stories(:one).tag_list = 'blog, ruby'
  stories(:one).save
  assert_equal [ stories(:one) ],
    Story.find_tagged_with('blog')
end
```

This test confirms that the functionality for finding stories by tag works as expected. After tagging a story, the test uses the `find_tagged_with` class method to retrieve a list of stories with the `blog` tag, and compares it with the list of stories that we expect to be returned.

Great, we're done! Let's go do some functional testing.

Testing the Controller

We need to add a few tests to our `StoriesControllerTest` to confirm that our tagging feature works correctly from a controller perspective.

Testing the Submission of a New Story with Tags

The first test confirms that the process of adding a new story with tags works:

14-stories_controller_test.rb (excerpt)

```ruby
class StoriesControllerTest < ActionController::TestCase
  : test methods…
  def test_should_add_story_with_tags
    post_with_user :create, :story => {
      :name => 'story with tags',
      :link => 'http://www.story-with-tags.com/',
      :tag_list => 'rails, blog'
    }
    assert_equal [ 'rails', 'blog' ], assigns(:story).tag_list
  end
end
```

In this test, we need to specify the tags as part of the `:story` hash. Remember, tags are submitted just like any other attribute in the story submission form:

```ruby
post_with_user :create, :story => {
  :name => 'story with tags',
  :link => 'http://www.story-with-tags.com/',
  :tag_list => 'rails, blog'
}
```

The assertion then ensures the `tag_list` method of the newly added `Story` returns the tags that we submitted:

```ruby
assert_equal [ 'rails', 'blog' ], assigns(:story).tag_list
```

Testing the Display of Tags on a Story Page

The next test checks whether a story's individual page displays its tags properly:

```
                                          15-stories_controller_test.rb (excerpt)
class StoriesControllerTest < ActionController::TestCase
  ⋮ test methods…
  def test_should_show_story_with_tags
    stories(:promoted).tag_list = 'apple, music'
    stories(:promoted).save
    get :show, :id => stories(:promoted).id
    assert_select 'p.tags a', 2
  end
end
```

In this test, we confirm that the container element on the story page contains an appropriate number of elements. We do this by counting the number of links within the p element that has a class of tags:

```
    assert_select 'p.tags a', 2
```

Testing the Display of the Story Submission Form

As we added a new field to the story submission form, we have to edit our StoriesControllerTest class so that the test_should_show_new_form test counts an additional paragraph element:

```
                                          16-stories_controller_test.rb (excerpt)
class StoriesControllerTest < ActionController::TestCase
  ⋮ test methods…
  def test_should_show_new_form
    get_with_user :new
    assert_select 'form p', :count => 5
  end
end
```

Now, let's move on and write some tests for our TagsController.

Testing the `show` Action of `TagsController`

To test our newly created `TagsController`, add the following test to the `TagsControllerTest` test case stored in **test/functional/tags_controller_test.rb**:

17-tags_controller_test.rb (excerpt)

```ruby
class TagsControllerTest < ActionController::TestCase

  def test_should_find_tagged_stories
    stories(:one).tag_list = 'blog, ruby'
    stories(:one).save
    get :show, :id => 'blog'
    assert_equal [ stories(:one) ], assigns(:stories)
  end

end
```

We start this test by assigning some tags to one of our stories, then call the `show` method of the controller to find all stories tagged with `blog`:

```ruby
stories(:one).tag_list = 'blog, ruby'
stories(:one).save
get :show, :id => 'blog'
```

The assertion then confirms that the `@stories` instance variable actually contains all the stories we expect it to:

```ruby
assert_equal [ stories(:one) ], assigns(:stories)
```

Testing the Display of Stories by Tag

The next test we need to add to our `TagsControllerTest` is the following:

18-tags_controller_test.rb (excerpt)

```ruby
def test_should_render_tagged_stories
  stories(:one).tag_list = 'blog, ruby'
  stories(:one).save
  get :show, :id => 'ruby'
  assert_response :success
```

```
    assert_template 'show'
    assert_select 'div#content div.story', :count => 1
  end
```

In this test, we put the template code through its paces. The `assert_select` call confirms that the resulting page contains the expected number of `div` elements with a `class` of `story`:

```
    assert_select 'div#content div.story', :count => 1
```

And that, dear reader, is the last test I'll make you write! Well, for this chapter, anyway.

Running the Test Suite ... Again!

To assure ourselves that all of these new tests (and our existing ones) pass, we'll run the whole suite again using `rake`, as illustrated in Figure 10.10.

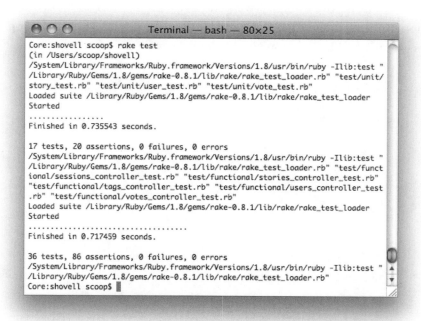

Figure 10.10. Running the test suite

```
$ rake test
```

If all of your tests passed, give yourself a congratulatory pat on the back for a job well done! And if there are any errors or failures, double-check your code against the code in the book and the book's code archive to see where you might have gone wrong. The error messages displayed in your console will help, of course. And if you get truly stuck, you could jump ahead to Chapter 11 to read about debugging your Rails application.

Summary

In this chapter, we had a brief look at using an existing Rails plugin to extend our application's functionality without reinventing the wheel. After installing the plugin and applying the necessary migration, we only had to add a single line of code to make use of the rich functionality provided by the plugin. When we'd ascertained how the plugin worked, we expanded the story submission form to take a comma-separated list of tags, and expanded several views to display the tag data.

Our work is not done yet, though—we still have a bit to learn about debugging our application, running integration tests, and configuring our environment for production; these topics will be the focus of the coming chapters.

Chapter 11

Debugging, Testing, and Benchmarking

Welcome to a chapter devoted to the very topics nobody likes to talk about: errors, bugs, flaws, and exceptions. These topics, however dismaying, are *de rigeur* for any comprehensive, hands-on technical guide—let's not pretend that development is perennially easy and always results in perfect, error-free code!

Once you begin developing applications on your own, the first lesson you'll learn—probably the hard way—is that bugs arise all the time, regardless of how proficient you are as a developer. It's your job to find and fix them, so you'd better be good at it!

Of course, the fun doesn't stop at bugs and errors. It may be that your finished application is not as speedy as you'd like. If this is the case, you'll need tools on hand to profile your application, so you can locate the bottlenecks responsible for slowing things down.

In this chapter, we'll explore all three topics.

Debugging Your Application

When you're building a web application, there are times you know exactly and immediately the cause of a problem and how to fix it. For example, if you notice a broken image on your web site, you'll instantly realize that you've forgotten to upload it, or that the path to the image is incorrect. With other bugs, however, you may not have the merest ghost of an idea what's happened. It's at times like these that knowing how to debug your code comes in *very* handy.

There are various approaches to debugging. The simplest involves printing out the values of some of the variables that your application uses while it runs, to gain a better idea of what's going on at each step in your code. A more complex approach involves complicated but powerful techniques—setting breakpoints, hooking into the running application, and executing code in the context in which you suspect it's misbehaving.

We'll begin our discussion with something simple: we'll look at the `debug` statement that's available for use within `ActionView` templates. Over the course of the next two sections, we'll work to squash a real, live bug in our Shovell application; I've gone against the developer grain and deliberately introduced problems into our existing, perfectly working application code so that we can get our hands dirty with a practical application. As you follow along, try to think of the potential causes for the problems we encounter.

Are you ready? Let's try our hands at a little debugging.

Debugging within Templates

I've deliberately broken our application by changing a specific line of code (obviously, I won't tell you which—that's the whole point of this section!). The result of this code change is that the story page for a newly submitted story throws an exception and no longer displays the story. Figure 11.1 shows how this bug appears in the browser.

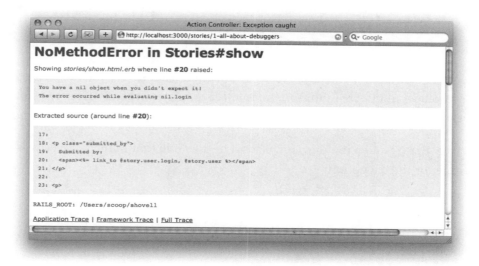

Figure 11.1. A mystery bug causing an error to display when we view a story

To complete this exercise, you'll first need to follow these steps to set up the purposefully buggy version of Shovell:

1. Copy the folder named **shovell-debug-01** from the code archive, and place it alongside your existing **shovell** application folder.

2. Start up your broken version of the Shovell application using the now familiar `ruby script/server` command.

3. Log in and add a new story to Shovell; I've given my story the name `All About Debuggers`.

4. Once you've submitted your new story, point your browser to http://localhost:3000/stories/1-all-about-debuggers.

When your browser has finished loading the page, you should see something very similar to Figure 11.1. Don't worry if the line number doesn't match exactly; as long as the error is the same, everything's working as expected.

Where do we go from here? How should we approach such an error? Let's begin by taking a closer look at the error message:

```
Showing stories/show.html.erb where line #20 raised:
You have a nil object when you didn't expect it!
The error occurred while evaluating nil.login
```

The obvious deduction here is that our application tried to call the `login` method on a `nil` object in our **show.html.erb** template. Understandably, Rails could not perform such an action, as the object `nil` certainly doesn't have a `login` method.

The error message also includes an excerpt of the code that Rails believes was responsible for the exception:

```
Extracted source (around line #20):

17: </p>
18: <p class="submitted_by">
19:   Submitted by:
20:     <span><%= link_to @story.user.login, @story.user %></span>
21: </p>
22: <p>
23:    <%= link_to @story.link, @story.link %>
```

The error message directs us to line 20 of the template, which is where the `link_to` helper tries to assemble a link to the user page associated with the user who originally submitted the story. This line also contains the call to the `login` method that raised the exception. We're calling the `login` method on the `user` object associated with the story that's currently being viewed:

```
20:     <span><%= link_to @story.user.login, @story.user %></span>
```

Rereading the error message, we get the impression that `@story.user` must actually must be `nil`. But what good are impressions in web application programming? No good at all. We need cold, hard facts!

Let's put two tasks on our to-do list:

- Confirm that `@story.user` is indeed `nil`.
- Find out *why* it is `nil`.

To tackle the first item on our list, let's change the parts of the template that raised the exception, in order to inspect the contents of @story.user. To do so, open the **app/views/stories/show.html.erb** template and change the following sections:

```
<p class="submitted_by">
  Submitted by:
  <%= @story.user.class %>
  <span><%# link_to @story.user.login, @story.user %></span>
</p>
```

I made two changes to the template. First, I added a statement to print the class of the @story.user variable to our browser. Then, I used the <%# %> syntax to comment out the link_to statement. If we don't do this, the application will continue to raise an exception when we reload the page, and we won't receive the output of the line we added. This line is now considered a comment, rather than a part of the working code, and as such it won't be executed.

When we reload the page, we see that @story.user is indeed nil, which explains the exception we're seeing. Figure 11.2 shows the results of our work. The first item on our to-do list is done!

Figure 11.2. @story.user visible in the rendered template

To find out *why* @story.user is nil, we'll need to follow the steps that lead to the user assignment when submitting new stories. Before we proceed, though, we should revert the changes that we just made to the **show.html.erb** template. Remove the statement that prints the class name, and make the link_to statement active again:

```
02-show.html.erb (excerpt)
<p class="submitted_by">
  Submitted by:
  <span><%= link_to @story.user.login, @story.user %></span>
</p>
```

When we implemented user authentication in Chapter 8, we started to populate this variable with the currently logged-in user available in the @current_user instance variable. Let's check the contents of this variable using the debug helper.

Add the following statement to the template that's being rendered for the new action—it's located in **app/views/stories/new.html.erb**:

```
                                             03-new.html.erb (excerpt)
<%= error_messages_for 'story' %>
<%= debug @current_user %>
<% form_for :story do |f| %>
  : form HTML...
<% end %>
```

The code I added between the `error_messages_for` and `form_for` statements is the debug helper provided by Rails:

```
<%= debug @current_user %>
```

The debug statement instructs Rails to output a YAML representation of the object that we pass as a parameter. In this case, because we're working from a view template, this output will be sent directly to the browser. Load the story submission form (http://localhost:3000/stories/new) in your browser with this debugging code in place, and you should see something that resembles Figure 11.3.

The output should remind you of our test fixtures—it's formatted in YAML, after all. The debugging content that's shown in addition to our regular template output is a representation of `@current_user` that contains the currently logged-in user.

The debug helper automatically wraps its output in a `pre` element. By default, the contents of a `pre` element are displayed by the browser as preformatted text in a monospace font.

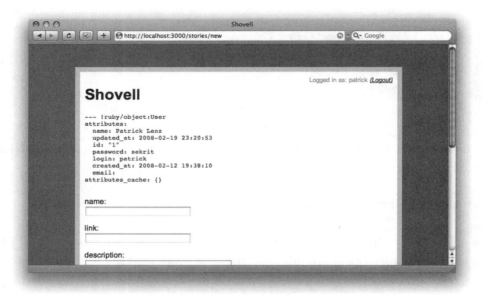

Figure 11.3. Looking at a YAML representation of @story

Within the YAML representation, you tell that what we're being shown is indeed a fully fledged user object which is appropriately stored in the referenced instance variable. (You can even spot the password, but don't tell anyone!) This means that the part of our code that fetches the user from the database via the ID that's stored in the session is indeed working fine.

Now the last place we can check is the place that is actually meant to make use of @current_user and the association between the User and Story classes to instantiate Story object with a prepopulated user_id: The create action of our StoriesController.

At this point, it's time for me to come clean about what causes our application bug: here's what the aforementioned controller action looks like:

```
                              shovell-debug-01/app/controllers/stories_controller.rb (excerpt)
def create
  @story = Story.new params[:story]
  # @story = @current_user.stories.build params[:story]
  : method body…
end
```

As you can see, the line that instantiates the new Story object has been replaced by one that uses the Story class directly instead of going through the association available via the @current_user object. As a result, no user will be assigned to the newly submitted story.

"But wait!" you might be thinking. "Wouldn't a test have caught this problem?"

Of course it would have.

Running the functional tests (using rake test:functionals) with the modified controller action in place, as it is above, would reveal a test failure, as Figure 11.4 shows.

The test that fails is the one that verifies that the submission of a new story stores the current user—obviously, it doesn't. The error message from the test even tells us that it expected a User object with a login of patrick; instead, it got a nil object.

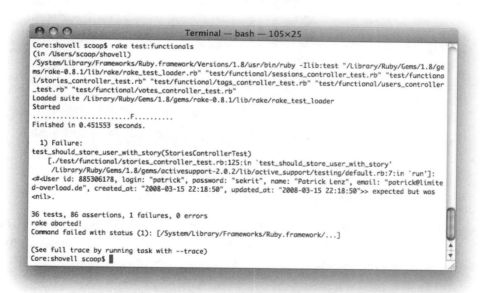

Figure 11.4. Functional tests failing and revealing the broken code

What lesson can we take from this exercise? Well, if you equip your code with proper test coverage from the beginning, you'll have an easy and efficient way to spot an error in your code later.

If you've been following along (you *have* been following along, right?), you'll need to either remove the story with the broken user association, or fix the user association through the console by changing its `user_id` to 1.

Debugging using ruby–debug

In the next example, we'll take a look at another problem that I've secretly introduced to our existing code. If you take a look at Figure 11.5, you'll notice that although we've provided a description for the new story we submitted, it doesn't show up on the final story page.

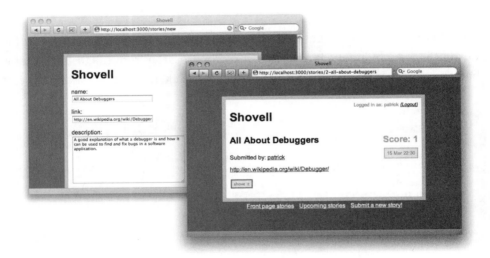

Figure 11.5. Story description missing from a newly submitted story

If you'd like to follow along with this example, copy the **shovell-debug-02 folder** from the code archive, and set it up using the steps we used to set up **shovell-debug-01** (I'll even wait for you!).

"Ha!" I hear you laugh. "I learned in the last section that I just need to run the test suite and it'll tell me what's wrong!"

While that's a great idea, the reality is that when we run the full test suite with `rake test` from the application root, every single test passes, as if nothing were wrong; Figure 11.6 shows the results of running the test suite.

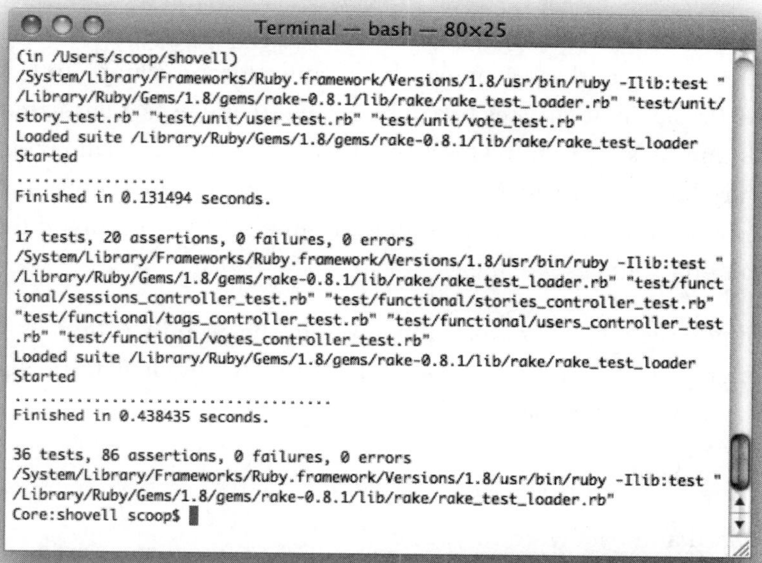

Figure 11.6. Running the test suite without errors

What happened here? We'll need to find out, but while we used statements to investigate specific objects and attributes in the previous example, in this case, we don't really know where to begin.

Meeting ruby–debug

When this book was first published, it included instructions on how to debug a Rails application using the Breakpointer client, which belongs to the third-party Breakpoint library. However, Breakpointer isn't compatible with the latest version of the Ruby programming language. Fortunately, a better alternative has since evolved: Rails core contributor and professional developer, Kent Sibilev has developed a tool that has been adopted as the official Rails 2 debugger with the blessing of the Rails Core Team, ruby-debug.[1]

ruby-debug is a worthy successor to the Breakpoint library, and is compatible with all the most recent releases of the Ruby language interpreter. Better yet, ruby-debug comes packed with many welcome shortcuts and powerful navigation commands

---

[1] http://rubyforge.org/projects/ruby-debug/

that make debugging Ruby scripts and Rails applications a joyful and rewarding experience.

While it would be beyond the scope of this chapter for me to explain how ruby-debug works its magic, it suffices to say that ruby-debug uses a natively compiled Ruby extension that's written in C. The result is that it performs amazingly well, even with very large Ruby scripts. For further reading on ruby-debug and many helpful articles and links to Ruby resources, I thoroughly recommend that you subscribe to Kent Sibilev's weblog.[2]

Unlike Breakpointer, which worked from a simple irb prompt, ruby-debug provides you with a more advanced shell, similar to that provided by GDB, the GNU debugger for the C programming language.[3]

In this shell you can:

- Step forward and backward in your code.

- Execute and skip lines of code, without copying and pasting them from your code editor window.

- List the actual source context at which you've stopped your application.

- Step into irb mode and make use of the same shell that's used by Breakpointer (if you're someone who finds old habits difficult to shake).

Installing ruby-debug

The following steps will configure your system for debugging with ruby-debug.

First of all, we need to install the ruby-debug library. Since it's distributed as a RubyGems package,[4] the installation is as easy as typing the following command (if you're on a Linux or Mac system, don't forget to add the prefix sudo):

```
$ gem install ruby-debug
```

[2] http://www.datanoise.com/ruby-debug/
[3] http://sourceware.org/gdb/
[4] http://rubyforge.org/frs/?group_id=126

The installation process should produce an output that looks similar to the one shown in Figure 11.7.

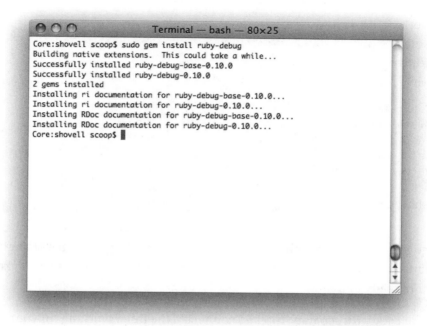

Figure 11.7. Installing ruby-debug

Now that we've successfully installed ruby-debug, we can place some hooks in our Rails application.

Adding ruby-debug to Your Application

Making a Rails application aware of ruby-debug is as simple as adding a command-line switch when starting up the application server (Mongrel or WEBrick) from your Rails application's root folder:

```
$ ruby script/server --debugger
```

At first glance, the console output won't look much different from what we're used to seeing when we run this command. However, keep a close eye on this window as we progress through this exercise.

Debugging an Application

So, let's crack the ruby-debug whip at this problem. First, add the `debugger` keyword to the new action in **app/controllers/stories_controller.rb**, like so:

04-stories_controller.rb *(excerpt)*

```
def create
  @story = @current_user.stories.build params[:story]
  if @story.save
    debugger
    flash[:notice] = 'Story submission succeeded'
    redirect_to stories_path
  else
    render :action => 'new'
  end
end
```

If you go ahead and try to submit a new story now, you'll experience "hanging browser syndrome," which indicates that your `debugger` statement has kicked in and you're ready to debug.

Instead of firing up a separate client to connect to the inner workings of your application, ruby-debug has opened this debugger shell right inside the terminal window in which you've fired up your application server, as Figure 11.8 indicates.

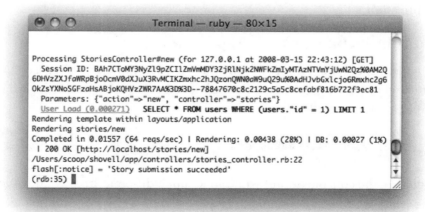

Figure 11.8. The ruby-debug interactive prompt appears within the server console

From this prompt, you can use a variety of commands to explore your application while it's paused mid-execution. Throughout this example, I'll indicate the ruby-debug shell prompt using the characters (rdb), and commands typed at this prompt will appear in bold, as follows:

```
(rdb) list
```

The ruby-debug Commands

What follows is a quick rundown of the most important ruby-debug commands, along with a brief description of what they do. Don't worry too much about remembering every last detail—the built-in help command will list all the available commands for you. You can also type help <commandname> to get help with a specific command.

backtrace

Displays a trace of the execution stack, similar to that which is displayed when your application raises an exception.

info break/break/delete

Displays a list of breakpoints that have been set in your application. break is used to set new breakpoints, and delete is used to remove existing breakpoints, from within the ruby-debug shell.

cont

Leaves the current debugger shell and resumes execution of the application until the next breakpoint is encountered.

irb

Invokes an interactive Ruby interpreter—similar to the shell used by the breakpoint library—at the current point of execution.

list

Displays the code fragments surrounding the current point of execution. (We'll make use of this command in a moment.)

method/method instance

Explores the available class methods and instance methods, respectively.

next/step

Continues execution one step at a time—a huge improvement over the capabilities of the Breakpoint library.

p/pp

Short for "print" and "pretty print" respectively, these commands can be used to evaluate Ruby expressions and display the value of variables to the console.

quit

Exits the debugger. Note that this command will also exit the application server if it was invoked from the command line, as demonstrated above. To just exit the current debugging session, use `cont`.

reload

Reloads the Ruby source files from disk. This command can be useful if you've changed class definitions and want to reload them dynamically without leaving the current debugging session.

For a list of all available commands and options, use the `help` command.

Moving Around in the Shell

Now that we've been dropped into a shell, it's time to make use of some of the commands we just discussed to get to the root of our problem—which, if you remember, is that our stories are displaying without descriptions.

First of all, let's find out exactly which point we're at in the execution of our story submission. This is the job of the `list` command, as shown in Figure 11.9.

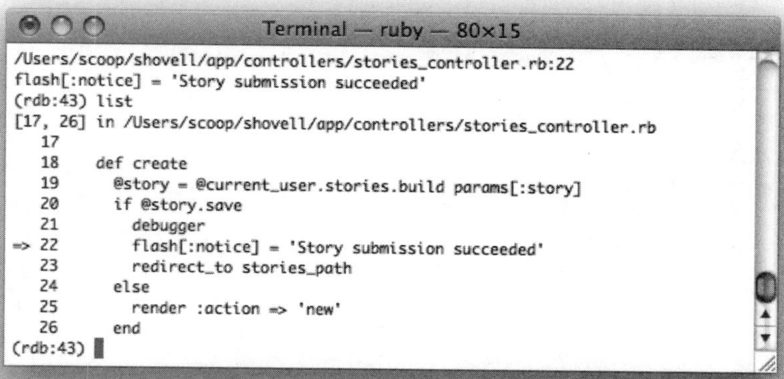

Figure 11.9. The `list` command displaying the current location in a paused application

As you can see, the `list` command displays a source code listing with an arrow pointing to the line of code that's next to be executed.

At this point, we can examine parts of the working environment, such as the `@story` instance variable or the params hash, from the `irb` shell. Type `irb` at the prompt, and let's investigate the `description` attribute of the `Story` object that's stored in our `@story` variable:

```
(rdb) irb
irb> @story.description
=> nil
```

The output that results from our inspection of this variable is shown in Figure 11.10.

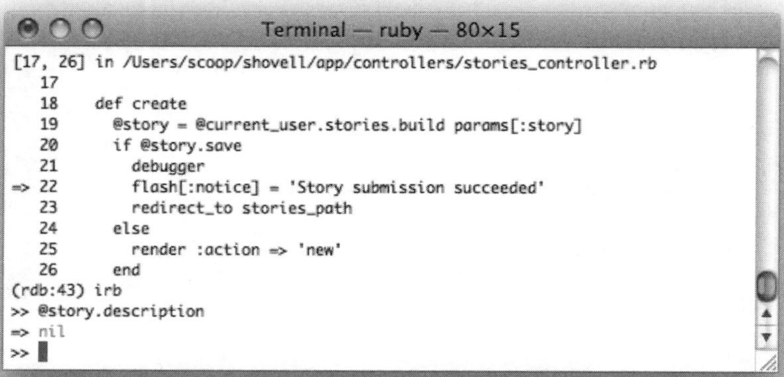

Figure 11.10. Using `irb` from within ruby-debug to inspect a variable

As you can see, even though we've entered a beautifully phrased story description into the form, the relevant `description` attribute of the new `Story` object is `nil`, or empty. But hang on a minute! Isn't there a command in ruby-debug that allows us to evaluate Ruby expressions and inspect variables without going through the hassle of using `irb`?

There sure is! Let's exit the `irb` shell (using the `exit` command) and continue poking around from outside the shell.

Back in the native ruby-debug shell, we can use the `pp` (pretty print) command to display the value of our story's description once it's populated through the web form:

```
(rdb) pp params[:story][:description]
```

If you type this into your ruby-debug shell, you'll see that it also returns nil: an empty object. So, as a last resort, let's take a peek at the full params hash, which contains the values of all the form fields that have been submitted, no matter which scope they reside in:

```
(rdb) pp params
```

The output of this command is shown in Figure 11.11.

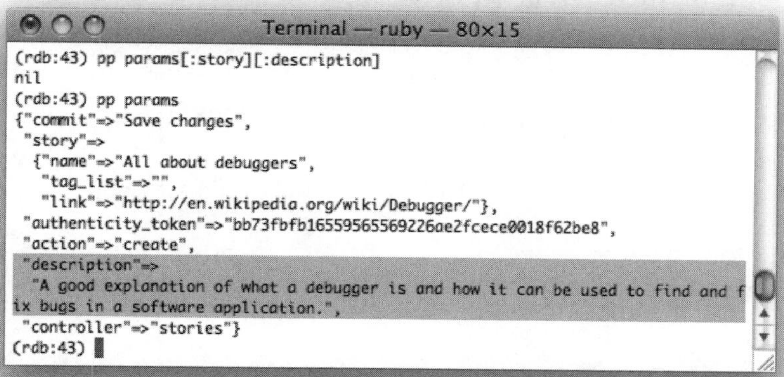

Figure 11.11. Using the pp command to inspect variables

As you can see, pp actually formats the output for us, making it more readable than the output we're used to seeing in the standard irb shell—hence the name "pretty." While this feature isn't exclusive to ruby-debug—the pp library can be loaded outside of ruby-debug as well—it's certainly convenient that ruby-debug makes use of it automatically.

The section I've highlighted in Figure 11.11 is the root of the problem. As you can see, the description is indeed present in the params hash, but it's not part of our story. While the Story's name and link attributes are sitting nicely together in the params[:story] hash, the description is sitting separately in params[:description].

Now, how did that happen? If we take a look at our form template (located in **app/views/stories/new.html.erb**), you'll see that I've "accidentally" used the wrong form field helper:

shovell-debug-02/app/views/stories/new.html.erb

```
# Wrong:
<p>
  description:<br />
  <%= text_area_tag :description %>
</p>
```

Instead of going through the `FormBuilder` object that the `form_for` helper provides and using the `text_area` helper, my code was calling `text_area_tag`. As a result, the description was ending up as a separate entry in the `params` hash, and our story was never receiving its value. This is what it should look like:

```
# Right:
<p>
  description:<br />
  <%= f.text_area :description %>
</p>
```

Discovering All the Fancy Tools in ruby–debug

Admittedly, we haven't had to use any of ruby-debug's more advanced features to debug this example problem. But when we're forced to debug more complicated code, ruby-debug's advanced features become really handy.

Let's first take a look at the stepping methods. To do so, we'll need to move our `debugger` statement into a method which contains a little more code than the previous example so that we can actually step through each line. The best candidate for this task is the `create` action of our `VotesController` found in **shovell-debug-02/app/controllers/votes_controller.rb**; here's a version of this method to which I've added the debugger statement (don't forget to remove it from our `StoriesController`):

05-votes_controller.rb *(excerpt)*

```
def create
  debugger
  @story = Story.find(params[:story_id])
  @story.votes.create(:user => @current_user)
  respond_to do |format|
    format.html { redirect_to @story }
    format.js
  end
end
```

To invoke the debugger in this new location, exit your current debugging session using the `cont` command. This will resurrect your stalled browser and allow you to continue browsing the Shovell application. Now, select a story from the Upcoming Stories queue and click the **shove it** button to engage the debugger once more.

Previously, we saw that the `list` command could be used to give us an indication of where in the source code our application was currently paused. When it's paused, we can use the `next` command to advance to the next line of code. Typing **next** will display the regular Rails log output for the following line, then return you to the ruby-debug prompt. From here, you can once again use `list` to check your new location in the application, as I've done in Figure 11.12.

```
● ○ ○          Terminal — ruby — 80×30
/Users/scoop/shovell/app/controllers/votes_controller.rb:7
@story = Story.find(params[:story_id])
(rdb:48) list
[2, 11] in /Users/scoop/shovell/app/controllers/votes_controller.rb
   2
   3       before_filter :login_required
   4
   5       def create
   6         debugger
=> 7         @story = Story.find(params[:story_id])
   8         @story.votes.create(:user => @current_user)
   9
   10         respond_to do |format|
   11           format.html { redirect_to @story }
(rdb:48) next
/Users/scoop/shovell/app/controllers/votes_controller.rb:8
@story.votes.create(:user => @current_user)
(rdb:48) list
[3, 12] in /Users/scoop/shovell/app/controllers/votes_controller.rb
   3       before_filter :login_required
   4
   5       def create
   6         debugger
   7         @story = Story.find(params[:story_id])
=> 8         @story.votes.create(:user => @current_user)
   9
   10         respond_to do |format|
   11           format.html { redirect_to @story }
   12           format.js
(rdb:48)
```

Figure 11.12. Using next to advance one line of code

To explore the methods provided by an object that you're curious about, you can use the `method` command. When executed with the optional `i` argument it will produce a list of the instance methods provided by the object you pass to it, sorted alphabetically:

```
(rdb) method i @story
```

An example using the @story object is shown in Figure 11.13.

Figure 11.13. Using the method command to display an object's instance methods

The method command can be used to list class methods, too. The following command will produce an alphabetically sorted list of class methods provided by the Story class, as shown in Figure 11.14:

```
(rdb) method Story
```

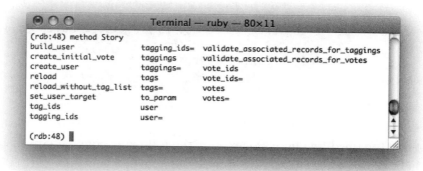

Figure 11.14. Listing the class methods for the Story class

Setting Breakpoints Mid-execution

While using the next command can be useful if you know exactly where to go poking around in your application, it can be less useful in a Rails application. The level at which the stepping occurs can in some circumstances be far too granular, and can result in your stepping through multiple lines of core library files instead of your own code.

To gain a little more control over where the debugger halts execution, you can manually set breakpoints at the locations you desire, without having to edit any files or stop the server. Breakpoints can be set by specifying either:

- a combination of filename and line number
- a class name and the name of an instance method or class method

As a practical example of setting manual breakpoints, we're going to move the halt point from its current location (inside the create action of VotesController) to the RJS template that's rendered when that same action is requested to render a JavaScript response—the result of our Ajax powered voting feature. We'll do all of this without ever opening a text editor, or stepping over every line between the current point of execution and the code of the RJS template.

The RJS template at **app/views/votes/create.js.rjs** reads:

```
                              /shovell-debug-02/app/views/votes/create.js.rjs (excerpt)
page.replace_html 'vote_score', "Score: #{@story.reload.votes.size}"
page[:vote_score].visual_effect :highlight
page[:vote_history].replace_html :partial => 'vote',
    :collection => @story.votes.latest
```

We can set a breakpoint at an arbitrary line of every file. For the sake of illustration, we'll set it at the third line here. So, execute the following command in the ruby-debug shell:

```
(rdb) break app/views/votes/create.js.rjs:3
```

You can now let go of the current breakpoint by typing the `cont` command in the ruby-debug shell. Execution will resume until the third line of the `create.js.rjs` template is executed, at which point the application will pause again.

To verify that we're paused exactly where we expect to be, type **list**. Figure 11.15 confirms that I've stopped my application at the beginning of the `replace_html` call dealing with the `vote_history` element.

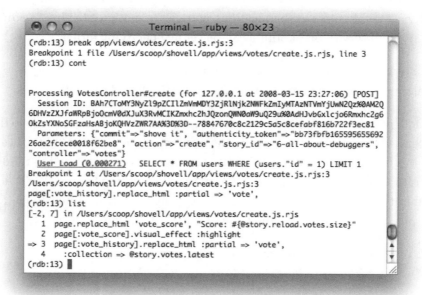

Figure 11.15. Stopping at a breakpoint that was set by specifying class and method name

A list of active breakpoints can always be obtained via the `info break` command.

Reloading Source Code

A Rails application, when run in development mode, automatically adopts all changes that are made to the source files without requiring you to restart the application server. ruby-debug includes a similar feature to avoid stale code passages from being displayed in the stack traces and listings output by the `list` command. To enable this feature type the following at the ruby-debug prompt:

```
(rdb) set autoreload
```

With this setting, ruby-debug will automatically reload your Ruby scripts from disk whenever necessary. There is a large performance cost, however. If this appears to slow down your development progress significantly, you can instead periodically invoke the `reload` command whenever you think you're getting stale representations of your code.

TextMate Integration

Those developers who develop their Rails applications on a Mac using the TextMate editor will be pleased to know that the author of ruby-debug is also a fan of Text-Mate.[5] Fortunately, ruby-debug ships with some nice hooks which you can use to integrate the debugger with the editor.

First of all, you can open the file in which your application is currently paused using the `tmate` command. This eases the round trips between your terminal window and your editor quite a lot.

I'd also recommend that you install the Ruby Debug Bundle for TextMate.[6] This package gives you ultimate control over setting breakpoints from within TextMate itself.

Once you've installed the bundle, you'll need to launch your application a little differently. Here's how to start your application server to take advantage of ruby-debug's remote debugging facilities (the $ indicates that we're typing this command from a terminal window):

---

[5] http://macromates.com/

[6] http://datanoise.com/assets/2007/1/27/Ruby_Debug.zip

```
$ rdebug --server script/server
```

Unlike the local debugging facility that we've been using thus far, you can safely minimize the terminal window in which you started your application server. We need to fire up a separate debugging client from a new terminal window to enable communication between TextMate and ruby-debug. Open a new terminal window and type the following command:

```
$ rdebug -c
```

You should see the "Connected" message shown in Figure 11.16. You'll need to leave this window open and accessible, as this will be the window that displays the ruby-debug console output once a breakpoint is encountered.

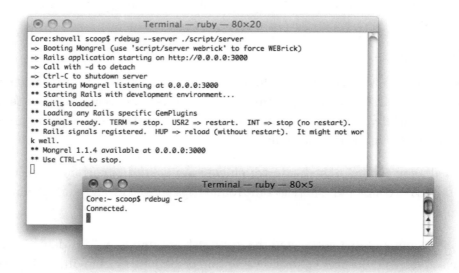

Figure 11.16. Using the TextMate Ruby bundle to connect to ruby-debug's remote debugging tool

As soon as that's accomplished, you can use the bundle's only keyboard shortcut, **Cmd+Shift+B**, to open up a menu of all the available commands, shown in Figure 11.17.

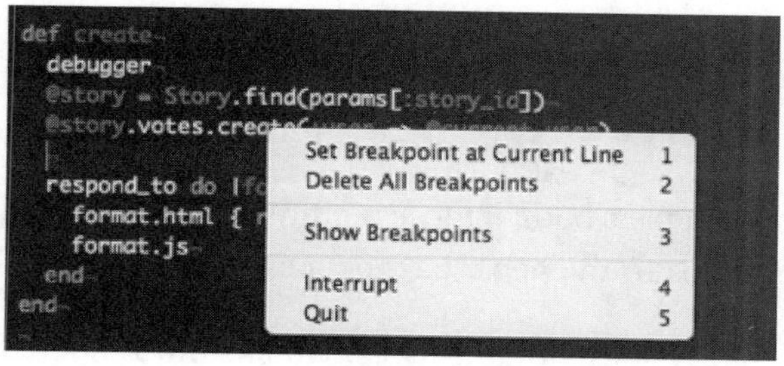

Figure 11.17. Displaying the TextMate Ruby Debug Bundle's menu options

You can use this menu to set a breakpoint at the position of the cursor in the current TextMate editing window. You can also show or delete all the breakpoints that have been set, or even interrupt or quit the debugging shell right from the convenience of your text editing window.

Using the Rails Logging Tool

Rails comes with an internal logging tool for writing custom event-triggered entries to your application's log file.

While logging events can certainly be useful for debugging purposes—especially in a production environment, where you don't want to scare your users with the output of debugging code—event logging can also be of general interest. For instance, log entries can reveal usage patterns for your application, such as the times at which maintenance jobs start and end, or the frequency with which external services are accessed.

We'll use the Rails logging tool to implement an **access log** for our application: a log of the pages requested by users who are logged in. While web server logs allow for comprehensive analysis, they don't contain any details of the specific user that requested the page; this information can be particularly useful, either to the marketing department (for their mysterious purposes), or when you're trying to diagnose a problem that was reported by a particular user.

To implement the access log, we need to:

1. Create a call to the Rails internal logging system.

2. Place this call in an appropriate location in our application code so that it's executed for every page. This location must allow the code to determine whether or not a user is logged in.

We have a location that meets both of these requirements: the `fetch_logged_in_user` before filter, which lives in the `ApplicationController` class.

To document the page requests of our users, we use the `logger` object, which is available at any point in a Rails application. `logger` is used to write a new entry to the environment-specific log file. By default, we operate in the development environment, so the `logger` object will write new entries to the bottom of the log file **log/development.log**.

Like logging functionality in Java or other platforms, Rails logging can deal with a variety of severity levels. When you log an entry, it's up to you to decide how severe the event you're logging really is. The most common severity levels are `debug`, `info`, `warn`, and `error`.

Each of the Rails environments has different default settings for the severity levels that are written to the log file. In the production environment, which we'll cover in depth in Chapter 12, the default is the `info` level; in the development and testing environments, events of every level of severity are logged.

Here's the `fetch_logged_in_user` action in **app/controllers/application.rb** with an added `logger` statement:

```
                                              06-application.rb (excerpt)
def fetch_logged_in_user
  return unless session[:user_id]
  @current_user = User.find_by_id(session[:user_id])
  logger.info "#{@current_user.login} requested
    #{request.request_uri} on #{Time.now}"
end
```

As you can see in the `logger` call above, we're using the `info` severity level to log these statements in all environments, including production. Specifying the severity level is simply a matter of calling the appropriately named instance method of the `logger` object.

The string that's written to the log file is actually a composite of three Ruby statements. First, we're logging the value of the `login` attribute for the current user:

```
logger.info "#{@current_user.login} requested
    #{request.request_uri} on #{Time.now}"
```

Then, we add the URL that the user requested (without the host and port; you'll see an example in a second), which is available from the `request` object that Rails provides:

```
logger.info "#{@current_user.login} requested
    #{request.request_uri} on #{Time.now}"
```

Lastly, the current date and time are added to the string:

```
logger.info "#{@current_user.login} requested
    #{request.request_uri} on #{Time.now}"
```

With these details in place, every page in our application will make an entry to the application log file. Here's a sample session, with all the clutter from the development log removed:

```
patrick requested /stories/new on Sat Mar 15 23:46:50 CEST 2008
patrick requested / on Sat Mar 15 23:47:24 CEST 2008
patrick requested /stories/bin on Sat Mar 15 23:47:26 CEST 2008
patrick requested /stories/1-my-shiny-weblog on Sat Mar 15
    23:47:29 CEST 2008
patrick requested /stories/1-my-shiny-weblog/votes on Sat
    Mar 15 23:47:38 CEST 2008
```

The `fetch_logged_in_user` method exits immediately if the current user hasn't logged in, so our log file displays only log entries from pages requested by users who were logged in when they used Shovell. Of course, you can customize log output to your heart's content, if this format doesn't suit your needs. For example, you could modify it to be more readable for humans, or more easily parsed by a Ruby script.

Overcoming Problems in Debugging

While we've added a considerable number of tests to our application code so far, we certainly haven't covered *every* aspect of the application.

Whenever you fix a problem during the development of your application, take a moment to add a test to your test suite that verifies that the problem has been fixed—just like we did in the last section. Following this approach will ensure that you never receive another bug report for the same problem.

Another approach is to write a test to verify the problem *before* you attempt to fix it. This way, you can be sure that as long as your test fails, the problem still exists. It's entirely up to you to determine your own approach to the task of debugging, but try to not move on from any problem without having added a new test for it to your test suite.

Testing Your Application

The test code that we've written so far for Shovell has dealt mostly with the isolated testing of controller actions and model functionality. To test scenarios which involve multiple controllers and multiple models, Rails also comes with a more thorough testing feature called integration testing.

Integration Tests

An **integration test** verifies the behavior of a number of controllers and models as a user interacts with the application. Integration tests tell a story about a fictitious user of our application—the user's login process, the links that person follows, and the actions that he or she takes.

When to Use an Integration Test

Some example scenarios that are ideally suited to testing via an integration test include:

- A visitor wants to submit a story, so he tries to access the story submission form. He is redirected to the login form because he hasn't logged in yet. After logging in using the login form, he's sent back to the submission form and submits a story.

■ A given user is the fifth user to vote for a particular story. She knows that the threshold for stories to appear on the front page is five votes, so once she's voted, she visits the front page to check that the story she voted for appears there.

■ A user submits a new story with a number of tags. After sending in her submission, she proceeds to the tag page for one of the tags she used on her submission, and checks that the story does indeed appear in the list.

As you can see, integration tests can be quite specific and detailed; writing Ruby test code to match the level of detail specified by the above scenarios is perfectly achievable.

Integration tests are highly dependent upon an application's business logic, so Rails doesn't offer a facility to automatically generate test templates like those we created for unit and functional tests. Let's begin writing our first integration test from scratch.

Creating Our First Integration Test

Returning to our rocking Shovell application, the first step we'll take is create a new file in which to store the test. Then, we'll set up a test case to implement the first of the scenarios that we just discussed: a user who is not logged in tries to submit a story. This scenario will be translated into Ruby code.

Every integration test class is stored in the **shovell/test/integration/** directory. Create a new file named **stories_test.rb** in this directory, and edit it to appear as follows:

07-stories_test.rb

```
require "#{File.dirname(__FILE__)}/../test_helper"

class StoriesTest < ActionController::IntegrationTest

  def test_story_submission_with_login
    get '/stories/new'
    assert_response :redirect
    follow_redirect!
    assert_response :success
    assert_template 'sessions/new'
    post '/session', :login => 'patrick',
        :password => 'sekrit'
    assert_response :redirect
    follow_redirect!
```

```
    assert_response :success
    assert_template 'stories/new'
    post '/stories', :story => {
      :name => 'Submission from Integration Test',
      :link => 'http://test.com/'
    }
    assert_response :redirect
    follow_redirect!
    assert_response :success
    assert_template 'stories/index'
  end

end
```

On the surface, this test resembles a regular functional test: the test performs an action, then asserts that the results of that action are as expected. In this case, the first action is to request a page; the test then verifies that the response code and the template used to render the page are as expected; it then continues with the rest of its actions.

However, instead of the get and post calls being based on specific controllers and their respective actions, page requests in an integration test take standard URLs (from which the domain is omitted). Why? Well, an integration test doesn't test a controller in complete isolation from its environment—it views the application as a whole, so other elements of the application, such as routing and the handover of control from one controller to another, are tested as well. So the first step of our test is to request the new Story form by using the appropriate URL and testing the response:

```
get '/stories/new'
assert_response :redirect
follow_redirect!
```

At this point, the test assumes that a redirect was issued after the last get call, which we're asserting using assert_response. It also assumes that the URL to which a user is redirected—the story submission page—is followed in the test. This introduces another new tidbit in this test code: the follow_redirect! statement.

Additionally, when we're verifying that an action renders the view template we expected, we must specify the path relative to the `app/views/` directory. Remember, we're not testing in isolation, so there's no "default" view directory:

```
assert_template 'sessions/new'
```

Other than that, the test consists of plain old functional test code.

Running an Integration Test

Let's run this test to make sure it passes as we expect. Like unit and functional tests, integration tests are run with a `rake` command:

```
$ rake test:integration
```

Integration tests are executed along with your unit and functional tests when running the `rake test` command. Figure 11.18 shows the outcome of our test.

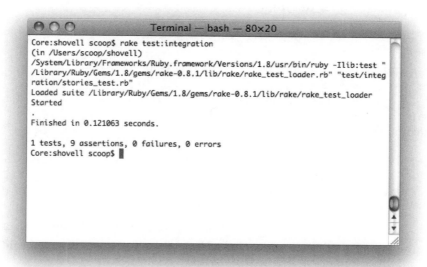

Figure 11.18. Running the integration tests

As you can see from this basic example, an integration test gives you the assurance that your application behaves independently of your functional and unit tests, and that all of your application's components are put through their paces in an automated manner.

Using Breakpoints in a Test

Just as we used ruby-debug to jump into the running application at a predefined point, we can also jump into the application from within a test. This technique can be useful for determining why a test is failing, or for gaining insight into the resources available when we're writing tests.

Using breakpoints in tests is equally as straightforward as using them in regular development mode: place the `debugger` statement at the point at which you want execution to halt. Just like it did in development, when you're using breakpoints in tests, ruby-debug presents you with the Rails console as soon as a `debugger` statement is encountered.

Here's an example of a breakpoint in action. I added a breakpoint to the integration test that we built in the previous section (as a reminder, this integration test is stored in **test/integration/stories_test.rb**):

08-stories_test.rb *(excerpt)*

```
class StoriesTest < ActionController::IntegrationTest

  def test_story_submission_with_login
    get '/stories/new'
    debugger
    : test method body…
  end
end
```

To make use of this in our testing environment, we need to make our test environment "ruby-debug aware." We do so by adding the following line to the **config/environments/test.rb** file:

09-test.rb *(excerpt)*

```
require 'ruby-debug'
```

Let's run our suite of integration tests using the command `rake test:integration`. We're presented with the Rails console immediately after the new session has been created—just after the test requests the submission form for the first time. At this point, we're free to explore the environment; below are examples of the characteristics of our code that can be revealed using the console.

Let's open an `irb` prompt:

```
(rdb) irb
irb>
```

First, let's look at the cookies that have been set for the user that the test is impersonating:

```
irb> cookies
=> {"_shovell_session"=>["session id…"]}
```

At the point at which the debugger appears, the user has not yet logged in, so no `user_id` value has been stored in the user's session:

```
irb> session[:user_id]
=> nil
```

We can log in using the same statement that our test uses a few lines down—the return value shown here is the numeric HTTP response code for a redirect (which happens to be 302). Enter this all on one line:

```
irb> post '/session', :login => 'patrick',
        :password => 'sekrit'
=> 302
```

The user's session now contains a `user_id` value, as this code and Figure 11.19 show:

```
irb> session[:user_id]
=> 885306178
```

```
Core:shovell scoop$ rake test:integration
(in /Users/scoop/shovell)
/System/Library/Frameworks/Ruby.framework/Versions/1.8/usr/bin/ruby -Ilib:test "
/Library/Ruby/Gems/1.8/gems/rake-0.8.1/lib/rake/rake_test_loader.rb" "test/integ
ration/stories_test.rb"
Loaded suite /Library/Ruby/Gems/1.8/gems/rake-0.8.1/lib/rake/rake_test_loader
Started
test/integration/stories_test.rb:9
assert_response :redirect
(rdb:1) irb
>> cookies
=> {"_shovell_session"=>"BAh7Bzo0cmV0dXJuX3RvIhEvc3Rvcmllcy9uZXciCmZsYXNooSUM6J0F
jdGlv%2S0AbkNvbnRyb2xsZXI6OkzsYXNoO0jpGbGFzaEhhcZh7AAY6CkB1c2VkewA%2S3D--8f03bf21
04ad26c3d5e6e4c46277f2be6820b3a3"}
>> session[:user_id]
=> nil
>>       post '/session', :login => 'patrick', :password => 'sekrit'
=> 302
>> session[:user_id]
=> 885306178
>> ▊
```

Figure 11.19. A breakpoint used in a test

Once again, ruby-debug can be a great timesaver if you need to explore the environment surrounding an action in order to write better and more comprehensive tests. Without using breakpoints, exploring the environment would only be possible in a limited fashion—for example, by placing lots of `puts` statements in your tests to output debugging messages and rerunning them countless times to get the information you need. Yes, it is every bit as laborious as it sounds.

With the breakpoints provided by ruby-debug, however, you can interact with your models as your application is being run, without modifying huge chunks of code. This process couldn't be easier, which means the barriers to writing tests are reduced even further.

Revisiting the Rails Console

We've used the `console` script frequently in previous chapters, mainly to explore features as they were being introduced.

The console can also be used to play with your application in **headless mode**, in which you can interact with your application from the console just as a browser would interact with it. In conjunction with breakpoints in tests, which we talked about in the last section, this technique can be a good way to play around with your application in anticipation of creating a new integration test once you've worked out exactly what you want to do.

When integration tests were introduced to Rails, with it came a new object that's available by default in the `console` script: the `app` object. This object can be thought of as providing you access to an empty integration test. You're able to `get` and `post` to URLs, you have access to the session and cookies containers, routing helpers, and so on—just like a regular integration test.

Let's have a go at using the `app` object from the `console` script. You should recognize a lot of the methods that we're using here from the integration test that we built earlier in this chapter.

Go ahead and open the Rails console (`$ ruby script/console`). Initially, we're interested to know what kind of object `app` really is:

```
>> app.class
=> ActionController::Integration::Session
```

Next, let's fetch the front page of our application using the `get` action:

```
>> app.get '/'
=> 200
```

The return value is the HTTP response code that indicates a successful page request. We've been using the `:success` symbol in its place in most of our tests until now.

Next, we'll use the `assigns` action to check the instance variable assignments that are made in the action we requested. In this case, we're looking at the number of elements in the `@stories` array:

```
>> app.assigns(:stories).size
=> 1
```

If we try to fetch the story submission form, we receive a redirect (HTTP code 302), as we're not yet logged in:

```
>> app.get '/stories/new'
=> 302
```

When we receive the redirect, we can look at the URL that the redirect is pointing to by use of the following construct:

```
>> app.response.redirect_url
=> "http://www.example.com/session/new"
```

It's easy to follow the redirect that was just issued using the `follow_redirect!` method:

```
>> app.follow_redirect!
=> 200
```

We can also use the `post` method to log in with a username and password, and follow the resulting redirect. However, Rails imposes security-related restrictions on who can talk to your application, even in the development environment. For that reason we need to explicitly switch off a feature called "request forgery protection," in order to allow the statement that follows to succeed:[7]

```
>> ApplicationController.allow_forgery_protection = false
=> false
```

Now it's time to log ourselves in:

```
>> app.post '/session', :login => 'patrick',
       :password => 'sekrit'
=> 302
>> app.follow_redirect!
=> 200
```

Note that we didn't look at the **app.response.redirect_url** before we accepted the redirection. Here's how you can check the last URL you requested:

```
>> app.request.request_uri
=> "/stories/new"
```

As it is, after all, an integration test, headless mode also provides you with access to the `session` and `cookies` variables:

---

[7] See http://en.wikipedia.org/wiki/Cross-site_request_forgery for more information about this security issue.

```
>> app.cookies
=> {"_shovell_session"=>"session id…"}
>> app.session[:user_id]
=> 1
```

Figure 11.20 shows a sample session in which the console is used in headless mode.

Figure 11.20. The console in headless mode

As you can see, headless mode is a great tool for checking out the possible ways in which you might develop an integration test. Once you're satisfied with your findings, you can open up your text editor and transform your console results into an automated test. Easy!

Benchmarking Your Application

As software developers, it's our job to know which part of our application is doing what. When an error arises, we can jump right in and fix it. However, knowing *how long* each part of our application is taking to perform its job is a completely different story.

Benchmarking, in software terms, is the process of measuring an application's performance, and taking steps to improve it based on that initial measurement. The benchmarking process usually involves **profiling** the application—monitoring it to determine where bottlenecks are occurring—before any changes are made to improve the application's performance.

While I won't cover the profiling and benchmarking of a Rails application in every gory detail (it's a topic to which an entire book could easily be devoted), I'll give you an introduction to the tools that are available for the job. Keep in mind that your first Rails application is unlikely to have performance problems in its early stages—the objective with your first application (or at least the first *version* of your application) should be to get the functionality right the first time; *then* you can worry about making it fast.

Taking Benchmarks from Log Files

When it's running in development and testing modes, Rails provides a variety of benchmarking information in its log files, as we saw briefly in the section called "Revisiting the Logs" in Chapter 6. For each request that's served by the application, Rails notes all of the templates rendered, database queries performed, and the total time taken to serve the request.

Let's examine a sample request to understand what each of the log entries means. This example deals with a request for the Shovell homepage:

```
Processing StoriesController#index (for 127.0.0.1 at 2008-03-16
01:04:42) [GET]
```

This line represents the start of the block of logging for a single page request. It includes:

- the names of the controller and action

- the IP address of the client requesting the page (127.0.0.1 being the equivalent of localhost)

- the time the request came in

■ the request method that was used (GET in this case)

Rails also logs the session ID of the request, as well as the parameters that the user's browser provided with the request:

```
Session ID: session id…
Parameters: {"action"=>"index", "controller"=>"stories"}
```

Each of the next three entries in our sample log file corresponds to a database query issued by the application. Each entry lists the time (in seconds) that the application took to execute the query:

```
Story Load (0.000660)   SELECT * FROM stories WHERE (votes_count >=
5) ORDER BY id DESC
Tag Load (0.000219) SELECT tags.* FROM tags INNER JOIN taggings ON
tags.id = taggings.tag_id WHERE ((taggings.taggable_type = 'Story')
AND (taggings.taggable_id = 6))
User Load (0.000244) SELECT * FROM users WHERE (users."id" = 1)
LIMIT 1
```

In the first of these log entries, Rails has asked the database for stories to display on the front page. The second query represents a request made by the acts_as_taggable_on_steroids plugin, to retrieve all tags for a particular story. The final line is a simple query fetching a particular User.

Each of the following lines corresponds to a rendered template; when Rails renders a layout template, it explicitly says so by logging Rendering within:

```
Rendering template within layouts/application
Rendering stories/index
```

A summary entry appears at the end of each page request:

```
Completed in 0.02248 (44 reqs/sec) | Rendering: 0.01632 (72%) |
    DB: 0.00091 (4%) | 200 OK [http://www.example.com/]
```

This summary contains totals for the time spent by each of the areas of the application that were responsible for serving the request. The total time taken to serve the request is mentioned along with the *potential* number of requests to this particular action that your application might be able to handle per second:

```
Completed in 0.02248 (44 reqs/sec) | Rendering: 0.01632 (72%) |
    DB: 0.00091 (4%) | 200 OK [http://www.example.com/]
```

This value should be taken with a grain of salt, however—in reality, calculating an accurate estimate of the number of requests that an application can handle in parallel involves more than simply dividing one second by the time it takes to serve a single request.

Additionally, Rails tells us the amount of time that was spent rendering templates and talking to the database—these figures are listed both in seconds, and as percentages of the total time that was spent completing the task:

```
Completed in 0.02248 (44 reqs/sec) | Rendering: 0.01632 (72%) |
    DB: 0.00091 (4%) | 200 OK [http://www.example.com/]
```

You don't need to be a mathematician to figure out that a whopping 24% is missing from these numbers! One of the reasons for this difference is that serving the request took only a couple of milliseconds. These numbers come from my version of Shovell, which is quite a small application, and the benchmark calculation gets a little wacky when it calculates time information using such small numbers. In the meantime, Figure 11.21 shows the log file from a complete page request.

For all the comfort and speed that Rails provides developers, it does have its drawbacks. The framework certainly requires a large amount of CPU time in order to do its job of making your life easy, which is another explanation for the missing milliseconds in the timing calculation above. However, the overhead used by the framework won't necessarily increase greatly as your code becomes more complicated, so with a larger application, these numbers become more accurate.

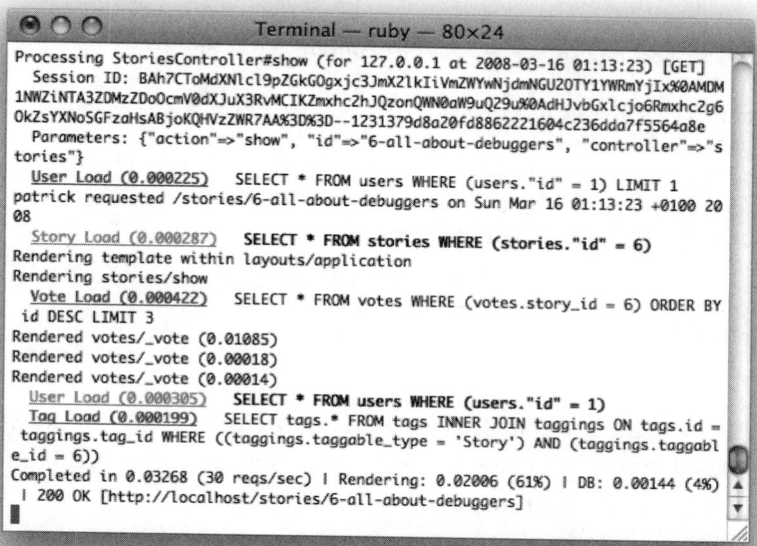

Figure 11.21. Benchmarking information in the log file

In any case, it's important to take a look at your log files every now and then to get an idea of your application's performance. As I said, take these numbers with a grain of salt—learn to interpret them by changing your code and comparing the new numbers with previous incarnations of the code. This will help you develop a feel for how your changes affect the speed of your application. You should not, however, use them as absolute measures.

Manual Benchmarking

While the default information presented by the Rails log files is great for providing an overview of how long a certain action takes, the log files can't provide timing information for a specific group of code statements. For this purpose, Rails provides the benchmark class method, which you can wrap around any block of code that you'd like to benchmark.

As an example, let's add benchmarking information for the story fetcher implemented in the fetch_stories method of our StoriesController, which is located in **app/controllers/stories_controller.rb**:

```
                                              10-stories_controller.rb (excerpt)

class StoriesController < ApplicationController
  ⋮ class methods…
  def fetch_stories(conditions)
    self.class.benchmark('Fetching stories') do
      @stories = Story.find :all,
        :order => 'id DESC',
        :conditions => conditions
    end
  end
end
```

As you can see, the `benchmark` class method simply wraps around the `Story.find` statement. As `benchmark` is a class method, rather than an instance method, we have to call it with a prefix of `self.class`:

```
self.class.benchmark('Fetching stories') do
  ⋮ code being benchmarked…
end
```

The textual argument provided to `benchmark` is the text that Rails writes to the log file, along with the timing information:

```
self.class.benchmark('Fetching stories') do
  ⋮ code being benchmarked…
end
```

When you request Shovell's front page or upcoming stories queue now (both pages make use of the `fetch_stories` method we just modified), you should find that the corresponding benchmark entries are added to the log file at **log/development.log**. The sample log file in Figure 11.22 shows how this looks—without all the other log clutter, of course.

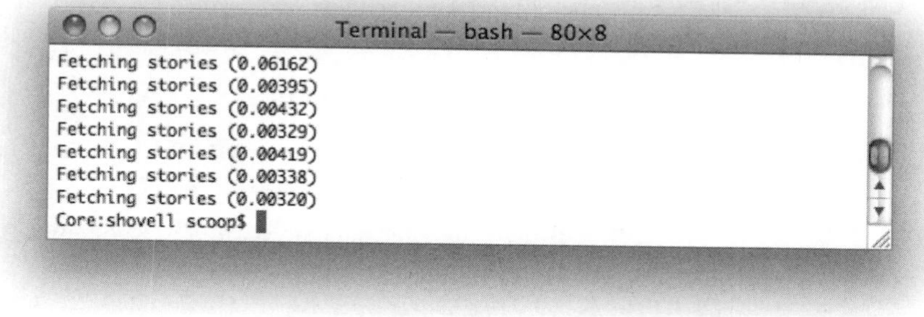

Figure 11.22. The output from manual benchmarking

Using manual benchmarks in this way can give you a feel for the amount of time required to execute certain parts of your code. Additionally, benchmark logs events with a severity of debug by default—as production mode does not log statements that have a severity of debug, benchmark statements in your code will not be calculated and won't slow your production application down.

Summary

In this chapter, we've dealt with some of the less glamorous—but very helpful—aspects of software development. We used debug statements to inspect certain objects in our views, we used the log files written by Rails to document certain occurrences in Shovell, and we looked at how the ruby-debug tool can be used to set breakpoints and explore our application at run-time.

We also covered the topic of integration tests—broad, scenario-based tests that have the ability to go beyond the isolated testing of models and controllers.

Finally, we talked briefly about the benchmarks that Rails provides by default, and explored a manual approach to benchmarking a specific group of statements.

In the next and final chapter, we'll take Shovell into production mode and discuss the options available for deploying a Rails application for the whole world to use!

12

Deployment and Production Use

When Rails applications start to fledge, you, as their guardian, have to take extra care to make sure they can fly ... although, admittedly, the term "roll" would be a little more correct in the Rails context!

In this final chapter, we'll review the variety of components involved in the process of deploying a Rails application to a production system. Following that, we'll look at fine-tuning an application's deployment so that it's able to cope with a moderate amount of traffic.

The Implications of "Production"

Back in Chapter 4, when we discussed the different environments Rails provides for each stage of an application's life cycle, we barely scratched the surface of what it means to flip the switch between the development and production environments.

In a nutshell, moving to the production environment results in four major changes to the way in which our application is run:

The Ruby classes that make up your application are no longer reloaded *on each request*.

Ruby's reloading of each class on each request is a nice feature of the development environment, because it allows you to make rapid changes to your application code and see the effects immediately. However, when your application's in production mode, the primary requirement is that it's *fast*, which isn't a goal that can be accomplished by reloading Ruby classes over and over again. To gain the effects of any changes you make to code while the application's in production mode, you'll need to restart the application.

The production environment doesn't log every single database communication that's executed by your application.

This restriction was put in place for performance reasons, and to save you from buying new hard drives just to store your log files. In the production environment, Rails logs items with a severity level of info or higher by default (skipping those with a severity of debug). While it may make sense to skip items with a severity of info later on, when our application first enters production we're still at a point at which the inner workings of our application are of interest, so we'll leave the default level of reporting unchanged for now.

Your application's users receive short, helpful error messages; they're not presented with the stack trace.

Obviously, the beautifully detailed stack trace that you investigate when you find an error in your code is not something you want users of your application to see. Fear not! Rails never throws stack traces at users while it's in production mode. Instead, you can use the Exception Notification plugin to dispatch an email to the administrators of the system to notify them of a potential problem in the code.[1] The email includes the same detailed stack trace you'd see in your browser if you were still in development, as Figure 12.1 illustrates. With the error notification taken care of, you can simply use a generic error page within your application to let users know that an error has occurred and the administrators have been notified.

---

[1] http://dev.rubyonrails.org/browser/plugins/exception_notification

```
Subject:  [ERROR] blog_posts#show (ActionView::TemplateError) "can't clone NilClass"
Date:  March 13, 2008 3:54:18 PM GMT+01:00

A ActionView::TemplateError occurred in blog_posts#show:

can't clone NilClass
On line #13 of app/views/layouts/application.rhtml
```

Figure 12.1. An example email resulting from the Exception Notification plugin

Caching is available for pages, actions, and page fragments.

To improve the performance of your application, you can cache its pages, actions, and even fragments of pages. This means that the fully rendered page (or fragment) is written to the file system as well as being displayed in the user's browser. The next request that's responded to by this page, action, or fragment is served without the data that it contains needing to be recalculated. Rails's caching features are especially useful in situations in which your pages don't contain user-specific content, and everyone sees the same pages.

In the following sections, we'll talk about the server software components that are well suited for production use and take a look at what we can do to make Shovell happy and healthy in a production environment.

Choosing a Production Environment

Common production setups comprise two parts: a "front-end" web server that's best suited to serving static content (such as CSS files, JavaScript, and images), and a separate "back-end" component that handles the dynamic pages generated by the Rails application. This process is depicted in Figure 12.2.

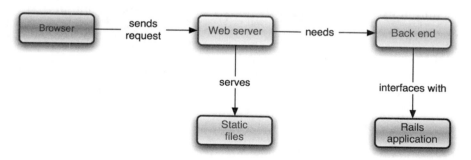

Figure 12.2. Architecture of a Rails application

I used those quotes around the terms *front-end* and *back-end* because on the Web these terms usually refer to the client and server respectively. However, in this case we're talking about two members of a web server team: the front-end server performs load balancing as well as serving static files, and the back-end component serves dynamic pages. Note that the back-end component is a persistent Ruby interpreter process—it never quits. As soon as the interpreter finishes servicing one request, it waits for the next.

The differences in the available back-end components can be described in terms of the protocol (or dialect) that the front-end web server has to speak in order to communicate with the Ruby process. We'll explore the back-end options in a moment, after we consider the available web servers.

Web Server Options

Back in the days when the World Wide Web wasn't dynamic at all—when everyone edited their web pages with a text editor and uploaded HTML files to a server connected to the Internet—web server software didn't have much else to do besides serving static content. For this reason, web servers are still very good at performing that task today.

Some things have changed, though. For instance, it's now much easier to make web servers communicate with the components that deliver dynamically generated pages, such as those created by web applications written in Perl, PHP, Python, and Ruby.

Let's take a look at three web server software packages that are available to use with Rails applications under the terms of various free software licenses.[2] Several commercial web servers which support Rails applications are also available, but for the sake of simplicity and relevance, we'll only look at open source options.

Apache

With more than 50% market share, the free Apache web server written and maintained by the Apache Software Foundation is certainly the de facto standard on the web server software market.[3] Apache is a good all-purpose, cross-platform web

---

[2] When we say "free software," we're referring to free software as defined by the Free Software Foundation [http://www.fsf.org/licensing/essays/free-sw.html].

[3] http://httpd.apache.org/

server. It's used by most web hosting providers, and therefore will be the server we'll use in the hands-on part of this chapter.

Apache has many strengths, one of which is the huge number of extensions that are available to expand its feature set. It also has a robust interface for back-end services, a useful URL rewriter, and extensive logging capabilities. It's available as free software under the Apache license.[4]

lighttpd

Often abbreviated to "lighty" since it's such a tongue twister, lighttpd is one of the more recent arrivals in the ever-expanding web server software market.[5] It was first created in 2003 by Jan Kneschke as a proof-of-concept that web servers could be secure and fast while treating kindly the resources of the hosting server. Since then, lighttpd has become a very popular choice among Rails developers who run it on their own servers; hosting companies, on the other hand, haven't yet embraced it for use in shared hosting environments.

lighttpd is free software under the BSD (Berkeley Software Distribution) license.[6] Apart from needing very little memory and CPU to do its job, lighttpd has excellent support for SSL, a flexible configuration file, and virtual-hosting capabilities.

nginx

Another relatively new player in this market is nginx (pronounced "engine x"), a high-performance HTTP and proxy server that was originally developed by Igor Sysoev to power several high-traffic sites in Russia.[7] Due to the fact that it only recently appeared on the radar outside of Russia, English documentation is sparse at the time of writing. However, many translation efforts have commenced.

Recent performance evaluations have revealed that nginx is indeed the leader of the pack in terms of raw speed, with Apache and lighttpd scoring second and third place, respectively. However, due to the lack of English documentation, many developers and hosting companies may not consider a switch to nginx for some time to come.

---

[4] http://www.apache.org/licenses/
[5] http://www.lighttpd.net/
[6] http://www.opensource.org/licenses/bsd-license.php
[7] http://nginx.net/

Apart from outstanding performance, nginx also offers excellent proxy and caching capabilities, SSL support, and flexible configuration options. nginx is also available under the BSD license.

Back-end Options

As we've already discussed, regular web servers excel at serving static files. However, in order to interface with our Rails application and handle dynamically generated pages, they need a server software component that's specifically designed for the task. This may be a software module that's shipped with the web server, or it may be one that's available as a third-party extension. Here's a list of the back-end component options that are currently available for Rails applications.

The mod_ruby Extension

Exclusively available for use on the Apache web server, the mod_ruby extension provides an embedded Ruby interpreter that executes Ruby (and Rails) scripts, which, in turn, serve dynamically generated content to the outside world.[8]

mod_ruby has never really been used as a production-quality back end for Rails applications because its architecture entails some major drawbacks which prevent multiple Rails applications from being run on the same server. This makes it an especially poor choice for shared hosting environments.

The SCGI Protocol

An abbreviation for Simple Common Gateway Interface, the SCGI protocol is commonly used to serve dynamic content provided by Python web applications.[9] It can also be used to serve content provided by Rails applications, but hasn't been widely adopted for this purpose.

Implementations of SCGI are available as a third-party extension for the Apache web server and support for the protocol is built into the lighttpd web server.

---

[8] http://www.modruby.net/
[9] http://python.ca/nas/scgi/

The FastCGI Protocol

When Rails became popular, FastCGI was the de facto standard for deploying Rails applications.[10] FastCGI, a variation of the Common Gateway Interface (CGI), operates by starting one or more persistent processes of the language interpreter (in our case, Ruby) when the application in question is started up. The web server then communicates with these processes through the FastCGI protocol to serve dynamic pages.

FastCGI is often used when the machine the web server is running on is separate from the machines running the application. The FastCGI processes are started on the application servers, and the web server is instructed to connect to those processes using TCP/IP.

Support for FastCGI is provided by third-party extensions for the Apache web server and is built into the lighttpd and nginx web servers, among others. Due to limitations that are present in the Apache extensions, FastCGI and Apache don't get along very well at times. Despite its excellent performance, FastCGI has been the victim of a number of stability problems, and is definitely a configuration headache.

Mongrel

One back-end component that uses a different approach to interface with the web server is Mongrel, created by Zed A. Shaw.[11] Unlike options such as SCGI and FastCGI, both of which use a rather complex communication protocol, Mongrel uses plain HTTP.

Due to Mongrel's pure-HTTP nature, it has replaced WEBrick as the default development server for Rails. While its performance isn't quite on par with that of FastCGI, it definitely outperforms WEBrick, boasts production-level robustness, and is *really* easy to use for Rails deployment.

Mongrel is compatible with every web server that's equipped with a proxy module to pass incoming HTTP requests on to other services. Apache, lighttpd, and nginx all have this capability.

---

[10] http://www.fastcgi.com/
[11] http://mongrel.rubyforge.org/

Because Mongrel already comes installed with Rails on most platforms, is so easy to use, and doesn't require complex protocols to interface with your preferred web server, it's an ideal choice for the hands-on part of this chapter. So, let's learn how to deploy Shovell using Apache and Mongrel!

Deploying Shovell

As you've seen, Rails applications can be deployed using various combinations of web servers and back-end services. Since most hosting providers use the Apache web server, and Mongrel is the simplest solution with decent performance (it definitely has the best speed to complexity ratio, bar none), we'll use this combination to deploy the Shovell application.

The hands-on part of this chapter will consist of a process that contains many steps. Our first task will be to configure Apache as a proxy to Mongrel to serve our application in production mode. This setup will be sufficient to handle a moderate amount of traffic to our application.

Moving to the Production System

The time has come to leave our development machine and switch to the machine that will provide a home to Shovell in production mode. Don't worry if you haven't found a hosting provider to host your Rails applications yet—you can just keep this section in mind for later reference.

Due to the fact that there are countless variations of server setups, we'll have to assume a few basics for the sake of this walk-through introduction:

- The operating system of the server is Linux.

- You either have superuser privileges (root) on the system, or know someone who does, even if that's your hosting provider's technical support team.

- Ruby and Rails have been installed on the server using a similar process to that outlined in the Linux section of the section called "Installing on Linux" in Chapter 2.

- Mongrel has been installed using the `gem install mongrel` command—see the note below.

- SQLite or MySQL has been installed and your databases (at least, the one configured for the production environment in **config/database.yml**) have been created.

- Apache Version 2.2 is installed and running.[12]

- The Apache configuration is stored in the directory /etc/httpd/ (if it's located elsewhere, you'll need to adapt the pathnames I mention).

- The Apache installation has the following extension modules available and enabled: mod_proxy, mod_proxy_balancer, mod_deflate, and mod_rewrite.

- You have access to the production system through a remote shell, preferably Secure Shell (SSH).

- You have the ability to upload files to the production system through either FTP or SSH.

- You have an available Internet domain name or a subdomain on which to host your application.[13]

Installing Mongrel

If you're a Windows or Mac OS X 10.5 user, you've been using Mongrel since the beginning this book, and if you're a Linux or MAC OS X 10.4 user you may have installed it using the RubyGems system as we mentioned previously in the section called "Starting Our Application" in Chapter 2.

However, it will also need to be installed on the production system if it's not already available. Execute the following command to install the Mongrel gem. It downloads the gem from the RubyForge servers, then installs it on your system along with its dependencies:

```
$ sudo gem install mongrel
```

If you don't have the required privileges to carry this out, you may need to seek help from the technical support department of your hosting provider.

---

[12] Versions 1.3 and 2.0 should work to a certain extent. However, the proxy_balance extension is only available in Version 2.2. Even the Apache Foundation recommends Version 2.2 as the *best you can get*, so why bother with anything else?

[13] Assuming domain.com is your domain name, shovell.domain.com would be a subdomain.

Okay, now that we have our assumptions clear, we can begin.

As we're starting out with a totally empty database on the production system, we need to recreate the database structure we've established on our development machine; you'll find it in the file **db/schema.rb**. Just to be sure that this file is up to date, run the following `rake` task on your development machine before you start to copy the files:

```
$ rake db:schema:dump
```

Assuming you see no errors when executing this command, your **schema.rb** file should now be up to date.

At this point, we need to transfer our application code to the production system. As I mentioned, we can achieve this task in a variety of ways. I'll use the file transfer capabilities provided by the SSH protocol to transfer the files; another common option involves the use of FTP.

In any case, you need to copy the full directory structure that houses Shovell to the production system (minus the files from the **log** and **tmp** subdirectories, which contain output from the application in development mode; that output isn't required to run the application in production mode). Where you place the application's directory structure doesn't really matter, either. I've put mine into the subdirectory **rails** in my user account's home directory, as depicted in Figure 12.3, so the full path to my application is **/home/scoop/rails/shovell**.

Once we've finished transferring the application code, we need to set up the database structure on the production system. Again, this can be accomplished with a `rake` task. However, this time, we need to prepare the production part of the environment, instead of the development and test parts.

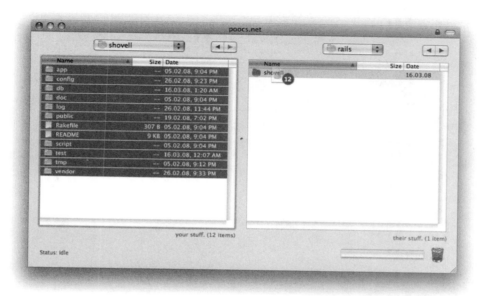

Figure 12.3. Transferring Shovell to the production system

All Rails scripts (in the **script** subdirectory) and all available `rake` tasks in your application will check whether an environment has been specified; if it hasn't, these scripts and tasks will assume you're using the `development` environment. To identify explicitly the environment you'd like to work in, you must declare the `RAILS_ENV` environment variable, as illustrated in Figure 12.4.

Let's set up the database structure in the production database (which is `db/production.sqlite3`, as configured in **config/database.yml**). Log into the production system through a remote shell like SSH, change directory to the application root (**/home/scoop/rails/shovell**, in my case), and execute the following command:

```
$ rake db:schema:load RAILS_ENV=production
```

```
○ ○ ○          scoop@flux: /home/scoop — ssh — 80×22
scoop@flux:~/rails/shovell$ rake db:schema:load RAILS_ENV=production
(in /home/scoop/rails/shovell)
-- create_table("stories", {:force=>true})
   -> 0.7262s
-- create_table("taggings", {:force=>true})
   -> 1.0228s
-- add_index("taggings", ["taggable_id", "taggable_type"], {:name=>"index_taggin
gs_on_taggable_id_and_taggable_type"})
   -> 0.0023s
-- add_index("taggings", ["tag_id"], {:name=>"index_taggings_on_tag_id"})
   -> 0.0925s
-- create_table("tags", {:force=>true})
   -> 0.0030s
-- create_table("users", {:force=>true})
   -> 0.0036s
-- create_table("votes", {:force=>true})
   -> 0.0724s
-- initialize_schema_information()
   -> 0.0036s
-- columns("schema_info")
   -> 0.0149s
scoop@flux:~/rails/shovell$ █
```

Figure 12.4. Creating the database structure

Why Not Use `rake db:migrate`?

But, I hear you cry, why aren't we using the `rake db:migrate` command that
we used during development to bring our database up to date? The simple reason
is that once the total number of migrations becomes sizeable, iterating over every
one to initially deploy an application can take quite a long time!

By specifying `RAILS_ENV=production` on the `rake` command line, we're instructing
`rake` to operate on the production database (and environment) instead of the development equivalents.

This environment variable is an application-wide, but slightly tedious, method of
specifying the desired environment. A few of the common Rails commands—for
example, `ruby script/console`—also take the environment name as a direct argument. Let's use the Rails console now to create an initial user for the production
version of Shovell:

```
$ ruby script/console production
```

The message `Loading production environment`, which displays when we execute this command, indicates that the console session is connecting to the production database. Next, let's create a new `User` object; the results of this command are shown in Figure 12.5:

```
>> User.create :login => 'patrick', :password => 'sekrit'
=> #<User id: 1, login: "patrick", password: "sekrit", …>
```

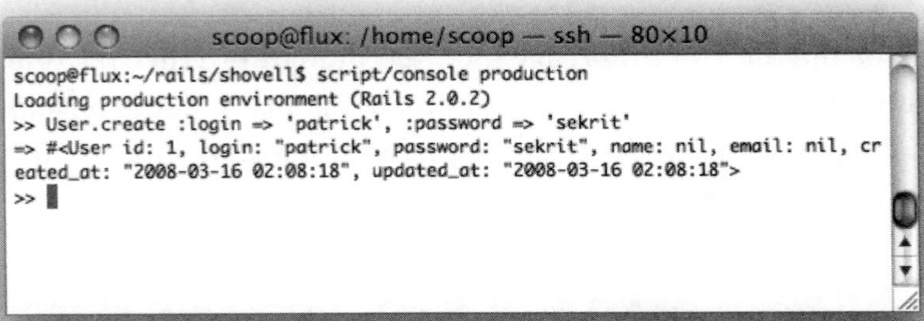

Figure 12.5. Creating a first production user

Armed with a ready-made production database, we can now launch Mongrel similarly to the way we have been launching it on our development machine. This command will ensure that both Mongrel and the application behind it are working on the production system. Execute the following command (if you're still in the Rails console, exit that first with the `exit` command):

```
$ script/server -e production
```

Yes, the `-e` argument is yet another syntax for specifying the environment we want to be in!

Mongrel will fire up and wait for requests on port 3000, just as it did on the development machine. However, our application is now running in the production environment, and will be quite a bit faster than it was in the development environment.

Depending on the firewall configurations employed by your hosting provider, you may or may not be able to connect to this port from the Internet. On a shared host, you may not even be able to *start* Mongrel on port 3000—it may be reserved for another user. In this case, you'll need to ask your web host's technical support team for a port number on which you can run your Rails application, then pass this port number to Mongrel using the -p argument:

```
$ script/server -e production -p 3333
```

Let's see how your application looks in production mode. Fire up a web browser and open http://*hostname*:3000/, where *hostname* is the fully qualified domain name of the production system. In my case, I'll connect to http://poocs.net:3000/.

You should see the Shovell front page pictured in Figure 12.6. No stories are listed as yet, because we left them in the development database on the development machine. However, you should be able to log in with the credentials of the user that you just created using the console. Excellent!

Figure 12.6. Shovell served by Mongrel

Setting up Apache

Although Shovell is now being served successfully by a single Mongrel process in production mode, a scenario in which our users have to type in an explicit port number in order to access the Shovell application is far from ideal.

Our next goal is therefore to set up Apache as a web server for Mongrel, so that Apache can pass incoming requests to the Mongrel process—technically referred to as a **proxy through**. This setup makes it possible to run multiple Rails applications (whether they be our own applications, or those of other users on the same system) on a single IP address: based on the configuration we give it, Apache decides which requests to forward to each application.

To set this up, we'll add the following configuration directives to the end of our Apache configuration file, **/etc/httpd/httpd.conf**:

```
<VirtualHost *:80>
    ServerName shovell.poocs.net
    ProxyRequests Off
    <Proxy *>
        Order deny,allow
        Allow from all
    </Proxy>
    ProxyPass / http://localhost:3000/
    ProxyPassReverse / http://localhost:3000/
</VirtualHost>
```

This is the simplest of all possible proxy configurations. Assuming that we're using the shovell subdomain of poocs.net, we instruct Apache to forward *every* request that comes in directly to the Mongrel process running on port 3000.

 Shared Hosting Configuration

Typically, the Apache configuration is split into many smaller files. However, in shared hosting setups, each user usually has his or her own configuration file, which is used for specific configuration directives concerning that user's own web sites and applications. In such cases, you should obviously put the directives mentioned in this section into the appropriate configuration file, rather than using the global one.

Don't be confused by the ProxyRequests Off directive. Apache's proxy module can be used as a forward *and* as a reverse proxy. A **forwarding proxy** acts as a middleman for your web browser when it connects to sites on the Internet, something typically used in a corporate environment. The proxy answers only those requests that originate from a known group of browsers (usually identified by their IP addresses) and forwards them on to an arbitrary number of web servers. A reverse proxy, on the other hand, serves as a front end to a known service, such as our Mongrel process. It handles incoming requests from an arbitrary number of browsers that may be scattered all over the planet.

The `ProxyRequests Off` directive turns off the forwarding proxy capabilities, while the `ProxyPass` and `ProxyPassReverse` directives turn the reverse proxy capabilities on.

To activate these configuration changes, we need to instruct Apache to reload its configuration file, which we usually achieve using the command `apachectl reload`.

For this setup to work flawlessly, we need to make sure the Mongrel process continues to run at all times, without us having to keep the terminal window open. Before the Linux and Unix folks scream "Use `screen!`," let me tell you that we can run Mongrel as a background process. We owe this ability to a helper script that was included when we originally installed Mongrel, the `mongrel_rails` command; now we can invoke the very same `script/server` command with the `-d` argument, like so:

```
$ mongrel_rails start -d -e production
```

You'll notice that you receive a short message about your Ruby version, and then the command exits and returns to the command prompt, looking as if nothing has occurred. Don't worry; now that this command has been executed, Mongrel is happily sitting in the background, waiting for requests. If you need to stop or restart your Mongrel process (don't forget, restarting is especially useful if you made changes to the application code, as a Rails application in production mode can't reload them on the fly), we just need to provide `mongrel_rails` with the appropriate argument:

```
$ mongrel_rails stop
$ mongrel_rails restart
```

Sure enough, using your browser to connect to your host URL—mine being http://shovell.poocs.net/—displays the Shovell front page shown in Figure 12.7.

Figure 12.7. Shovell proxied through Apache

Well done: you've successfully deployed your application!

Alternatives for Session Storage

When you start thinking about performance and load distribution, the next logical step is to consider the performance of the session container.

As we discussed in Chapter 9, Rails creates a new session for every visitor, logged in or not, by default. Each session is stored in a cookie by default, contained in the user's browser.

However, the situation becomes awkward when you either want to store additional information in the session (or the flash) or when you need to create more advanced features like user online statistics or server-side session expiration, which is outright impossible with cookie-based sessions.

For this reason, Rails supports alternative session storage containers, two of which we'll look at in this section.

The `ActiveRecord Store` Session Container

The most popular option after the cookie-based default, the `ActiveRecord Store` session container stores all session data safely within a table in your database. While this is not as fast as other options, using `ActiveRecord Store` allows sessions to be accessed from multiple machines—an essential feature for applications that are large enough to require multiple servers. It's also very straightforward to configure. These abilities make `ActiveRecord Store` the preferred option for applications that attract low-to-medium levels of traffic, so let's configure Shovell to use it now.

First, we need to make room in our database for the session data. Rails provides a shortcut for this job in the form of a `rake` task, and in so doing removes any need for manual table creation. As we're still on the production system, we need to include the production environment option explicitly:

```
$ rake db:sessions:create RAILS_ENV=production
```

This command will create a new migration file that contains the Ruby code necessary to create an appropriate `sessions` table which will hold our session data. The migration can then be applied using the regular `rake` task `db:migrate`:

```
$ rake db:migrate RAILS_ENV=production
```

Figure 12.8 shows the output of these migrations being applied.

Next, we need to let Rails know that we want to use the `ActiveRecord Store` instead of the default file-based session container. We can tell it the good news via the **config/environment.rb** file; simply remove the comment mark in front of the following line:

```
config.action_controller.session_store = :active_record_store
```

You then need to open the **app/controllers/application.rb** file and remove the comment before the `protect_from_forgery :secret` value:

```
protect_from_forgery  :secret => 'random string...'
```

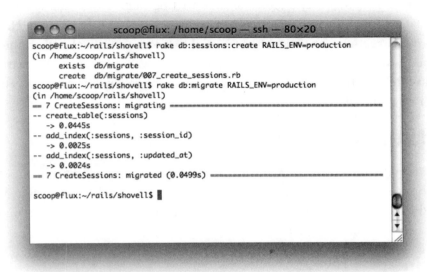

Figure 12.8. Creating the sessions table

As soon as you restart the application (using `mongrel_rails restart`), sessions will be stored in the SQL database.

Be aware that the changes you make to **config/environment.rb** will have global effects. If you want to limit this configuration change to a specific environment (for example, you want it to affect the production environment only), add the line above to the environment-specific configuration file located at **config/environments/production.rb**. If you make the change on your development machine (or copy the application code back and forth between it and your production server), be sure to run the migration in order to add the sessions table to your development database.

The MemCached Store Session Container

Another popular option for session storage is the `MemCached Store` session storage container.[14] With `MemCached`, a piece of software originally developed by Danga Interactive for the LiveJournal blog-hosting service, sessions are stored in the available memory on your server—nothing is ever written to disk.

---

[14] http://www.danga.com/memcached/

This approach is obviously a lot faster than writing each session to the hard disk or to a database (which will eventually be written to a hard disk as well). However, the setup instructions for `MemCached` are slightly more complicated than the `ActiveRecord Store` option we saw above, and the software provides little extra value for an application the size of Shovell. I'll leave you to review the setup instructions on the Ruby on Rails Wiki.[15]

Further Reading

We've done it! Our application is ready for initial public consumption, and the hands-on parts of this book have come to an end. However, I'd like to alert you to a few additional Rails features and extensions that may come in handy in your future encounters with Rails applications.

Caching

Depending on the project budget and the availability of hardware, every Rails application can only serve so many dynamic pages at any given time. If your app happens to receive traffic numbers that exceed these limits, you'll have to consider your options for tackling this problem.

Rails' built-in caching options vary in their levels of granularity. The simplest of all possibilities is to cache whole pages in the form of HTML files. What Rails does in such cases is to take the output that's sent to the browser, and store it in a file on the server's hard disk. This file can then be served directly by Apache without even bothering Mongrel, provided your setup is configured appropriately. This saves Rails from regenerating page content over and over again even though the content may not have changed between successive requests for the same page. Another option allows you to cache the outputs of single actions and even fragments of views (a sidebar, for example).

Caching can do wonders to improve your application's performance. However, take care to ensure that the relevant sections of the cache are flushed when pages change, otherwise your users will receive outdated content. Additionally, using cached pages may not be feasible if your application depends on a lot of user-specific con-

---

[15] http://wiki.rubyonrails.com/rails/pages/HowtoChangeSessionStore

tent—for instance, in an application whose page content changes depending on who's using it.

The Rails documentation for the caching feature is available online.[16]

Version Control and Deployment Management

Software development projects usually progress at a rapid pace—a truth that's even more relevant in the case of web applications. There are no strict version numbers; new features are continuously being implemented while, at the same time, bugs are fixed. Updated source code must be deployed easily and quickly. Developer resources typically need to be distributed across projects in a flexible manner.

And developers make mistakes. Not on purpose, of course—but we're all human.

Version control and deployment systems have been developed to address these issues; popular options include Subversion[17] and Capistrano.[18]

Subversion

Subversion is a general-purpose version control (or source control) system that's available for free under an open source license. This package is highly recommended for use in any software development project.

Using Subversion, you can access the project code at any point in time and you can view any code revision that was made to your project. All changes are tracked, and no modification is irreversible or destructive. Subversion also allows for the easy updating of a given copy of the project's code (for example, the copy that resides on the production system) with changes that were made elsewhere (on your development machine, perhaps).

Capistrano

Capistrano is a deployment and management system that was written in Ruby by Jamis Buck, one of the Rails core members. Capistrano can be used only with projects that are version controlled through a system such as Subversion.

---

[16] http://ap.rubyonrails.com/classes/ActionController/Caching.html

[17] http://subversion.tigris.org/

[18] http://www.capify.org/

Capistrano is designed to assist you in a number of ways:

- It facilitates the deployment of application code to your production server, along with the necessary maintenance tasks (such as restarting the Mongrel processes after the code has been updated).

- It provides a means by which you can revert to the last "known good" code base if errors appear, or put up a maintenance banner when you need to perform database repairs.

- It supports the deployment of application code to *multiple* servers simultaneously.

Errors by Email

We've talked briefly about the fact that Rails will never annoy your users with extensive stack traces if an error occurs in your application. Instead, it will display a polite message to inform the user that the request couldn't be processed successfully. The default templates for these messages can be found in `public/404.html` and `public/500.html`.

But what if you want to *fix* such errors instead of silently ignoring them? You could certainly comb through your log files every day, checking for unusual activity. Better yet, you could install the `exception_notification` plugin, which hooks into your application and sends you an email whenever something unusual happens.

The plugin can be installed using the `script/plugin` utility. Documentation that explains how to customize its behavior is available online.[19]

Summary

In this final chapter, we've plowed through the variety of options available for deploying Rails applications to production systems.

We opted to use the combination of Apache and Mongrel to deploy Shovell. We took the Shovell application code to the production system, initialized the production database, and started serving requests with a single Mongrel process. It doesn't get much easier than that!

---

[19] http://dev.rubyonrails.org/svn/rails/plugins/exception_notification/README

Once Shovell was running happily in its new environment, we looked at some alternative session storage containers and found that the `ActiveRecord Store` suited our needs by storing session data in our SQL database.

Finally, I provided a few pointers to more advanced information on some particularly relevant aspects of Rails application development and deployment.

I hope you've found value in the time you've spent with this book, and that you're now able to go forth and build upon what you've learned. Now's the time to get out there and use your knowledge to build an application that changes the Internet!

Index

THE ART &
SCIENCE
OF CSS

BY **CAMERON ADAMS**
JINA BOLTON
DAVID JOHNSON
STEVE SMITH
JONATHAN SNOOK

CREATE INSPIRATIONAL STANDARDS-BASED WEB DESIGN

THE PRINCIPLES OF
BEAUTIFUL
WEB DESIGN

BY JASON BEAIRD

SIMPLY JAVASCRIPT

BY **KEVIN YANK**
& CAMERON ADAMS

EVERYTHING YOU NEED TO LEARN JAVASCRIPT FROM SCRATCH

THE CSS
ANTHOLOGY
101 ESSENTIAL TIPS, TRICKS & HACKS

BY **RACHEL ANDREW**
2ND EDITION

ESSENTIAL READING FOR ANYONE USING CSS

THE ULTIMATE

CSS

REFERENCE

Tommy Olsson & Paul O'Brien